The Ethics of the Story

The Ethics of the Story

Using Narrative Techniques Responsibly in Journalism

David Craig

ROWMAN & LITTLEFIELD PUBLISHERS, INC.
Lanham • Boulder • New York • Toronto • Plymouth, UK

ROWMAN & LITTLEFIELD PUBLISHERS, INC.

Published in the United States of America
by Rowman & Littlefield Publishers, Inc.
A wholly owned subsidiary of The Rowman & Littlefield Publishing Group, Inc.
4501 Forbes Boulevard, Suite 200, Lanham, Maryland 20706
www.rowmanlittlefield.com

Estover Road
Plymouth PL6 7PY
United Kingdom

Copyright © 2006 by Rowman & Littlefield Publishers, Inc.

Excerpts from *Dallas Morning News* articles are used by permission of the newspaper.
Oregonian excerpts © 2006, *The Oregonian*. All rights reserved. Reprinted with
   permission.
Excerpts from *Los Angeles Times* articles and other *Times* materials are used by permission of the newspaper.

British Library Cataloguing in Publication Information Available

Library of Congress Cataloging-in-Publication Data Available

ISBN-13: 978-0-7425-3776-7 (cloth : alk. paper)
ISBN-10: 0-7425-3776-5 (cloth : alk. paper)
ISBN-13: 978-0-7425-3777-4 (pbk. : alk. paper)
ISBN-10: 0-7425-3777-3 (pbk. : alk. paper)

Printed in the United States of America

Contents

Acknowledgments

Special thanks to Peter Gross for encouraging me to pursue this project and for helping me navigate through the publishing process. Thanks to Linda Steiner, Mark Fackler, Charles Self, and Kathryn Jenson White for their ideas and encouragement. I also appreciate the good work of graduate assistants Ted Satterfield and Erin Sigler.

My thanks to the University of Oklahoma Research Council and the Gaylord College of Journalism and Mass Communication for their financial support. And thanks to the newsroom managers at the *Dallas Morning News, Los Angeles Times,* and *Oregonian* for allowing me to visit—and to the journalists I interviewed for their time and thoughts.

Most of all, I want to thank my wife and daughter. To Barbara, thank you for typing when my arms gave out, for helping me find the right words when I couldn't, and for praying and listening from start to finish. To Elizabeth, thanks for finding computer commands I'd never heard of, for displaying a great eye for detail, and for making me laugh at the right moments.

Introduction:
Ethics Paragraph by Paragraph

The story may be a deadline piece about a house fire or a four-day series on life in an intensive-care unit. It may be a straightforward account of an investigation into police practices or an analysis of presidential candidates' positions. In all of these cases, writers and editors face ethical choices—from the angle or theme of the story down to the individual word, phrase, or paragraph. The thinking behind these choices is largely invisible to the public, but together they shape what the public learns about people and issues.

This book explores these choices through the eyes of journalists at three large newspapers: the *Los Angeles Times*, the Portland *Oregonian*, and the *Dallas Morning News*. It includes the perspectives of writers, copy editors, assigning editors, and top-level managers. These sixty journalists[1] have worked with lengthy features, in-depth investigations, and columns. They have covered government, politics, business, sports, and the joys and grief of people's everyday lives. Some have won or helped others win Pulitzer Prizes.

A careful look at the ethics of journalists' everyday choices is important to journalists and students, to those who study and critique journalism, and to society. All of the storytelling devices writers employ and editors evaluate have ethical implications. They may illuminate or obscure truth—or sometimes they may do both, as in the case of anecdotes used to open many stories and dramatize issues. They may stir compassion among members of the public to address a community problem or meet an individual need—or they may outrage readers, as with a careless choice of an inflammatory label for an individual or group. Choices about matters such as anecdotes, description,

1

quotations, and attribution are a daily part of the work of news and feature writers.

Ethical choices are particularly evident in narrative writing, which has appeared in newspapers and magazines, in books, on the World Wide Web, and in television news magazines. Narrative journalism, which applies the literary techniques of fiction storytelling to journalistic writing (usually features),[2] leaves journalists with challenging choices—such as how much to explain the sources of description, quotations, and other information in a story that is supposed to read as engagingly as a novel yet be as factually credible as a news story. Powerful narratives may provide insight about a person's suffering or the essence of a complicated issue. But at a time when many in the public are skeptical of the truthfulness of journalists,[3] and when journalists have been embarrassed by high-profile fabrications such as Jayson Blair's at the *New York Times*[4] and Jack Kelley's at *USA Today*,[5] ethical scrutiny of the techniques used in narrative is particularly important.

Although the ethical implications of journalistic writing techniques are significant, little of the writing and discussion about ethics in recent years has systematically critiqued these devices from an ethical perspective. In the past two decades, media scholars, other media critics, members of the public, and journalists themselves have talked and written a great deal about journalism ethics—though the word "ethics" has not always been used. Recent media criticism has been variously fueled by books offering measured evaluation of ethics by professors and professionals;[6] more sharply critical popular books;[7] venues for professional discussion such as the Poynter Institute for Media Studies and its website;[8] media watchdog groups of various political stripes such as the Media Research Center[9] and Fairness and Accuracy in Reporting;[10] radio and television talk programs;[11] Jon Stewart's satirical *The Daily Show*;[12] and Internet blogs reflecting a variety of viewpoints.[13]

Discussion outside universities and journalism training centers like Poynter may not often be based on formal principles of ethics, but sometimes it does point to specific concerns about the framing and wording of stories. In addition, as later chapters will note, newspaper readers sometimes raise specifics of framing and wording with public editors or other representatives of newspapers. In many cases, the motives of intentional bias that the public or watchdog groups impute to journalists are probably absent—though their decisions, like everyone else's, are inevitably shaped by their backgrounds and worldviews. The interviews, as well as my own experience as a newspaper copy editor, suggest that good journalists go out of their way to be fair, to an extent that would probably astonish many critics. But the criticisms underline the fact that ethical choices are embedded in the techniques of writing.

Writing about ethics by professionals and professors has, for all of its attention to cases and principles, dealt relatively little with the ethics of the daily choices about technique in writing and editing. Among professionals, thoughtful narrative writers and editors have provided important exceptions, grappling with issues such as how to signal the sources of information adequately while maintaining the flow of a powerful story.[14] Scholars who study journalistic writing have written about the ethics of quotations[15] and the reconstruction of events.[16] But most ethical attention has gone to cases that involve questionable decisions or clear lapses—such as Blair's and Kelley's and, two decades earlier, the fabrication of a Pulitzer Prize–winning story by *Washington Post's* Janet Cooke—or to choices beyond the details of writing and editing.[17]

The absence of discussion of good ethical decisions is especially glaring. It is also destructive because it helps to perpetuate public perceptions that journalists are sloppy, biased, and uncaring—and leaves both journalists and students lacking good models from which to learn.

Day-to-day choices about journalistic technique are important beyond what they mean for individual journalists and for students or observers of journalism. They are ultimately important for the life of a democratic society and the building of community and culture. Taken together, the truthful and compelling use of journalistic storytelling devices helps to nurture a form of communication that not only provides credible information for citizens about public issues but also has the potential to inspire them to press for change and hold officials—as well as corporate leaders and other professionals—accountable for their actions. In addition, by helping to provide stories that foster understanding of the lives of others, journalistic techniques can help build and sustain a sense of connectedness among members of a community. Ultimately, the language of journalism plays a key role in making the meaning that creates and sustains culture itself.[18]

The newspapers represented by the journalists in this book are not perfect, and they are not immune to the profit pressures squeezing journalistic resources across the country—as evidenced by the layoffs of about sixty journalists[19] at the *Dallas Morning News* the month after interviews were completed there.[20] The newspapers and the journalists who work for them also face the daily challenge of living up to the high standards they profess for reporting and writing—a point underlined by a dispute over issues of accuracy and interpretation in an *Oregonian* narrative article as this book was being completed.[21] However, all three newspapers have done in-depth narrative and investigative work in recent years, and they have many talented writers and editors on staff.[22] The journalists interviewed represent a wide range of experience and age. Together, they offer an unusual look at the best—though not perfect—practices of journalism.[23] With journalists facing intense pressure from business interests, a fragmenting audience, and a skeptical public, it is important to look closely at these practices because they could become rare exceptions if not examined and sustained.

Although the journalists interviewed work for newspapers, the issues that they raise are relevant to the practice of broadcast and web journalism, as well as magazine and nonfiction book writing. Regardless of the medium and the format of presentation, journalists wrestle with choices about the techniques raised in this book as they seek to tell stories.

This book provides insight into how journalists think—and therefore adds to a stream of books in the past three decades that have examined the process and practices of journalistic work from a variety of perspectives.[24] But the examination of journalists' thinking will also lead to detailed suggestions about how professionals can handle the ethical issues associated with writing stories.

Chapter 1 focuses on the power of journalistic storytelling and on two key ethical issues in journalists' work: truth and compassion. Both the questions in the interviews and the evaluation of what the journalists said are connected to these two issues—though the discussion of ethics is not limited to them.[25] Truth and compassion are principles with long histories in ethical thought and current use in journalism ethics, and they help to shed light on what these writing techniques can do for readers.

Chapters 2 to 7 focus on the journalists' perspectives on several issues of writing technique: anecdotes, description, attribution, quotations and paraphrasing, word choice and labeling, interpretation and analysis, and voice. The chapters explore the ethical implications of their thinking and practices from the vantage point of ethical principles and some insights of media scholarship. The chapters include numerous examples from the interviewees' work to make the discussion useful for students and professionals and provide detailed evaluation for media researchers. Chapter 8 steps back and looks at lessons for the practice of journalism and the future of the profession.

Notes

1. One of the interviewees, *Los Angeles Times* readers' representative Jamie Gold, does not write or edit but influences the writing and editing process at the paper through her in-house communication of reader feedback.

2. Journalists tend to think of this kind of work when they hear the term "narrative." Media scholars tend to think of narrative more broadly—encompassing all

forms of journalistic storytelling and, in the widest sense, all of the forms of communication that contribute to a society's understanding of itself. The writing techniques discussed in this book are part of narrative in all of these senses.

3. More than half (53 percent) of respondents in a 2004 survey by the Pew Research Center for the People and the Press agreed with the statement, "I often don't trust what news organizations are saying." Almost half (48 percent) said they believed that people who decide on news content are "out of touch." See "News Audiences Increasingly Politicized: Online News Audience Larger, More Diverse," Pew Research Center for the People and the Press, people-press.org/reports/display.php3 ?ReportID=215 (accessed May 24, 2006).

4. See Jill Rosen, "All About the Retrospect," *American Journalism Review* (June–July 2003): 32–35 and Dan Barry, David Barstow, Jonathan D. Glater, Adam Liptak, and Jacques Steinberg, "Correcting the Record; Times Reporter Who Resigned Leaves Long Trail of Deception," *New York Times*, May 11, 2003, 1-1 (Late Ed.-Final), web.lexisnexis.com.

5. See Jill Rosen, "Who Knows Jack?" *American Journalism Review* (April–May 2004): 29–38; and Bill Hilliard, Bill Kovach, and John Seigenthaler, "The Problems of Jack Kelley and USA TODAY," www.usatoday.com/news/2004-04-22-report-one _x.htm.

6. These books include broad critiques of journalistic norms such as Clifford G. Christians, John P. Ferré, and P. Mark Fackler, *Good News: Social Ethics and the Press* (New York: Oxford University Press, 1993) and Jeremy Iggers, *Good News, Bad News: Journalism Ethics and the Public Interest* (Boulder, Colo.: Westview Press, 1998); theory-based case books such as Philip Patterson and Lee Wilkins, *Media Ethics: Issues and Cases*, 5th ed. (Boston: McGraw-Hill, 2005) and Clifford G. Christians et al., *Media Ethics: Cases and Moral Reasoning*, 7th ed. (Boston: Pearson Education, 2005); and more professionally based critiques such as Bill Kovach and Tom Rosenstiel, *The Elements of Journalism: What Newspeople Should Know and the Public Should Expect* (New York: Crown Publishers, 2001) and Leonard Downie Jr. and Robert G. Kaiser, *The News About the News: American Journalism in Peril* (New York: Alfred A. Knopf, 2002).

7. For example, Bernard Goldberg, *Bias: A CBS Insider Exposes How the Media Distort the News* (Washington, D.C.: Regnery, 2001); Bob Kohn, *Journalistic Fraud: How The New York Times Distorts the News and Why It Can No Longer Be Trusted* (Nashville, Tenn.: WND Books, 2003); and Eric Alterman, *What Liberal Media? The Truth About Bias and the News* (New York: Basic Books, 2003).

8. Poynter Institute for Media Studies, www.poynter.org (accessed June 5, 2006).

9. Media Research Center, www.mediaresearch.org (accessed May 29, 2006).

10. Fairness & Accuracy in Reporting, www.fair.org (accessed May 29, 2006).

11. Although the quality, accuracy, and tone of the discussion vary, these programs contribute to public perspectives on media work. News coverage is a topic of discussion on radio, for example, on *The Rush Limbaugh Show* from a conservative perspective and *The Al Franken Show* from a liberal one. Discussion of media work

occurs on television, for example, on the *NewsHour* on PBS and on more critical shows such as Fox News's *The O'Reilly Factor*.

12. The website for the program, shown on Comedy Central, is at www.comedy central.com/shows/the_daily_show/index.jhtml (accessed May 29, 2006).

13. Media news blogs include I Want Media, www.iwantmedia.com (accessed May 29, 2006), Romenesko's Media News, www.poynter.org/column.asp?id=45 (accessed May 29, 2006), and others reflecting liberal or conservative viewpoints.

14. Harvard University's Nieman Program on Narrative Journalism—www.nieman .harvard.edu/narrative (accessed May 24, 2006)—and the conferences, discussion, and articles growing out of it have explored ethical issues in narrative. For an example of discussion of ethics connected with the Nieman conferences, see poynter .blogs.com/narrative/narrative_after_jayson_blair (accessed May 24, 2006). For a quick historical overview of debates over the ethics of nonfiction narrative, see Roy Peter Clark, "The Ethics of Narrative Journalism: A Continuing Debate," Poynter Online, poynteronline.org/content/content_view.asp?id=4718&sid=32 (accessed May 24, 2006).

15. G. Michael Killenberg and Rob Anderson, "What Is a Quote? Practical, Rhetorical, and Ethical Concerns for Journalists," *Journal of Mass Media Ethics* 8, no. 1 (1993): 37–54.

16. Russell Frank, "'You Had to Be There' (and They Weren't): The Problem with Reporter Reconstructions," *Journal of Mass Media Ethics* 14, no. 3 (1999): 146–58.

17. Many books—for example, Jon Franklin, *Writing for Story: Craft Secrets of Dramatic Nonfiction by a Two-Time Pulitzer Prize Winner* (New York: Plume, 1994) and James B. Stewart, *Follow the Story: How to Write Successful Nonfiction* (New York: Simon & Schuster, Touchstone, 1998)—have dealt with issues of writing technique and form, but these have not focused on ethics. The interviewees themselves did not always think of the techniques we discussed in ethical terms. Roy Peter Clark and Christopher Scanlan, *America's Best Newspaper Writing: A Collection of ASNE Prizewinners*, 2nd ed. (Boston: Bedford/St. Martin's, 2006) includes a chapter on "Ethical Journalism and the Craft of Honest Writing." For a brief discussion of ethics and news stories, see Carole Rich, "Ethics of the News Story," in *Journalism Ethics: A Reference Handbook*, ed. Elliot D. Cohen and Deni Elliott (Santa Barbara, Calif.: ABC-CLIO, 1997), 45–50.

18. Christians, Ferré, and Fackler, in *Good News*, 113–15, discuss how narratives including news stories help to create communities. James W. Carey, in *Communication as Culture: Essays on Media and Society* (Boston: Unwin Hyman, 1989), argues that communication is crucial in forming "an ordered, meaningful cultural world" (18–19).

19. Robert W. Mong Jr., e-mail messages to author, January 25 and 27, 2005.

20. Profits suffered partly because of a scandal involving overstatement of the paper's circulation figures. See Charles Layton, "The Dallas Mourning News," *American Journalism Review*, April–May 2005, www.ajr.org/Article.asp?id=3836 (accessed May 24, 2006).

21. A narrative written by Pulitzer Prize winner Tom Hallman, Jr., and edited by Jack Hart—both interviewed for this book because of their commitment to excellence in narrative—was questioned by the subject of the piece, Mark Provo, over its accuracy and its characterization of him. The newspaper agreed that the story, "The Riddle in Room 114," included one factual error and acknowledged that "there were a few places where the interpretation" of Hallman's notes "should have been more precise," but said "the overall tenor of the story was accurate." See Peter Bhatia, "This Week's Note from Us: Mark Provo," *Oregonian*, May 28, 2006, A2 (Sunrise Ed.), infoweb.newsbank.com. Hart responded to Provo's contentions on the *Oregonian* Editors' Blog, www.oregonlive.com/weblogs/editors/index.ssf?/mtlogs/olive_editor/archives/2006_05.html#144034 (accessed May 24, 2006). For the article, see "The Riddle in Room 114," *Oregonian*, May 7, 2006, http://www.oregonlive.com/news/oregonian/index.ssf?/base/news/1146880510272131.xml&coll=7 (accessed May 24, 2006).

22. The *Oregonian* is nationally known for its narrative writing and has done strong investigative work as well. It is also known for its innovation in newsroom organization and management. The *Dallas Morning News* has done in-depth investigative journalism and some narrative as well and is strong in religion coverage, sports, and business. The *Los Angeles Times* has done outstanding investigative and narrative work and is known in the industry for its general excellence. All three papers have large staffs of assigning editors and rigorous copy desks.

23. The interviewees do not represent an exhaustive list of the many excellent journalists at the three papers, but the conversations provided an in-depth look at many viewpoints across a variety of writing forms, beats, and backgrounds. The interviews focused mostly on narrative writing and editing at the *Oregonian*; on investigative, narrative, and political writing at the *Los Angeles Times*; and on a wide array of work at the *Dallas Morning News* including religion, sports, and business in addition to investigative and narrative. All but four interviews were conducted in person at the newspapers, and most interviews lasted from one to one and a half hours.

24. These works include Edward Jay Epstein, *News from Nowhere: Television and the News* (New York: Random House, 1973); Gaye Tuchman, *Making News: A Study in the Construction of Reality* (New York: Free Press, 1978); Mark Fishman, *Manufacturing the News* (Austin: University of Texas Press, 1980); Herbert J. Gans, *Deciding What's News* (New York: Vintage Books, 1980); Todd Gitlin, *The Whole World Is Watching: Mass Media in the Making and Unmaking of the New Left* (Berkeley: University of California Press, 1980); John H. McManus, *Market-Driven Journalism: Let the Citizen Beware?* (Thousand Oaks, Calif.: Sage, 1994); James S. Ettema and Theodore L. Glasser, *Custodians of Conscience: Investigative Journalism and Public Virtue* (New York: Columbia University Press, 1998).

25. I assume that ethics encompasses matters of moral duty or responsibility and benefit or harm. Ethical concerns may be rooted in a variety of sources—professional, social, religious, or philosophical—that journalists and other humans bring to their daily choices. Chapter 1 addresses some of the roots of truth and compassion.

CHAPTER ONE

The Power and Ethics of the Story

Powerful journalistic stories, from the articles of the muckraker era of the early 1900s to investigations of recent decades,[1] have had significant impact on public life and policy. Narrative features about the lives of hurting people[2] have helped readers empathize with others' lives and struggles—and sometimes shed light on broader social problems. Explanatory pieces[3] about complicated subjects have added to public understanding. In all of these cases, the power of the journalism is built on well-used techniques. A compelling story can shape—for good or ill—the way a reader understands people, events, and issues. The power of the story underlines the importance of the ethical choices writers and editors make about the details of narrative technique. This chapter will illustrate the power of journalistic storytelling with examples from award-winning work in Los Angeles, Dallas, and Portland, Oregon. Then it will step back and place this power against an important backdrop: the broader significance of stories in human life and communication. Finally, to set up the discussion of techniques in the rest of the book, it will explore two important ethical issues relevant to evaluation of writing and editing: truth and compassion.

The Power of Journalists' Stories

All of the journalists interviewed for this book have played a role in crafting powerful stories—as writers, editors, or both. Taken together, their work provides a wealth of examples of engaging writing. Among the most high-profile pieces are stories that won Pulitzer Prizes. Here are three examples.

The Narrative Power of "Enrique's Journey"

Los Angeles Times staff writer Sonia Nazario told the story of Enrique, a boy who traveled to the United States alone from Honduras as a teenager in search of his mother. She had gone seeking work when her son was young, and he tried—eight times—to get to the United States to see her. "The Boy Left Behind: Enrique's Journey," published in six parts in the fall of 2002, retraced the steps he took as he hopped freight trains, endured a beating, and eluded authorities. In telling his story, she pointed readers to the broader migration of which Enrique was a part: thousands of children traveling from Central America and Mexico in the face of great danger, often—like Enrique—searching for their mothers.

Nazario spent three months, along with photographer Don Bartletti, traveling north through Mexico. They rode the tops of trains, hitched rides with truckers, and interviewed and photographed people Enrique had met—along with many others. Nazario also talked with Enrique in Nuevo Laredo, Mexico, where she first found him, and in North Carolina, where he was reunited with his mother. Her in-depth reporting enabled her to craft a narrative with great descriptive power. The third chapter of the series opens this way:

> Enrique wades chest-deep across a river. He is 5 feet tall, stoop-shouldered and cannot swim. The logo on his cap boasts hollowly, "No Fear."
>
> The river, the Rio Suchiate, forms the border. Behind him is Guatemala. Ahead is Mexico, with its southernmost state of Chiapas. "Ahora nos enfrentamos a la bestia," immigrants say when they enter Chiapas. "Now we face the beast."
>
> Painfully, Enrique, 17, has learned a lot about "the beast." In Chiapas, bandits will be out to rob him, police will try to shake him down, and street gangs might kill him. But he will take those risks, because he needs to find his mother.[4]

The vivid detail of the opening paragraph gives the reader an immediate picture of the obstacles Enrique faced and the against-the-odds nature of his journey. The rest of the passage places the reader more fully in the scene and adds context that underscores the danger he faced. Nazario talked about how her reporting enabled her to describe the scene powerfully:

> The chapter was about getting through Chiapas, and so he's once again been kicked back to the border, across the border into Guatemala. So it seemed like a natural place to start, with him going across this river one more time and starting the journey into Chiapas again. And I was able to give it that immediacy both by crossing the river myself and seeing both sides of it, and talking

to other immigrants who had done it and talking to him about his experience doing it. So like most of these scenes I try to experience it in every way possible to try to be able to write about it very authoritatively.[5]

In addition to vivid description, creative attribution of information contributed to the power of the story, as well as its credibility. Nazario made attribution sparing in the stories themselves, allowing them to move more quickly. But she and her editor, Richard E. Meyer, at the urging of *Times* editor John S. Carroll, developed endnotes after each day's segment to provide rich detail about sources of information. For example, they included this note for the passage above:

Crossing the Rio Suchiate: drawn from interviews with Enrique, other immigrants who made the crossing and Nazario's observations as she crossed on a raft. Facing Chiapas state, "the beast": from Father Flor Maria Rigoni, a Catholic priest at the Albergue Belen migrant shelter in Tapachula, Chiapas.[6]

As Meyer put it, "Now anyone could find out where everything in the story came from—which is to say, they could find out how Sonia knew everything she knew."[7] By moving much attribution out of the stories but detailing it in notes, they enhanced the power of the story while also showing more skeptical readers that the reporting was solid. Nazario said readers responded positively to the notes.

This series, which won the 2003 Pulitzer Prize for feature writing, touched readers deeply, as evidenced by emotional calls and e-mails they received—some from people who had made similar journeys themselves. It also prompted discussion in the area. As Meyer's letter nominating the series for the Pulitzer put it:

Ministers based sermons on it. The Rev. J. Edwin Bacon Jr., at all Saints Church in Pasadena, told his large congregation that the poor people who helped Enrique were "an oasis of grace . . . and a community of saints." A murmur of agreement spread through the church.

Teachers taught from it. Entire classes wrote to thank Nazario for writing it. At Anaheim High School, 600 students went to the auditorium to talk about it. Roberta Dieter's English students plastered their classroom with posters showing its chapters and the lessons they learned.[8]

The stories, focused on an individual but connected with a broader issue, illustrate how thoughtful use of journalistic techniques can help to touch people's hearts and deepen their understanding.

The Explanatory Power of "The French Fry Connection"

Oregonian reporter Richard Read faced a different kind of challenge: how to explain the Asian economic crisis of the late 1990s and its impact on the Pacific Northwest simply and clearly. Economic problems were causing havoc in Asian countries and damaging businesses in the Northwest. Individuals were hurt, but the impact went well beyond individuals, and the reasons for the crisis were complicated. So Read chose a product to which nearly everyone could relate: the frozen french fry. He built his four-part narrative, "The French Fry Connection," around the progress of a load of fries from a Washington farm through shipment to the Far East and ultimately to a McDonald's in Singapore. He also described the economic pain of Indonesia, which was torn by riots.

Read uses vivid description in places to strengthen this explanatory narrative, but much of its power lies in passages that spell out the larger meaning of the story. For example:

> Sixteen months after the economic blaze ignited in Thailand, Asia's fires still smolder, flaring unexpectedly as far away as Russia and Latin America, still threatening to cause a world conflagration.
>
> But the global economy is so new, so unchecked and so crudely understood that the world's leading economists can't agree on how to douse the flames. Jittery investors dash for the exits with each new sign of smoke, upsetting stock markets and compounding uncertainty.
>
> The example of the Northwest french fry illustrates one sure truth: The global economy is ubiquitous to the point that there's no going back. Countries and regions can no more shut it out than rebuild the Berlin Wall or resurrect the Soviet Union.[9]

Read provides analysis for the reader built on extensive Asian reporting experience and knowledge of world trade. Because of his background and the in-depth reporting he brought to the series, he is able to comment straightforwardly and confidently about the meaning of the global economy—without loading the story down with attribution to experts or qualification of what he knows. Read, the newspaper's senior writer for international affairs and special projects, explained his approach this way:

> It's based on eight years of reporting in Asia and watching all the developments during that time, and it's based on, in this specific story, interviewing a lot of experts on everything from the potato industry to foreign exchange markets to trade officials. And I could write a story in which I go through and quote all of them and explain what they say—and if they have differing opin-

ions, bounce their opinions off against each other—and make some of the same points. My idea was condense it all based on all those interviews without having to show the reader the plumbing. And I suppose at this point if somebody's gone through three parts with you and they're still reading, hopefully they've decided that you're credible enough that they'll bear with you when you just state this without attribution. I couldn't have done anything like this at the beginning of my career as a cops reporter or even a city hall reporter.[10]

By taking an approach that did not "show the plumbing" but rested on strong reporting, Read was able to discuss a complicated issue clearly.

The series won the 1999 Pulitzer Prize for explanatory reporting. Responses from dozens of readers showed that the series had succeeded in engaging people's interest and educating them about this complex topic. Managing editor Jack Hart recounted one reaction in his Pulitzer nomination letter: "'I normally skip over articles like this,' wrote one woman, 'because they're so boring.' She was scrambling to find Day 1 after she stumbled across Day 2 and plunged into the rest of the series." Another reader said, "It made people who weren't aware of business understand what this is all about."[11]

The Investigative Impact of "Violence Against Women"
The *Dallas Morning News* used powerful writing in 1993 to draw attention to violence against women around the world—as far away from its audience as China and as close as Dallas. In a series of fifteen articles that ran from March to June that year, reporters described how—among other things—girls or women were sold into prostitution in Thailand, beaten in Brazil's culture of machismo, raped by Serb attackers in the former Yugoslavia, and mutilated through the custom of female circumcision in Africa. Accusations of sexual abuse by Dallas police and other violence against U.S. women brought the series closer to home. Reporters also explored movements toward reform in Canada and Sweden.

The series, which won the 1994 Pulitzer Prize for international reporting, was powerful not only because of the strong reporting behind it, but also because of its use of writing techniques. For example, a story by Pam Maples about violence against U.S. women opened this way describing the abuse one woman suffered from her husband:

ANN ARBOR, Mich.—Her heart pounded, and a shiver ran through her body. Sandy Henes closed her eyes tight, held her breath and waited to die.

Not today. Maybe tomorrow. Maybe next week.

Sometimes he kicked her with steel-toed boots. Sometimes he hit her with his fist. Sometimes he penetrated her vagina with the barrel of a loaded handgun.

The threat was always the same: I can kill you just like that. And nobody will care.[12]

The power of this horrifying description would grab the attention of even a casual reader. Talking about this opening, Maples—now the newspaper's assistant managing editor for projects—said, "What I was trying to do was find something that would be real, on one level, real clear and real simple, but on another level would have sort of that punch in the gut to pull the reader in." She wanted to bring home to readers the fact that this kind of violence happens in the United States, too, and it is not just strangers who do it.[13] The story ended with a quote from Henes that was similarly powerful:

"I get up every day, and I don't know if he's going to be outside my door or outside my office," she says.

"In my soul, I don't think this will be over until I have to kill him. I hope I'm wrong, but I just feel like the day will come and it will be him or me. And it's not going to me. It's never going to be me again."[14]

Maples said she thought this quote took readers back to the scene at the opening, showing the woman had changed from being a victim who expected to die to someone resolving that she was not going to die.

Another story in the series brought home the power of the writer's voice. It did something unusual for a newspaper, inserting first-person reflection by the reporter, Victoria Loe (now Victoria Loe Hicks), about the violence she herself had suffered. The story, in which she interviewed a chronic sex offender named Koy Bass, also included her reaction to interviewing him. Near the end, she quoted Bass: "I'm not looking for any sympathy or understanding or anything," he said. "If they're angry at me, that's OK. And if they want to talk about it, that's OK, too." Then she closed this way:

I am angry, and I want to talk about it.

I am angry at every man who is still hurting women. I hold them accountable. I am angry at our society, which tells men it is permissible to hurt women because women are less than men. I hold it accountable.

I am angry that women are expected to live crippled by fear, self-hatred, despair, isolation or guilt so that our culture not be brought to account for its sins. I am angry that anyone would dare to tell us our suffering is our fault. It is not our fault.

We have a right—a human right—to live as full equals, respected and free from fear. We have a right to keep talking about these crimes, and about our anger, until the crimes stop.

Koy Bass has a full-time job. His job is not to victimize women.
My job is not to be a victim. My job is to stay angry.[15]

In this case, stepping out of the detached news voice to comment directly underlines for readers the gravity of the problem the story is addressing. It also discloses the reporter's standpoint as someone who was clearly not a detached observer on this topic.[16]

The Morning News's Ralph Langer, in the letter nominating the series for a Pulitzer Prize, said the stories brought responses of shock and anger from readers, both men and women. But beyond that, they drew the interest of government officials from Austria, Canada, and the United Nations, as well as from advocacy groups. The series coincided with a petition drive to make the issue of violence against women a priority at the United Nations' World Conference on Human Rights held in June 1993. It "gave momentum to a rising tide of sentiment that carried the issue to the conference and its agenda."[17]

Through a variety of thoughtful uses of writing techniques, "Enrique's Journey," "The French Fry Connection," and "Violence Against Women" gave readers important insights in compelling ways. However, lengthy narrative series and investigative articles are not the only kinds of stories that use writing techniques powerfully. As chapters 2 through 7 in this book will show, writers across a variety of beats—including politics, religion, education, the arts, and sports—use devices such as anecdotes, description, and quotations in ways that strengthen their work. Columnists, among others, use word choice and voice to enhance the impact of their pieces. The assigning editors and copy editors who work with writers also influence the power of their writing. Upper-level newsroom managers, particularly with longer and more sensitive pieces, may shape their work, too. For all of these writers and editors, the choices they make every day about the details of technique shape their readers' understanding of the world.

A Step Back: The Broader Power of Stories

Scholars in recent years have thought deeply about the power of stories and realized that journalistic storytelling, and narratives in general, are crucial building blocks for society and people's understanding of it. Historian Hayden White has written: "To raise the question of the nature of narrative is to invite reflection on the very nature of culture and, possibly, even on the nature of humanity itself." Humans, he says, naturally want to narrate, and it is "inevitable" that accounts of how things happened will take the form of stories.[18] Communication scholar Walter R. Fisher's narrative paradigm views humans as *homo narrans*: storytelling is at the core of who they are. Whether they are giving the history of an event, sketching a biography, explaining, or making an argument, people are telling stories to themselves and to one another to create meaning in human life.[19] Readers of news articles, features, analyses, and columns, then, are taking in fragments of meaning— whether from anecdotes and description or statements of explanation—that together help to shape the world in which they think and act.

Some current scholarly perspectives place a particularly strong emphasis on the importance of narrative. Communitarianism, which emphasizes the mutual connections and concern among people in society, views the stories that individuals tell as key elements in the construction of a good and just world. The news media, in the communitarian ethic of Clifford G. Christians, John P. Ferré, and P. Mark Fackler, can help build mutual understanding and change communities by providing truthful stories—particularly stories that highlight injustices:

> A press nurtured by communitarian ethics requires more of itself than fair treatment of events deemed worthy of coverage. Under the notion that justice itself—and not merely haphazard public enlightenment—is a *telos* of the press, the news-media system stands under obligation to tell the stories that justice requires.[20]

Deciding what justice requires may be a matter of intense debate in a diverse society, but communitarian ethics makes considering the question— and trying to provide answers through stories—a priority. "Enrique's Journey" is an example of a narrative that, in the communitarian view, uses the power of storytelling in the service of portraying the complexities of justice and human need.

Feminist thinking has also pointed toward the importance of narratives. For feminist scholars such as Carol Gilligan and Nel Noddings, caring relationships are a crucial aspect of life and ethics.[21] Narratives—be they stories told among individuals or stories about their lives told in newspapers—are ethically significant in the context of this perspective because they can help to nurture and sustain the web of relationships and responsibilities that is central to individuals' lives.

On a feminist reading, portrayals of women in the media—news or entertainment—are also crucial to society's broader understanding or misunderstanding of women and their needs. Therefore, series such as the *Dallas Morning News*'s "Violence Against Women," by bringing voices and problems of women into the open, are narratives of potentially profound importance.

Postmodernist thinking—though it cannot be defined as a single perspective—highlights the importance of narrative in an even deeper way. In postmodern philosophy, narrative is, in a sense, all that there is. There is no truth about the world deeper than what individuals and society agree is true. As Richard Rorty put it:

> It is central to the idea of a liberal society that, in respect to words as opposed to deeds, persuasion as opposed to force, anything goes. This openmindedness should not be fostered because, as Scripture teaches, Truth is great and will prevail, nor because, as Milton suggests, Truth will always win in a free and open encounter. It should be fostered for its own sake. *A liberal society is one which is content to call "true" whatever the upshot of such encounters turns out to be.*[22]

If understandings of the world built through language are all that we have, then journalistic and other narratives are crucial in shaping the kind of worldviews and society that prevail. Even if one does not go so far as a thoroughgoing postmodernist would toward abandoning notions of a greater truth, this view underlines the importance of language in shaping people's understanding of the world.

Study of narrative from a variety of perspectives has exploded in recent decades. Since the 1920s, scholars of narrative theory or "narratology"—from areas as diverse as linguistics, anthropology, literary criticism, and film theory—have paid rigorous attention to the structure of stories.[23] In recent years, the objects of their study have expanded to include narratives as diverse as music videos, advertisements, jokes, and people's accounts of their day—as well as journalism.[24]

Researchers who study the content of news have reflected in a variety of ways on the power of journalistic storytelling. For example:

- James S. Ettema and Theodore L. Glasser have pointed to the power of narrative form—in particular, the narratives of investigative journalism—to frame the morality of situations of terrible wrongdoing. Investigative reporters may enhance the audience's sense of moral outrage by portraying citizens as, to at least some degree, innocent victims. In one instance, a reporter writing about jail rapes "used two narrative strategies to evoke outrage at the victims' plight: highlighting cruelly ironic details of the victims' experiences and privileging the victims' accounts of those experiences."[25] The establishment of innocence was set against failures of the system responsible for the jail conditions. At the same time, Ettema and Glasser argued, the narrative form stressed the plight of individuals in this story and others rather than in-depth exploration of the system failures. They thus pointed to the limitations as well as the power of the form.

- Michael Schudson has argued that the form of news stories carries messages about the nature of the U.S. political system. Stories about the president's State of the Union message since 1900 have, for example, underlined the preeminence of the president by emphasizing the message and its content, not the response of Congress. These stories have also transmitted assumptions about the proper role of journalists—such as the view that journalists should provide analysis of the meaning of such events.[26] On the other hand, Phyllis Frus argues, when journalists avoid interpretation and try to practice objective journalism—"allowing facts to 'speak for themselves'"—there is a different kind of exercise of power: people's emotional response is narrowed and their current understanding of the social world is maintained.[27] In both cases, narrative technique carries social power.

- Carolyn Kitch, analyzing newsmagazines' coverage of the terrorist attacks of September 11, 2001, and their aftermath, underlined the cultural power of journalistic narratives. Through many devices, including reporter commentary and anecdotes of survival and heroism, the magazines aided in the nation's mourning and its evaluation of the meaning of these events. In the end, journalistic images and language helped to create a larger cultural story of courage, redemption, and pride.[28]

Journalistic stories, then, help to create or maintain a society's understanding of itself, its political and social system, and its vulnerabilities and injustices. The devices of news, of features, and of analysis and commentary are key pieces in the building of this understanding. The power of journalistic techniques—evident both in examples of influential stories and in the insights of scholars—underlines the value of thinking carefully about how they are used.

Two Ethical Lenses for Looking at Stories

Writers, assigning editors, and copy editors make choices every day—even every hour—about how to use writing techniques to get across the point of a story or column most fully and accurately. When the subject is a suffering individual or a community problem, journalists face choices about how to portray the person or issue in a sensitive way—and how to give readers reason to care. As the interviews for this book showed, journalists do not always think about decisions of technique explicitly as ethical choices. As one put it, they are issues of craft but they also have an ethical dimension.[29] Decisions about how to express a point fully and accurately relate to the ethical issue of truth. Choices about how to portray a person or issue in a sensitive and compelling way connect with the issue of compassion. Given the potential power of journalistic techniques, it is important to view them through these ethical lenses, not just through the lens of craft.[30]

Truth and compassion will be used in later chapters to help evaluate the choices that writers and editors make about techniques and the impact of those choices. In formal ethical terms, this kind of discussion is based on ethical duties—deontological ethics—because it uses two dimensions of ethical responsibility to evaluate the work of journalists. However, the principles are used here with an eye to evaluating not only the rightness of choices but also their consequences—for example, whether a particular use of analytical writing provides more truth about an issue to readers or an anecdote stirs greater compassion. And, more generally, in discussion of techniques, journalists' views on the benefits and dangers or difficulties of journalistic techniques will be presented. Because the discussion will consider such benefits and dangers, it also has—in formal ethical terms—a consequentialist element.[31]

To set the stage for the ethical discussion in the rest of the book, the following two sections examine truth and compassion in more detail, place them in the context of scholarly and professional thinking, and begin to illustrate how these principles shed light on ethical choices about journalistic techniques.

Truth

Truth has been a key concern historically in philosophy since the ancient Greeks. As philosopher Sissela Bok put it:

> "Truth"—no concept intimidates and yet draws thinkers so powerfully. From the beginnings of human speculation about the world, the questions of what truth is and whether we can attain it have loomed large. Every philosopher has had to grapple with them. Every religion seeks to answer them.[32]

Although it would be impossible to recount its history comprehensively here,[33] this long livelihood is worth noting because it underlines the priority that thinking members of society have placed on its pursuit. The priority here, though, is to place truth in its current context—the context in which the journalists interviewed create and evaluate accounts of the world.

Postmodernism, a major part of the intellectual backdrop of the early twenty-first century, runs radically counter to professional journalism's professed desire to—in the words of the Society of Professional Journalists (SPJ) Code of Ethics—"seek truth and report it."[34] In the words of Hilary Lawson, "If relativism initiated an unsettling of truth and objectivity post-modernism is an attempt to engage in the complete dismantling of the edifice."[35] If the world is built on images and words, and not on a deeper reality, it is difficult to justify a broad claim to pursue truth as a professional. As noted earlier, postmodernism does underline the importance of narratives for shaping the world in which people live. But it calls into serious question whether journalists can evaluate their work in terms of how it advances or hinders understanding of truth.

Despite the postmodernist critique of truth, however, scholarly cases for its importance and use are still being made. An interesting recent argument applied to communication comes from Clifford Christians,[36] drawing on the work of German philosopher Hans Jonas.[37] He argues that humans' natural regard for the sacredness and preservation of life provides a "protonorm" that creates a oneness of purpose among humans. Although this valuing of life is present regardless of whether people stop to reflect on ethical principles, Christians says that on reflection, "we recognize that it entails such basic ethical principles as human dignity, truth, and nonviolence."[38] In this view, the importance of communicating truth rests on something deeper than philosophical debate.

Truth is a value whose recognition crosses cultures and religions. It is fundamental, for example, to Arab Islamic and Latin American communication, to Buddhist thought, and to communication among many Native tribes including the Shuswap of Canada.[39]

Professional journalists[40] and journalism organizations have consistently held up truth as an important ethical value. It is the first of four ethical values listed in the Society of Professional Journalists Code of Ethics,[41] and it or related ideas appear in codes of other U.S. journalism organizations such as the Radio-Television News Directors Association[42] and the National Press Photographers Association.[43] Truth also shows up widely in journalism ethics codes elsewhere in the world. A study of codes in Europe, North Africa, the Middle East, and Muslim Asia found that "'Truth,' 'accuracy,' and 'objectivity' are almost consensual cornerstones of journalism ethics as documented in professional codes."[44]

In professional usage, truth encompasses accuracy, honesty, lack of distortion or misrepresentation, and fairness.[45] It also implies thoroughness in both depth and breadth of reporting. Truth means reflecting a variety of views and the voices of people who may not have power or official status. As the SPJ Code says, expressing an oft-stated goal of journalism, "Give voice to the voiceless."[46]

Whether pursuing truth means striving for objectivity is likely to prompt more debate among journalists. Ettema and Glasser note that objectivity was dropped as a stated goal in the most recent revision of the SPJ Code in 1996. At the same time, they contend that even investigative reporters, whose business is to bring moral wrongdoing to public light, might still regard themselves as able to weigh facts in a disinterested way apart from values.[47] However, journalists who see themselves as able to be objective run up against a wall of criticism of the notion of objectivity that has been built over decades by scholars inside and outside media studies. These scholars have raised a wide range of issues including the influence of individuals' standpoints on the world, the limitations of language, organizational pressures on journalists, and the perpetuation of current social injustices.[48]

Still, the difficulties connected with objectivity do not require journalists to abandon truth as an ethical responsibility because truth encompasses more than objectivity. The notion that journalists should pursue truth and tell truth to their audiences—even if this can be done only incompletely and imperfectly—can help to foster thoughtful evaluation of how journalists use writing techniques. Truth is the primary principle underlying the discussion of journalistic techniques in the rest of this book, though the discussion will continue to explore its limitations, too. Issues of truth are relevant across all of these techniques—for example, in choices about how to attribute information about scenes, how to represent a speaker's words in quotes, and when to spell out the meaning or significance of an event in the writer's voice rather than from sources. Many interviewees mentioned truth—or related ideas such as accuracy, context, honesty, and fairness—as the most important ethical issue related to journalistic writing.

Compassion

Compassion is more evidently relevant in relation to some techniques than others, but it is still a core ethical concern, too. Among the key sources of thinking about this ethical value historically and currently have been religions. Without glossing over the great differences in many of their basic teachings, Xinzhong Yao notes that religions have considerable common ethical ground: "From the Buddhist 'Five Prohibitions' to the Judaic 'Ten Commandments' (except for the theological items), from Christian 'agape as neighbour-love' to the Confucian 'jen as loving all,' we find a common condemnation of selfishness, egoism and indifference to others' suffering, and a common praise of sincerity, altruism and idealism."[49] In Confucianism, for example, the idea of *jen* calls for exercising unconditional love toward one's family and, extending outward, to all others. The teaching of Jesus called for love for one's neighbor—echoing a command of the Jewish scriptures—and even loving one's enemies. A model of compassion toward others is displayed in Jesus' parable of the Good Samaritan, in which a man crossed ethnic boundaries and went out of his way to care for another man left beaten beside a road. This kind of teaching placed a high priority on care for human needs. Journalists such as investigative reporters who highlight injustices and serious needs—and narrative writers who tell the stories of hurting individuals—do not always do so out of religious motives, but religious perspectives strongly support their work. Clifford Christians's "proto-norm" of respect for life also provides ethical support for such an exercise of compassion—without reference to religious foundations—because compassion naturally grows out of respect for life.

Similarly, feminist scholars have emphasized what has often been called an ethic of care, which places a priority on the care that develops and is exercised in relationships with others—rather than placing ethics in the realm of abstract rules.[50] Gilligan, commenting on how a woman she interviewed regarded activities of care, wrote: "The ideal of care is thus an activity of relationship, of seeing and responding to need, taking care of the world by sustaining the web of connection so that no one is left alone."[51] This perspective, like communitarianism, makes mutual concern central to the exercise of ethics.

The ethical value of compassion is also connected with the notion of minimizing harm. Avoiding harm to others—sometimes formally called "nonmaleficence"—has long been a concern in medical ethics.[52] It has also been an important part of professional thinking about journalism ethics in recent years, as evidenced in the SPJ Code of Ethics. Under that heading, the code urges journalists to "treat sources, subjects and colleagues as human beings deserving of respect" and to exercise "compassion for those who may be affected adversely by news coverage." Journalists should be particularly sensitive "when dealing with children and inexperienced sources or subjects." They should be careful in dealing with grieving people and respect the privacy of people who are not officials or others seeking public attention.[53] Concerns about privacy are common to codes of journalistic ethics in a number of other countries, too.[54]

In relation to the ethics of journalistic writing techniques, compassion is relevant both to decisions that a writer or editor may make about treatment of topics and story sources and to the ways that writing devices may stir compassion among readers. Though few interviewees mentioned it directly as an ethical issue, it was implied in concerns of a number of them about care toward people who are not used to being in the media spotlight and toward sources in sensitive investigative pieces, and in a desire to connect emotionally with the audience through stories. Considering how writing may stir compassion is an important issue for evaluating narrative techniques because of the strong emotional hold that powerful narratives may create, especially since they often focus on the struggles of individuals.

Caution is warranted in the application of compassion as an ethical value. For one thing, it may not be clearly relevant in stories that do not have a strong emotional component and do not focus on an individual's or a community's problems. Beyond that, if it is carelessly applied, it can compromise another ethical value of journalism: independence. Writers and editors may, in the larger public interest, publish potentially hurtful information over the objection of a source. The best journalists are sensitive to how their work affects others without being enslaved by that concern. Compassion is an implicit goal in much news (including investigative) and feature writing. If the journalist did not want the reader to care about the topic and the people, there would be little point in writing the story. It is still up to the reader whose compassion is stirred to respond or not respond.

Chapter 2 will examine a technique that raises important issues of compassion as well as truth: anecdotes.

Notes

1. See David L. Protess et al., *The Journalism of Outrage: Investigative Reporting and Agenda Building in America* (New York: Guilford Press, 1991); Judith Serrin and William Serrin, eds., *Muckraking! The Journalism that Changed America* (New York: New Press, 2002); Cecelia Tichi, *Exposés and Excess: Muckraking in America, 1900/2000* (Philadelphia: University of Pennsylvania Press, 2004).

2. For examples, see recent Pulitzer Prize winners in the feature writing category at www.pulitzer.org (accessed May 24, 2006).

3. See winners in the explanatory journalism category at www.pulitzer.org.

4. Sonia Nazario, "Defeated Seven Times, a Boy Again Faces 'the Beast,'" *Los Angeles Times*, October 2, 2002, A1 (Home Ed.), infoweb.newsbank.com.

5. Sonia Nazario, telephone interview by the author, March 11, 2005.

6. "Note About Sources for Chapter Three," *Los Angeles Times*, October 2, 2002, A20 (Home Ed.), infoweb.newsbank.com.

7. Richard E. Meyer, remarks prepared for presentation at Nieman Conference on Narrative Journalism, Harvard University, December 2004.

8. Richard E. Meyer, January 24, 2003, letter nominating "Enrique's Journey" for 2003 Pulitzer Prize in feature writing.

9. Richard Read, "Strands in a Broken Web," *Oregonian*, October 21, 1998, A1 (Sunrise Ed.), infoweb.newsbank.com.

10. Richard Read, interview by the author, June 25, 2004, Portland, Oregon.

11. Jack Hart, January 26, 1999, letter nominating "The French Fry Connection" for the 1999 Pulitzer Prize in explanatory reporting.

12. Pam Maples, "Bringing Fear Home: U.S. Women Face Pervasive Threat of Violence, Often at the Hands of Husbands, Boyfriends," *Dallas Morning News*, June 6, 1993, 1A (Home Final Ed.), infoweb.newsbank.com.

13. Pam Maples, interview by the author, September 14, 2004, Dallas.

14. Maples, "Bringing Fear Home."

15. Victoria Loe, "Confronting Trauma: Question of 'Why?' Haunts Victims of Rape, Physical Abuse," *Dallas Morning News*, June 13, 1993, 1A (Home Final Ed.), infoweb.newsbank.com.

16. For more detailed discussion of Victoria Loe Hicks's approach to this story, see chapter 7.

17. Ralph Langer, letter nominating "Violence Against Women" for the 1994 Pulitzer Prize in international reporting.

18. Hayden White, "The Value of Narrativity in the Representation of Reality," *Critical Inquiry* 7, no. 1 (Autumn 1980): 5.

19. Walter R. Fisher, "Narration as a Human Communication Paradigm: The Case of Public Moral Argument," *Communication Monographs* 51 (March 1984): 6–7. For more on his development of the narrative paradigm, see Walter R. Fisher, *Human Communication as Narration: Toward a Philosophy of Reason, Value, and Action* (Columbia: University of South Carolina Press, 1987).

20. Clifford G. Christians, John P. Ferré, and P. Mark Fackler, *Good News: Social Ethics and the Press* (New York: Oxford University Press, 1993), 93. For an overview of communitarian media ethics and communitarian theory in general, see David A. Craig, "Communitarian Journalism(s): Clearing Conceptual Landscapes," *Journal of Mass Media Ethics* 11, no. 2 (1996): 107–18.

21. Carol Gilligan, *In a Different Voice: Psychological Theory and Women's Development* (Cambridge, Mass.: Harvard University Press, 1982); Nel Noddings, *Caring: A Feminine Approach to Ethics and Moral Education* (Berkeley: University of California Press, 1984).

22. Richard Rorty, *Contingency, Irony, and Solidarity* (Cambridge, Eng.: Cambridge University Press, 1989), 51–52 (italics in the original). "Liberal" here does not mean politically liberal versus conservative. It refers instead to a democratic society that is built on the free exchange of ideas.

23. Sarah Kozloff, "Narrative Theory and Television," in *Channels of Discourse, Reassembled: Television and Contemporary Criticism*, ed. Robert C. Allen (Chapel Hill: University of North Carolina Press), 67–68.

24. Mark Currie, *Postmodern Narrative Theory* (New York: St. Martin's, 1998), 1–2.

25. James S. Ettema and Theodore L. Glasser, *Custodians of Conscience: Investigative Journalism and Public Virtue* (New York: Columbia University Press, 1998), 116.

26. Michael Schudson, *The Power of News* (Cambridge, Mass.: Harvard University Press, 1995), 53–71.

27. Phyllis Frus, *The Politics and Poetics of Journalistic Narrative: The Timely and the Timeless* (Cambridge, Eng.: Cambridge University Press, 1994), 92.

28. Carolyn Kitch, "'Mourning in America': Ritual, Redemption, and Recovery in News Narrative After September 11," *Journalism Studies* 4, no. 2 (2003): 213–24.

29. Victoria Loe Hicks, interview by the author, September 14, 2004, Dallas.

30. Thanks to Dr. Edmund Lambeth of the University of Missouri School of Journalism for pointing out the lens analogy in earlier personal conversations about media scholarship.

31. Because of its concern for providing examples of excellent work, this discussion also implies the kind of concern for cultivation of practical wisdom that is emphasized in Aristotle's ethics of virtue—although the perspective of this book is not primarily virtue-based. In addition, compassion may be viewed as part of the ethics of care rather than a matter of duty.

32. Sissela Bok, *Lying: Moral Choice in Public and Private Life*, 2nd ed. (New York: Vintage Books, 1999), 5.

33. Barry Allen, *Truth in Philosophy* (Cambridge, Mass.: Harvard University Press, 1993), though not offering a comprehensive account of truth's philosophical history, talks in some depth about key shifts in views of truth in philosophy.

34. Society of Professional Journalists Code of Ethics, www.spj.org/ethics_code .asp (accessed May 24, 2006).

35. Hilary Lawson, "Stories about Stories," in *Dismantling Truth: Reality in the Post-Modern World*, ed. Hilary Lawson and Lisa Appignanesi (London: Weidenfeld and Nicolson, 1989), xii.

36. Clifford G. Christians, "The Ethics of Being in a Communications Context," in *Communication Ethics and Universal Values*, ed. Clifford Christians and Michael Traber (Thousand Oaks, Calif.: Sage, 1997), 3–23. See also Clifford Christians and Kaarle Nordenstreng, "Social Responsibility Worldwide," *Journal of Mass Media Ethics* 19, no. 1 (2004): 3–28. For additional justifications for truth as an ethical value in communication, see Dietmar Mieth, "The Basic Norm of Truthfulness: Its Ethical Justification and Universality," in Christians and Traber, *Communication Ethics*, 87–104.

37. Hans Jonas, *The Imperative of Responsibility: In Search of an Ethics for the Technological Age*, trans. Hans Jonas with David Herr (Chicago: University of Chicago Press, 1984).

38. Christians, "The Ethics of Being," 12–13.

39. Christians and Nordenstreng, "Social Responsibility Worldwide," 22; Thomas W. Cooper, *A Time Before Deception: Truth in Communication, Culture, and Ethics* (Santa Fe, N.M.: Clear Light Publishers, 1998), 135.

40. Wesley G. Pippert, a long-time wire service reporter, offered a thoughtful discussion of truth in *An Ethics of News: A Reporter's Search for Truth* (Washington, D.C.: Georgetown University Press, 1989).

41. Society of Professional Journalists Code of Ethics.

42. Code of Ethics and Professional Conduct, Radio-Television News Directors Association, www.rtnda.org/ethics/coe.html (accessed May 24, 2006).

43. National Press Photographers Association Code of Ethics, www.nppa.org/professional_development/business_practices/ethics.html (accessed May 24, 2006).

44. Kai Hafez, "Journalism Ethics Revisited: A Comparison of Ethics Codes in Europe, North Africa, the Middle East, and Muslim Asia," *Political Communication* 19, no. 2 (2002): 225–50.

45. All of these elements are reflected in subpoints in the Society of Professional Journalists Code of Ethics.

46. Society of Professional Journalists Code of Ethics.

47. Ettema and Glasser, *Custodians of Conscience*, 9–10.

48. For a review of critiques of objectivity in media studies, see Meenakshi Gigi Durham, "On the Relevance of Standpoint Epistemology to the Practice of Journalism," *Communication Theory* 8, no. 2 (May 1998): 117–40. See also, for example, Ettema and Glasser, *Custodians of Conscience*; Carlin Romano, "What? The Grisly Truth About Bare Facts," in Robert Karl Manoff and Michael Schudson, eds., *Reading the News* (New York: Pantheon, 1986), 38–78. For a vigorous defense of objectivity, see Michael Ryan, "Journalistic Ethics, Objectivity, Existential Journalism, Standpoint Epistemology, and Public Journalism," *Journal of Mass Media Ethics* 16, no. 1 (2001): 3–22. For a broader philosophical discussion of the problem of objectivity, see Joseph Margolis, "Objectivity as a Problem: An Attempt at an Overview," *Annals of the American Academy of Political and Social Science*, vol. 560, *The Future of Fact* (November 1998): 55–68.

49. Xinzhong Yao, *Confucianism and Christianity: A Comparative Study of Jen and Agape* (Brighton, Eng.: Sussex Academic Press, 1996), 11.

50. See, for example, Gilligan, *In a Different Voice*; Noddings, *Caring*; Mary Jeanne Larrabee, ed., *An Ethic of Care: Feminist and Interdisciplinary Perspectives* (New York: Routledge, 1993); Daryl Koehn, *Rethinking Feminist Ethics: Care, Trust and Empathy* (London: Routledge, 1998); and Vanessa Siddle Walker and John R. Snarey, eds., *Race-ing Moral Formation: African American Perspectives on Care and Justice* (New York: Teachers College Press, 2004).

51. Gilligan, *In a Different Voice*, 62.

52. Tom L. Beauchamp and James F. Childress, *Principles of Biomedical Ethics*, 5th ed. (New York: Oxford University Press, 2001).

53. Society of Professional Journalists Code of Ethics.

54. Hafez, "Journalism Ethics Revisited."

Anecdotes

Journalists for both print and broadcast media often use anecdotes about individuals to illustrate larger points, particularly in leads. Feature writers use them to provide insight about the life of a person they are portraying in depth. Five decades ago, Rudolph Flesch urged writers to try to draw readers into stories by using anecdotal leads about everyday people trying to overcome obstacles.[1] The anecdotal-lead approach was popularized by the *Wall Street Journal* and copied by newspapers around the country.

Anecdotal leads have become so popular that some journalists see them as overused. Dean P. Baquet, managing editor of the *Los Angeles Times* until he became editor in August 2005, said: "I just think sometimes writers and editors, to show that they can write and edit, will overdo it. On occasion I'll pick up the paper and almost every story has an anecdotal lead. And that's pretty monotonous." Worse, they can cover up for poor reporting. As Baquet put it: "I think that sometimes people use anecdotal leads as crutches. I don't have the story, but I've got this hell of an anecdote, so I'm going to use that as my lead and then sort of do a lot of mush around it."[2] Anecdotal leads may also tax the patience of busy readers. *Times* readers' representative Jamie Gold, who fields complaints and praise from the audience, said readers used to complain about them—and some still do despite efforts to reduce their length. "I can't count how many letters I get and got from readers saying whatever happened to who, what, when, where, and how? Lots of e-mails and letters along those lines."[3]

Still, there are good reasons for writers to use anecdotal leads if they approach them thoughtfully. Michael Merschel, an assistant features editor at the *Dallas Morning News*, noted that anecdotal leads can become formulaic: "'Bill Smith was angry about his property taxes.' Quote: 'I sure am angry about my property taxes.' Lead: 'But the city council raised property taxes again.'" At their best, however, anecdotes can help newspapers serve readers: "The internet has us beat on speed and TV has us beat on images, and we're never going to catch up. But we can give context and we can give writing that lets people really digest what's going on. We can't do it if we're using writing gimmicks, but we can if we're using thoughtful writing."[4]

Thoughtfully crafted anecdotes carry power. It is that power that calls for careful consideration of their ethical implications—not so they can be discarded as a technique but so they can be used in ways that serve readers best. This chapter will examine the power of anecdotes, explore their ethical benefits and difficulties, and suggest some ways they could be used better. The discussion will focus on anecdotal leads but will extend to other uses of anecdotes, including whole stories that explore the lives and struggles of individuals through vivid scenes.

The Power of Anecdotes

Gina Kolata, a science reporter for the *New York Times*, pointed to both the power and the difficulties of anecdotes in a 1997 interview:

> I think anecdotes are actually almost too powerful. I always call it the "tyranny of the anecdote." You have to be really careful with anecdotes because people will remember the anecdote and it will mean more to them than anything else you say. So you have to be very, very careful, I think, about how you use them, but I think that they're so powerful that they sort of cry out to be used if they can.[5]

Journalists' instincts about the power of anecdotes have been supported by research on the use of examples about individuals, such as anecdotes, in places including news coverage. Studies have found that examples do shape people's perceptions of social issues. Among the findings:[6]

- Using examples can overwhelm the influence of broader figures or statements about how frequent or typical an event is.[7] In one study, subjects shown an article about a welfare recipient and an interview with a prison guard changed their minds about the population as a whole, regardless of what kind of information they received about how typical the case was.[8]

- Different distributions of exemplars have differing effects on how people perceive issues. Researchers varied the ratio of examples to counterexamples in a story about keeping off weight after dieting. The audience's perception of how commonly people regained weight proved most accurate when the examples represented the situation in the broader population.[9] Another study found that the perception of majority and minority opinions on public issues followed the distribution of examples.[10] Other scholars found that changes in the kinds of exemplars used in a news report on the plight of family farmers altered readers' perceptions of how prevalent family farm failures were.[11]

- Using examples from extraordinary or highly emotional cases also affects what the audience perceives. Researchers found that estimates of the frequency of deaths in carjackings increased as exemplars were tilted more and more toward the unusual case of a fatal carjacking.[12] A study of television news stories[13] found that examples using emotional victims fostered perceptions that problems of food poisoning and random violence were more severe than when unemotional or no victim examples were used.

- Using quotes in examples influences audiences, too. Direct, one-sided personal testimony in print reports changed perceptions of amusement park safety.[14] Personal testimony about the plight of family farmers swayed readers' views on the issue.[15]

Taken together, research on the power of examples underlines the importance of carefully considering the ethical choices involved in anecdote use.

The Ethics of Anecdotes

A number of ethical benefits and difficulties with anecdotes became clear in the interviews with journalists. These comments from writers and editors connect with the ethical concerns noted in chapter 1: truth and compassion.

Ethical Benefits
Well-crafted anecdotes engage readers' interest in stories that they might otherwise pass over. They simplify issues and shed light on how they affect people. They provide insight into people's lives and may foster empathy for their struggles and needs. In these ways, they provide truth with greater texture and have the potential, at least, to stir compassion among readers.

Drawing in Readers and Simplifying Issues

The time pressures of people's daily lives and the lure of competing news sources make it hard to get their attention—especially attention that lasts long enough for them to gain significant insight about an issue or a person. Done well, leads that focus on people can give readers a reason to stick with a story they might otherwise throw aside after the first few paragraphs.

Los Angeles Times investigative reporters Scott Glover and Matt Lait, who work as a team, tried to draw readers into a story on a prison killing in this way:

> WASCO, Calif.—When Gary Avila arrived at Wasco State Prison two months ago, the 18-year-old was ushered into an 8-by-10 cell that was already home to another inmate—a psychiatric patient who had been deemed too dangerous to share a cell with anyone.
>
> By the time dawn broke on Avila's first night behind bars, he was dead, a bloody bedsheet looped around his neck.
>
> Inside the cell, Paul Posada paced back and forth, mumbling to himself.
>
> "Yeah, I did it," Posada allegedly told a prison lieutenant minutes after the discovery of Avila's body. "He messed up."[16]

As Lait put it in discussing their approach:

> It's a more gripping top than "An 18-year-old youth was killed in prison Friday night." You're putting him in there—you're painting the dimension of the cell, 8 by 10. In there was essentially a crazy man who shouldn't be in there with anybody else. I think his age, the fact that it's his first night in prison kind of draws you in there. With a bloody bedsheet wrapped around his neck—that kind of stuff I think would draw you into the story a little bit more than a straight hard news lead.[17]

Glover noted that a hard news lead might lose readers who are not sympathetic to what happens to prisoners.[18]

Although some busy—or unsympathetic—readers might still decide to stop reading, this approach has the potential to draw people in by showing them an injustice against one young person, not just a set of dry facts. They may leave the story with some truth about prison life that they did not know before.

Anecdotes are particularly useful for drawing readers into stories about complex issues because they can simplify difficult topics. Leo C. Wolinsky, the *Times*'s deputy managing editor and later managing editor, cited the alternative minimum tax as an example of a topic that would be difficult for readers to navigate. "How do you get somebody to read something like that? And if you do, how do you get them to identify what the heck it is? So if you can give a human example of something, you can get them into it. I think that there is an advantage there—if used properly."[19] In ethical terms, it more fully meets the responsibility of truth telling[20] by clarifying readers' understanding about a topic and giving them reason to read on and learn more.

Humanizing the Truth: How Trends and Issues Affect People
A good anecdote is also ethical in that it reflects some broader truth that a story is trying to convey. As Vernon Loeb, California investigations editor for the *Los Angeles Times*, put it, a well-chosen anecdotal lead is "the microcosm of the story."[21] In stories about issues and trends, anecdotes are powerful devices partly because they are so effective at showing how an issue that might seem distant to readers—such as dangerous practices in prisons—affects real people. Showing the truth about human impact enlivens stories whether they are about police, government, business, or education.

Andy Dworkin, a medical writer for the *Oregonian*, said anecdotes can help show the impact of medical developments beyond doctors or researchers:

> In some cases it's a lot easier to get access to the researchers or the doctors that have a stake of some sort in talking to you. We're talking about the condition and you can lose sight of the fact that there are always patients or research subjects who are part of the equation also and are affected by all of this. . . . You can write entire stories about medicine without—and medical research— without really mentioning patients. You can mention viruses and doctors and researchers, and you never have to bring a patient in. And so that is an important part of the story that can get left out if you don't focus it back on patients. And anecdotes are a powerful way to focus it back on patients. Even though it's just one person standing in for the broader category it does make people think about that and the way it affects them.[22]

By showing how medical developments affect the lives of patients and their families, reporters reflect the truth of these developments more fully.

A *Times* series about conservators—for-profit guardians who manage the affairs of elderly people—provides an example of an anecdotal lead that captured the essence of a story by showing human impact. The series opened with this lead:

> Helen Jones sits in a wheelchair, surrounded by strangers who control her life.
> She is not allowed to answer the telephone. Her mail is screened. She cannot spend her own money.

A child of the Depression, Jones, 87, worked hard for decades, driving rivets into World War II fighter planes, making neckties, threading bristles into nail-polish brushes. She saved obsessively, putting away $560,000 for her old age.

Her life changed three years ago, when a woman named Melodie Scott told a court in San Bernardino that Jones was unable to manage for herself. Without asking Jones, a judge made Scott—someone she had never met—her legal guardian.

Scott is a professional conservator.

It was her responsibility to protect Jones and conserve her nest egg. So far, Scott has spent at least $200,000 of it. The money has gone to pay Scott's fees, fill Jones' house with new appliances she did not want and hire attendants to supervise her around the clock, among other expenses.

Once Jones grasped what was happening, she found a lawyer and tried, unsuccessfully, to end Scott's hold on her. "I don't want to be a burden to anyone," she told a judge, almost apologetically. "I just wanted to be on my own."

Jones' world has narrowed. She used to call Dial-A-Ride and go to the market, or sit in her driveway chatting with neighbors.

Now she spends her days watching television in her living room in Yucaipa, amid pots of yellow plastic flowers and lamps with no shades. The caretakers rarely take her from her house, except to see the free movie each Friday at the local senior center.

"I'm frustrated, because I don't know my way out," she said, sitting within earshot of one of Scott's aides. "There must be a way out."[23]

Loeb said that lead tells in microcosm the much larger story of older people's lives being taken over by conservators without their knowledge.[24] Reflecting on the ethics of this kind of lead, Loeb said, "The idea is you want people to read this stuff because we think it is important." Therefore, he sees it as ethically defensible to look for a powerful device as long as that device is factually accurate and fairly represents what is happening to people in a story—rather than portraying an isolated tragic moment.[25]

Providing Insight about Individuals' Lives and Struggles

Just as anecdotes humanize broader issues and developments in news stories or trend pieces, they also provide insight about individuals in feature stories. Sometimes the anecdotes are in the lead, but they may also be scenes throughout a story—or they may make up the whole story.

Vivian McInerny, a feature writer for the *Oregonian*, used this lengthy but vivid lead about a couple's choice to allow their unborn child with Down syndrome to live:

Ultrasounds, blood samples and white-coated conversations in grave voices stole most of the morning, leaving Tacee Webb emotionally exhausted and physically famished. Heath Webb drove around Legacy Emanuel Hospital & Health Center looking for a place to eat. They ended up at Red Robin.

Colorful balloons bobbed on ribbons. Laughter spilled out from the kitchen. Waitresses with name tags and service smiles carried bottomless baskets of steak fries. Everywhere they looked that February day in 2003, Tacee and Heath saw happy families with perfect babies.

They slid into a booth, talking in whispers to carve out some privacy.

"How could this be happening to us?" Tacee remembers thinking.

At Tacee's age—30—the odds were in favor of delivering a normal, healthy baby. But results of the amniocentesis test were conclusive: The baby she was carrying had Down syndrome.

Heath, 29, pushed aside the ketchup and packets of sugar to make room for the armful of books the doctors had given them. Four of the books explained Down syndrome in technical terms. There was a picture book for Palace, Tacee's 6-year-old daughter from a previous marriage, about having a sibling with Down syndrome. A sixth book offered a terrible hint of what their future could hold: It was about grieving an unborn child.

Over half-empty bowls of teriyaki rice and lip-smudged water glasses, Tacee and Heath laid out their most intimate fears. Could they be good parents to a Down syndrome child? Were they selfish to consider terminating the pregnancy? Could a retarded person share in the hopes and dreams that make us fully human? Or was their child doomed by a chromosomal fluke to wander, lost, in a kind of twilight half-life?

When Tacee and Heath stood to leave, they looked back at one of those happy families with a perfect baby at a nearby table. They noticed something for the first time: The baby had Down syndrome.

The Webbs don't attend formal church services. But seeing that particular baby served as a reminder that perceptions shift and change, emotions soar and crash, and that a good life is not so much about finding balance as it is riding the ups and downs with grace.[26]

McInerny said this scene of contrasts provided insight about the couple, their view of the world, and their struggle:

They're in this very boring, routine restaurant and very happy little balloons bobbing on strings and they're going through this turmoil, personal turmoil, and the juxtaposition of that I thought was really interesting, it was absolutely true. And Tacee, the woman, was very aware of it, that they had chosen this very odd place to have this very heavy conversation, and then the fact that in this surreal scene they see a Down syndrome kid. . . . And it was like an omen. And it was such a perfect story to open because it was really what they were about, searching for this dilemma, what's right, what's ethical about having this child, and then they were thrown what they saw as little omens. . . . It tells the truth of who they are, dealing with all this turmoil while life goes on and every-thing's normal. And the connection that they have, and the way they view the world, that they would look for omens.[27]

This anecdote, then, provides more than an engaging opening; it sets up the rest of the story by giving readers a kind of truth about this couple. The lead deepens people's insight about who they are and how they struggled.

For writers and editors who work with narrative features, the use and im-pact of anecdotes are part of the broader issue of how to tell stories that give insight into people's lives and struggles. Often these stories contain multiple scenes that are each anecdotes—woven together to provide a nuanced per-spective on who a person is. That perspective may connect with issues and struggles that are common to humans.

Tom Hallman, Jr., a narrative writer at the *Oregonian*, won the 2001 Pulitzer Prize for feature writing for "The Boy Behind the Mask," a series about Sam Lightner, a boy with a deformed face, and his choice to have sur-gery to try to change his appearance. The first of the series' four parts in-cludes this scene about his visit to a high school open house as a fourteen-year-old:

"Ready for this, Sam?" asks David Lightner, a weathered jewelry designer who saves money by riding a motorcycle 25 miles to work. Sam nods his head and replies with a garbled sound, wheezing and breathless, the sound of an old man who has smoked too long and too hard.

"OK," his father replies. "Let's go."

His sister and brother watch from the window as Sam and his parents walk to a Honda Accord that has 140,000 hard miles on the odometer. The boy gets in the back seat, and the Honda backs down the driveway.

Just a few blocks from home, Sam senses someone looking at him. After a lifetime of stares, he can feel the glances.

The Accord is stopped at a light, waiting to turn west onto Northeast Sandy Boulevard, when a woman walking a poodle catches sight of him. She makes no pretense of being polite, of averting her eyes. When the light changes, the woman swivels her head as if watching a train leave a station.

Grant High School's open house attracts more than 1,500 students and par-ents. Even though they've come early, the Lightners must search for a parking place. Sam's father circles the streets until he finds one nearly 15 blocks from the school.

The family steps out onto the sidewalk and walks through the dark neigh-borhood. As Sam passes under a streetlight, a dark-green Range Rover full of teen-age boys turns onto the street. A kid wearing a baseball cap points at the boy. The car slows. The windows fill with faces, staring and pointing.

Sam walks on.

Soon, the streets fill with teen-agers on their way to Grant. Sam recognizes a girl who goes to his school, Gregory Heights Middle School. Sam has a secret crush on her. She has brown hair, wavy, and a smile that makes his hands sweat and his heart race when he sees her in class.

"Hi, Sam," she says.

He nods.

"Hi," he says.

The boy's parents fall behind, allowing their son and the girl to walk side by side. She does most of the talking.

He's spent a lifetime trying to make himself understood, and he's found alternatives to the words that are so hard for him to shape. He uses his good eye and hand gestures to get his point across.

Two blocks from Grant, kids jam the streets. The wavy-haired girl subtly, discreetly, falls behind. When the boy slows to match her step, she hurries ahead. Sam lets her go and walks alone.

Grant, a great rectangular block of brick, looms in the distance. Every light in the place is on. Tonight, there are no shadows.

He arrives at the north door and stands on the steps, looking in through the windowpanes. Clusters of girls hug and laugh. Boys huddle under a sign announcing a basketball game.

Sam grabs the door handle, hesitates for the briefest of moments and pulls the door open. He steps inside.

He walks into noise and laughter and chaos, into the urgency that is all about being 14 years old.

Into a place where nothing is worse than being different.[28]

This scene is only one—the second—in a story that links these anecdotes to provide insight about Sam, his life, and his struggles. Readers found the stories so powerful that the newspaper received more than 3,500 phone calls, letters, and e-mails in response.[29]

Managing editor Jack Hart, who was the primary editor on "The Boy Behind the Mask," said a story narrative such as this tries to "tap some larger thematic truth. The trick is in showing readers that it applies to them in some way. And by telling them through the eyes of a protagonist you can show them how it applies to them." Hart talked about the larger truth about humanity that emerges from Sam's story:

Here's a kid who's incredibly deformed, one of the worst facial deformities you can imagine. How do you get readers to relate to him? Well, in a larger sense this is a story about acceptance—acceptance by the outside world, and acceptance by one's peers, and acceptance of yourself—and maturity. It's a coming-of-age story. It's learning to accept yourself that's the key sign of maturity in that story. So readers need to be able to, first of all, feel empathy and sympathy for a kid who is hideously deformed. And two, see that he may be an extreme example of a problem but he is an example of a problem that we all face, at least in American society where, as you get to a certain age, the judgments of your peers become very important to you and a source of anxiety to you. So, every reader who went from middle school or junior high into high school can understand on a really felt level what Sam's complication is. So, I think having a character like that allows you to achieve that sense of identification. It's not an abstraction. It's not just somebody providing you with information. You can share an emotional reality that illustrates something that applies, in the best work, to all human beings in all places in all times.[30]

Hallman reflected on the kind of truth that emerges from a story like this:

There are certain core elements about the way we live and the way we are as humans that I try to get at, too, in my stories, and that's about how you live and how you feel and how you move through the world. I think those truths ring true with readers and they know it's right because they've lived that or it just feels right. So it's not necessarily the factual kind of truth as much as the emotional truth.[31]

Hart's and Hallman's comments show how both truth and compassion are wrapped up in the message of an anecdote or a story built on anecdotes. Through powerfully told anecdotes and larger narratives, readers can gain insight about our common humanity—but it is not bare intellectual knowledge; it is wrapped up with the compassion that comes from identifying emotionally with a person's joys and struggles.

Extended narratives multiply the potential power of single anecdotes by giving readers insight into multiple facets of a person's life. Beatriz Terrazas, a feature writer at the *Dallas Morning News*, noted that features about individuals can provide context about the lives of ordinary people—and the meaning of those lives—that short news stories cannot. Discussing a two-part narrative she did on two teenagers who died in a car accident,[32] she said it would have been easy to do a quick-hit story focused on drinking. "Drinking was a very small part of what those kids did. The context of their lives was much, much bigger, as it is with any person, and I think you can run into trouble with that. And I think that's why a lot of people have issues with the way we tell stories in journalism." She said her intent was "to show people that these two kids had meant something to this community."[33] She did that by going into depth about their lives and relationships, including anecdotes about them that took the picture beyond a caricature of teenagers who like to party.

Anecdotes, then, can do ethical good by showing readers why they should invest the time to gain truth of any kind from a story and can help to clarify that truth for readers. Beyond that, they can stir compassion as readers see the human impact of broad issues and trends, and as they look in-depth through a narrative lens at the lives and difficulties of individuals.

Ethical Difficulties

Although anecdotes carry power to do ethical good, they can create ethical problems, too—especially if they are used without careful thought. They may be interesting without reflecting the larger point of a story. They may poorly represent an issue or a person and skew the picture that readers take away. A powerfully written anecdote may bias people about an issue if it represents only one side, and even a more balanced one may be so engaging that it narrows the focus from a broader issue. At worst, anecdotes can leave a publication vulnerable to errors or even falsification.

Not Reflecting the Larger Point

One of the problems that journalists noted most often in the interviews is that an anecdote may not reflect or develop the larger point of a story. To provide truth that takes the story forward, an anecdote must do more than read in an interesting way.

Henry Fuhrmann, senior copy desk chief for business and more recently a deputy business editor at the *Los Angeles Times*, put it this way:

> It's got to work as an interesting scene, but it's got to help tell the story—can't just be gratuitous. It's got to be, if it's an anecdote in a story about John Kerry, it's got to be telling of a human being that we're talking about. It's got to somehow speak to a larger truth about him, or explain something that we later learn about him that we're telling about. It's got to be instructive. Otherwise it's just empty calories. It's not filling. I'm all for empty calories—I mean you've got to entertain here and there—but not always, and certainly not in a more serious story where you choose to use or write an anecdote to start out. It's got to fit into the larger theme.[14]

Sue Goetinck Ambrose, a science writer for the *Dallas Morning News*, said she does not use anecdotes at all. They would seldom work in her stories because she usually writes about laboratory research that may not even involve humans. But she is concerned that anecdotes will not convey enough information about the developments she covers—developments that take space to explain well. She said this in discussing an article about possible unintended results from the addition of folic acid to American diets:[35]

> I could have started out this folic acid story about a woman who had a baby with spina bifida and then after that she took her folic acid and her next two babies were healthy—and that has happened—and then moved into the point, well, where some researchers are wondering whether folic acid also does that thing. But how useful would that have been because it would take up a lot of space? I could really convey the message in one or two sentences, and you might just pull in some readers who think they're going to read about this woman and then they're not. It's kind of a red herring to me because there's a lot more in the story and you might lose readers that want to read about possible implications for cancer, autism or miscarriage—which I also went into in the story—if you push that further down in the story.[36]

Her comments underline the point that while, on one hand, an anecdotal lead may draw a reader into a story about a complex issue, limitations of space may make it more important to invest the space ensuring that all of the important issues in the story are covered.

Skewing the Picture

Anecdotes can skew the truth that readers take away from stories. They can fail to represent a broader issue well by focusing on a person whose situation is not typical or does not fit the facts of the rest of the story. They may oversimplify a situation. They may even convey an extreme case.

Roy Peter Clark, a senior scholar and writing teacher at the Poynter Institute for Media Studies, has questioned the notion that writers should focus on a figure who is typical: "As a writer, I reject the idea of the 'ordinary person.' I'm not sure any character should be chosen for a story because he or she is 'ordinary.' Sometimes a writer will 'cast' a character because he or she seems representative, and other times because the character is extraordinary."[37]

A blanket decree that anecdotes must always include the most typical person available would be foolish because it would point writers away from stories such as Sam Lightner's that look at people who are in some way unusual but offer insight or even inspiration to readers. Still, it is important ethically, especially for anecdotal leads that set up broader issues, to think carefully about the difficulties that lack of representativeness can create—as research on the power of examples suggests.

In practice, it is hard—sometimes impossible—to find people who fully represent an issue. Michael Arrieta-Walden, public editor of the *Oregonian* and later senior editor for online, pointed to a lead that illustrates the difficulty. The story, about a conflict between the Bush administration and the state over Oregon's medical-marijuana law, opened this way:

Travis Paulson was heading into the kitchen one recent morning to fix break-fast for himself and his 84-year-old mother, Loretta, when he noticed what appeared to be black-clad "ninja warriors" in his back yard.

It turned out to be a house call from the U.S. Drug Enforcement Administration. The agents took the marijuana plants Paulson had nurtured in a fiber-glass-walled grow area to heights of 12 feet, his day planner, laptop computer, checks intended for deposit, $3,300 in cash and several firearms from underneath his mother's bed.

According to Paulson, one of the agents remarked, "Gee, you're pretty obvious at what you're doing." To which Paulson, who has an Oregon license to grow medical marijuana, replied, "Why wouldn't I be?"

Because the federal government does not recognize Oregon's 1998 law permitting residents to grow marijuana for medicinal purposes. DEA [Drug Enforcement Administration] officials say they're simply enforcing federal laws.

The raid, which marked the second time in a year DEA agents have seized marijuana cultivated in Oregon for medicinal uses, is part of a larger conflict between the Bush administration and Oregon voters.[18]

Arrieta-Walden said the lead was supposed to exemplify the federal crack-down on medical-marijuana growers—a crackdown that some Oregonians saw as unfair. But later the story notes that the U.S. Drug Enforcement Administration said Travis Paulson was growing many more plants than he was allowed under the Oregon law. "So," Arrieta-Walden said, "that to me is an example where you need to choose anecdotes really carefully to represent your idea"—an example that was "off by, in this case, maybe 10 or 15 degrees." He pointed out that the anecdote could have been used in a richer way to highlight "a thorny issue"—that some people are truly growing marijuana for medical benefits while others have "side businesses."[39]

Although it is important to choose an anecdote that represents an issue as well as possible, it is also important not to adjust the anecdote to fit the needs of the broader story. Michael Finnegan, a state politics reporter for the *Los Angeles Times* who also covered the 2000 and 2004 presidential campaigns, said it is very difficult to find "a clean anecdote that tells exactly what is most convenient for the story you're telling." As an example, he cited this lead:

SACRAMENTO—In the gilded state Senate chamber one morning, Sen. Gloria Romero (D-Los Angeles) bemoaned the liquor industry's sway in the Legislature. She named booze lobbyist Aaron Read as a key opponent of her push to raise liquor taxes by $700 million a year.

But days later at a nearby restaurant, there was Read—who wants lawmakers to spare liquor as they look for ways to relieve the state's fiscal woes—in a crowd of lobbyists at a reception for Romero's reelection campaign. The door charge, for tamales and quesadillas, was $1,000, and a police group lobbying against budget cuts had bought Read a ticket.

These may be tough times for teachers facing layoffs and patients who fear hospital cuts. But the state fiscal crisis has been a boon to members of the Legislature in at least one respect: Lobbyists are responding to requests for campaign money with piles of $1,000 checks from clients seeking budget favors.[40]

Finnegan said the lead was " a little bit tortured" because the liquor lobbyist showed up at the fund-raiser, but a police group, not the liquor companies, had paid for his ticket.

It's more difficult for the reader to have the police thrown in there, and yet we wound up doing that when we were editing the story because it just wasn't fair otherwise. It made it look like the liquor company or the lobbyist himself were paying for that ticket. I think that often anecdotes have complications like that where it would be nice or convenient if the liquor company had paid for that ticket, but it didn't. . . . I think that we have an obligation to be very careful about what we choose as anecdotes, and make sure we're not leaving out something that's relevant and makes it not quite as clean as the journalist might like it to be.[41]

Finnegan's comments show the difficulty of carrying out the ethical obligation to be truthful in anecdotes—in particular, making them representative of an issue without distorting their details and oversimplifying the situation in the anecdote.

Another ethical difficulty from the standpoint of truth telling arises from some journalists' tendency to emphasize the extreme or unusual. Steve Blow, a Metro section columnist at the *Dallas Morning News*, said considering context is important when choosing anecdotes: "I think: have we really given an accurate portrayal of an event if we go and latch on to the most extreme person there? You know it makes for a vivid lead and a great photograph, but have you really accurately captured an event if you start out by talking about the most outrageous character there?" As an example, he cited stories about gay pride parades, in which journalists may tend to focus on the most flamboyant-looking person. More generally, he worries that portraying extremes may make readers cynical:

I think our training and our instinct is always just go for the wild, and I think readers in a way come to expect that maybe; they're going to read about it. Then it sort of creates a little bit of a cynicism, I guess, that they're going to read in a political debate, they're going to read about the maybe 45 seconds of emotional give and take. They really may have shed no light on anything but it was "Voices were raised"—that's going to become the lead. And then perhaps some really meaningful dialogue or exchange of information will be down in the body of the story, and so we just have to be careful not to succumb to that.[42]

Distortion of the broader picture of an event or issue, then, may diminish not only the opportunity that readers have to gain understanding, but also their interest in doing so.

Creating Bias

The power of anecdotes to stir compassion among readers can also create ethical problems because an emotionally engaging anecdote may slant a story toward one viewpoint at the expense of readers' understanding of other perspectives on an issue.

Frank Christlieb, a senior copy editor on the news copy desk at the *Dallas Morning News*, noted that it is difficult to use anecdotes well in stories about sensitive political issues. "You almost have to get both sides into that lead anecdote or else you're not being fair. I think that's something that is a challenge that reporters face and that copy editors face, recognizing that something is, right off the bat, is not balanced."[43] Jake Arnold, a copy editor at the *Oregonian*, cited health care stories as a place where empathy can obscure balanced understanding of an issue:

> If, for instance, you're writing a health care story—something about budgeting and health care—and you decide to humanize it, and you write about the person who just lost their health care, you've just slanted the story. It's no longer about the budget; it's about that family losing their money. Yes, that is the reality of the story, that if we cut health care a bunch of families are going to lose, but you're not getting both sides of the story. You're not getting the side of the story where Joe Smith's taxes aren't going up. There's always more to the story than just the guy down the block loses health care.[44]

Bob Steele, who has directed Poynter's ethics program and served as an ethics consultant in newsrooms, has noted that stories with anecdotes focusing only on, for example, a victim of industrial pollution are not authentic because they neglect the fact that many other people have a stake in the issue.[45] Sandra Mims Rowe, editor of the *Oregonian*, stated the problem this way in an interview:

> It's trite in terms of how much journalism has used the poor mother who's losing this or that service or benefit to personify something, and that again . . . doesn't take into account what choices the agency or the bureaucrats made

when they started that particular program and what other programs they might have dropped. It doesn't take into account the arguments of those who believe that this particular government service or that one is inefficient.[46]

Rowe believes that journalism—beyond just the anecdotal lead—does not always fully portray the choices that people and institutions face and the competing values that are at issue in those choices.

Some readers do indeed see bias in anecdotes. Steele was quoted in *Quill* magazine commenting on a finding of the American Society of Newspaper Editors Credibility Project. He said some readers "believe anecdotal leads can improperly frame a story, giving inappropriate weight to the anecdote that opens the story," and that, for example, "stories about human services that start with an anecdotal lead about a recipient of government funding are inherently slanted and biased."[47]

Gold, the *Los Angeles Times* readers' representative, said some readers do complain about stories that put a face to a subject as showing sympathy for one side. She mentioned a story with this lead as an example:

> With three sons and her mother to care for, Flora Andrade finds that her wages as a Santa Monica hotel housekeeper run out long before her family's needs do.
> "I can't pay for my rent, my bills, my food," she said. "It's just too little."
> That is why the Guatemala-born Andrade, 41, is risking the ire of her employer, the Doubletree Guest Suites, to speak out for Measure JJ, a referendum on Tuesday's ballot that would enact a "living wage" for thousands of workers in the city's coastal and downtown tourism zone.[48]

Gold said a couple of readers complained that the lead and the story as a whole seemed to be framed to portray the woman as a victim and imply that "anyone who didn't want to vote for higher wages was a heel." Such complaints, even if they come from a few readers, underline the importance of carefully weighing whether an anecdote—perhaps by stirring compassion— poses a barrier to truth in the sense that it may sidetrack readers from understanding the breadth of what is at stake in an issue.

It is impossible for any individual to convey all of the parties or views at stake in an issue, and a story must rely on more than an anecdote to cover this breadth. But Arrieta-Walden, who heard reader feedback at the *Oregonian* in his role as public editor, offered a caution that is nonetheless important to consider: "Invariably when you choose an anecdote you are choosing a certain perspective. . . . You're saying this is how I see the story and I'm saying this is the most important, and that this person's experience is the most important. And so having done that, in some ways again are you conveying or signaling a bias to folks by having done that?"[49] On sensitive issues such as abortion or gay marriage, it may be particularly difficult for journalists to craft an anecdote that rises above claims of bias—perhaps bias in opposite directions—by people with different viewpoints on an issue.

Dworkin, the *Oregonian* medical writer, pointed out that anecdotes about people's medical problems may stir compassion to the point that some needy patients—those who are subjects of news coverage—may receive help while others do not, especially when the newspaper mentions that there are financial needs.

> Because we're writing lots of medical stories, lots of patients involved and there are many more people who probably are having financial troubles making ends meet. And we don't put that in and people will be stirred to compassion. But we don't always make it easy for them to help out when we do that. And so it's selective who gets that benefit. A lot of it depends on how much you focus on the individual case.[50]

The very fact that newspapers and broadcast stations do stories that highlight specific individuals' medical needs is a sensitive issue ethically because focusing on one person may neglect the needs of someone who has greater needs—a concern that medical ethicists might point out.[51] It is impossible for journalists to write about all needy people, but they will minimize ethical problems by being careful to place them in the broader context of needs of people with the same condition and, where possible, other medical needs.

Narrowing the Focus from an Issue

Dworkin also pointed to another problem with anecdotes: they may help keep readers from focusing on the broader issue in the story at all.

> I think that there's an assumption that readers are very interested in people and in human stories, which is why we use the anecdotes, but sometimes they may be more interesting than the broader themes that we're trying to explain. . . . When you move past the anecdotal lead and try to move into something else, you might lose the reader and they won't get to the broader topic or when they think back on the story they won't remember it.[52]

These comments echo the argument by the *New York Times*'s Kolata that "people will remember the anecdote and it will mean more to them than anything else you say."[53] They also fit with the findings of the psychological studies that found examples can dominate people's minds compared with the influence of broader figures or statements about events.[54]

Opening the Door to Inaccuracy or Falsification

At the most basic level of ethical concern, the truthfulness of anecdotes can be abused to the point of falsification. Richard Nelson, a national copy editor at the *Los Angeles Times* who has worked at four newspapers, said:

> I have read things before thinking: that does not pass the smell test. That does not have the ring of truth. People don't act that way. And that's a peril, I think, with anecdotes because if the writer wants to be clever, the writer wants to write a nice lead or a nice beginning . . . it doesn't always work. And I think it actually opens up the possibility of more ethical lapses. Look at Jayson Blair.[55]

Because of their allure as engaging ways of drawing readers in, abuse of the truthfulness of anecdotes is a temptation reporters and editors need to guard against carefully.

Short of falsification, issues of truth can arise with anecdotes the reporter did not witness but develops based on what the subject said. Melissa McCoy, the *Times*'s assistant managing editor for copy desks and later deputy managing editor,[56] said:

> If the reporter sees what's related in an anecdotal lead with his or her own eyes, it's very different, I think—when the reporter sees it, you just take it on faith that it's right. The reporter saw it, experienced this moment with the subject, and is relating what happened and has written it in an anecdotal-lead style. If the anecdote is relayed to the reporter through the subject, now the reporter has to have faith in the subject. And now the copy editor or editor has to have faith in the reporter and the subject. And how do you relay that information to the reader in such a way that you're making it extremely clear that the reporter didn't witness it and that the subject may be going very far back in time in relaying it? It's kind of like a paraphrasing of memory.[57]

In some anecdotes, it may be important to say directly to readers how a reporter knows what he or she knows. In others, it may be enough to allow readers, as McCoy put it, to take a "journey" with the writer without using direct attribution—an issue to be discussed more fully in chapter 3. However, she also said it is important for copy editors to keep their guard up and critically evaluate the work of all writers—"superstars" or not.

Using Anecdotes Better

Both the ethical benefits and the difficulties connected with anecdotes point to the need for journalists, students, and researchers to think carefully about how they can be used most truthfully and in a way that harnesses their potential to stir compassion in the most constructive way possible.

The interviews with reporters and editors point to a number of ideas for using anecdotes more effectively and ethically. This chapter will close by examining some of the best.

Shorten or Eliminate the Anecdotal Lead

At a time when readers are busy and media competition is keen, writers and editors need to look for opportunities to shorten anecdotes or even eliminate them if necessary to draw people in quickly. Editors know that, on news section fronts, they have only a few paragraphs to work with before the story jumps. As Frank Smith, the deputy copy desk chief on the news copy desk at the *Dallas Morning News*, put it, they want the point of a news story to be "crystallized" on the front of the section.[58]

Don Frederick, national political editor for the *Los Angeles Times*, said, "We use anecdotal leads still a fair amount because we have the writers who can pull it off. But they've got to be really sharp, they've got to be really focused."[59] As an example, he talked about a story from the 2004 presidential election campaign that opened with these two paragraphs:

NORMAL, Ill.—Ordinarily, neighbors would no more discuss their political leanings than pass around their bankbooks. Impassioned conversation usually stops at Illinois State University basketball.

But this year is different: People can't remember the last time they felt so worked up about an election.[60]

The story follows with four single-paragraph anecdotes about people showing their political passions—such as Guy Hanna, who "planted not one handmade red, white and blue wooden elephant on his corner front lawn, but nine." The writer had turned in the story with the sentence about Illinois State basketball after the examples. Once editors realized the layout would push that sentence onto the jump, they talked with her and moved it up because it vividly expressed the key point of the story.

Sometimes an anecdotal lead can be cut altogether if the story works well without it. Arnold, in his work as a copy editor at the *Oregonian*, has occasionally raised questions about whether anecdotal leads are needed:

Sometimes you'll have an anecdotal lead that's only a couple of sentences, maybe a paragraph, and then the real start of the story is the second graph. There have been times where I've talked to an editor and said: You know what? This just doesn't have anything to do with the story. Can we just start at the second graph? And the *Oregonian* is a good newspaper and they've done that here.[61]

Do a Whole Story, not Just an Anecdote

The opposite approach also has an important place. Extended narratives about individuals' lives and struggles may connect deeply with readers—as Hallman's stories on Sam Lightner did. But even for stories about issues and trends, an in-depth look at an individual can powerfully illustrate a broader problem. Rowe, the *Oregonian's* editor, said:

> I think frequently anecdotal leads also don't get to the heart of the matter. So they may be interesting, telling, but not really representative or show understanding. And the stories that I've seen it best end up where it's not an anecdotal lead. It's a story about an issue and we know that person is so much the right example, so much the perfect illustration and we know so much about every facet of it, that you really are telling the full story and at the same time bringing out the issues and the conflicting viewpoints and the choices that people make, because so many issues are about choices rather than black and white.[62]

She cited a story that reporter Ted Sickinger did about how the Oregon economy had changed.[63] He did it not by focusing on dry facts and statistics but by showing the changes in the life of one person. "A lesser reporter or one who hadn't spent months finding the perfect person would have had a person as an anecdotal lead and may have had a couple of other quotes from them. This is a much fuller story in the same way that Rich Read used the potato to show about what was happening in the Eastern economy"[64] (as discussed in chapter 1). A story that portrays an issue in this way takes diligence in reporting as well as skill in writing, but it gives readers deep insight in an engaging way.

Integrate the Anecdote Better with the Story

One way to tie an anecdote better to a story's broader point is to return to it at the end of the story. Bryan Denson, a reporter who has done investigative and narrative writing at the *Oregonian*, said reporters setting a scene early in a story can use a "narrative hook" to signal to readers, "'Hey, we're just getting your attention here. We're going to give you a full exploration of the issue here and then we're going to bring you back.'"[65] Denson pointed to the *Wall Street Journal* as an example of a place where writers have effectively used this kind of hook.

Look for Someone Who Reflects the Range of a Subject

Although it is difficult, where possible writers should look for people who reflect more than one facet or side of an issue so the complexity or range of the topic is better represented. The *Oregonian's* Dworkin gave an example from medical writing:

> So if there is a medical treatment that's really promising but also has a terrible side effect in 20 percent of patients, if I can find somebody who's had the benefits but also experienced the side effect, that's better in my mind. Because that will let me, even if I don't necessarily put that all at the top, I can stay with that same person throughout the story, use the same anecdote of the same character I've introduced and get the multiple features in it.[66]

Applying this idea to issues stories, a reporter might look for one person who is undecided on an issue and is carefully weighing both sides, or someone who has experienced both positive and negative consequences of a policy decision.[67]

Explain How the Anecdote Is and Isn't Representative

Another way to represent the truth about a topic more fully in an anecdote is to explain how this person's situation is not typical as well as how it is. Dworkin noted that the standard approach to an anecdotal lead calls for stating the lead, then saying how it represents the broader trend. But it is also important to consider how a person—for example, someone having a medical procedure—is different from the typical case. Otherwise, the reporter's portrayal may leave wrong impressions about the broader picture.[68]

Check the Fit of an Anecdote with a Trusted Source

Glover and Lait, the investigative team at the *Los Angeles Times*, are strong supporters of doing read backs, as are several other reporters interviewed. Read backs involve double-checking story passages for accuracy and context by reading to sources quotes or other material they have given a reporter for the story. Glover described how read backs might help with anecdotal leads:

> If you read something past someone and they say, "Well, I mean if you're intending for this to represent X, I really don't think that works because Y is true." And that is something that a reporter might not see. You're not seeing it from all angles, and if you're dealing with a source who's part of the story or someone who has a bigger-picture view, they might be able to steer you away from that.[69]

Glover and Lait are careful not to give sources veto power or make them de facto editors, but they value the knowledge that sources can provide. "If something was wrong, or out of context, I'd rather know prior to publication than after publication," Lait said.[70] And Glover noted that in investigative reporting, the stakes are high when it comes to accuracy in a lead:

> You choose to go with an anecdotal lead and it might be something that's seemingly benign information, but if you get something wrong—the tiniest of facts—in that lead, or if for whatever reason it doesn't work, the proposition it stands for is not supported in the story and you don't see that, you open yourself to just tremendous criticism. Someone can pull on a seemingly inconsequential fact and wave that around saying, "They can't even get this right, this guy's type of work," that kind of thing.[71]

Read Critically and Question Inconsistencies

Editors can help to spot errors and worse problems in anecdotes. McCoy of the *Times* pointed out that some mistakes and falsified information are difficult for copy editors to spot—as her review of *New York Times* corrections showed would have been true for Jayson Blair's stories. But she pointed back to Janet Cooke's 1980 *Washington Post* story "Jimmy's World" about a child drug addict—the story that won a Pulitzer Prize but was then exposed as a hoax. She said some people have argued that an excellent copy editor could have stopped the story from being published by spotting numerous inconsistencies—including a statement in the opening paragraphs that "Jimmy" was eight years old and in fourth grade.[72]

Factual inconsistencies such as these should ideally be caught before they reach the copy desk. But if other editors have missed them, the copy desk serves an important ethical purpose in its role as the last check in the editing process.

Pat Mullarkey, who reads behind copy editors as a slot at the *Oregonian* and has worked with large narrative projects, emphasized the need for an atmosphere of constructive communication about questions in stories. "You have to have good dialogue between the desk, the writer, and the editor. Otherwise you're setting yourself up for a big mistake. If it's adversarial, it's going to set a bad precedent" as happened in the Jayson Blair and Jack Kelley cases. "You've got to have open communications where people aren't defensive. Just explain what your thinking was on it and have discourse on it."[73]

If writers and editors communicate openly about problems in anecdotes, the worst problems this device may create are more likely to be prevented and more of their potential is likely to emerge.

Notes

1. Rudolph Flesch, *The Art of Readable Writing*, 1st ed. (New York: Harper, 1949).

2. Dean P. Baquet, interview by the author, October 5, 2004, Los Angeles.

3. Jamie Gold, interview by the author, October 7, 2004, Los Angeles.

4. Michael Merschel, interview by the author, September 13, 2004, Dallas.

5. Gina Kolata, telephone interview by the author, April 29, 1997. Quoted in David A. Craig, "Covering the Ethics Angle: Toward a Method to Evaluate and Improve How Journalists Portray the Ethical Dimension of Professions and Society" (Ph.D. diss., University of Missouri–Columbia, 1997).

6. This summary of research findings on anecdotes is adapted from the review of literature in David A. Craig, "The Promise and Peril of Anecdotes in News Coverage: An Ethical Analysis," *Journalism and Mass Communication Quarterly* 80, no. 4 (Winter 2003): 802–17. Adapted with permission of the Association for Education in Journalism and Mass Communication.

7. Daniel Kahneman and Amos Tversky, "On the Psychology of Prediction," *Psychological Review* 80 (July 1973): 237–51; M. Hammerton, "A Case of Radical Probability Estimation," *Journal of Experimental Psychology* 101 (December 1973): 252–54; Don Lyon and Paul Slovic, "Dominance of Accuracy Information and Neglect of Base Rates in Probability Estimation," *Acta Psychologica* 40 (August 1976): 287–98.

8. Ruth Hamill, Timothy DeCamp Wilson, and Richard E. Nisbett, "Insensitivity to Sample Bias: Generalizing from Atypical Cases," *Journal of Personality and Social Psychology* 39 (October 1980): 578–89.

9. Dolf Zillmann, Joseph Perkins, and S. Shyam Sundar, "Impression-Formation Effects of Printed News Varying in Descriptive Precision and Exemplifications," *Medienpsychologie: Zeitschrift fur Individual- und Massenkommunikation* 4 (September 1992): 168-85, 239-40. Summarized in Dolf Zillmann and Hans-Bernd Brosius, *Exemplification in Communication: The Influence of Case Reports on the Perception of Issues* (Mahwah, N.J.: Lawrence Erlbaum, 2000), 63–65.

10. Hans-Bernd Brosius and Anke Bathelt, "The Utility of Exemplars in Persuasive Communications," *Communication Research* 21 (February 1994): 48–78.

11. Dolf Zillmann et al., "Effects of Exemplification in News Reports on the Perception of Social Issues," *Journalism and Mass Communication Quarterly* 73, no. 2 (Summer 1996): 427–44.

12. Rhonda Gibson and Dolf Zillmann, "Exaggerated versus Representative Exemplification in News Reports," *Communication Research* 21 (October 1994): 603–24.

13. Charles F. Aust and Dolf Zillmann, "Effects of Victim Exemplification in Television News on Viewer Perception of Social Issues," *Journalism and Mass Communication Quarterly* 73 (winter 1996): 787-803.

14. Rhonda Gibson and Dolf Zillmann, "The Impact of Quotation in News Reports on Issue Perception," *Journalism Quarterly* 70 (Winter 1993): 793–800.

15. Rhonda Gibson and Dolf Zillmann, "Effects of Citation in Exemplifying Testimony on Issue Perception," *Journalism and Mass Communication Quarterly* 75 (Spring 1998): 167–76. Aside from the studies on exemplification, studies of framing effects have found that episodic and human-interest frames—in which anecdotes are often an element—affect audiences' thinking in important ways. See, for example, Shanto Iyengar, *Is Anyone Responsible? How Television Frames Political Issues* (Chicago: University of Chicago Press, 1991) found that episodic framing, focusing news coverage on individuals and events, tends to prompt television news audiences to attribute responsibility for issues to individuals rather than social factors. Patti M. Valkenburg, Holli A. Semetko, and Claes H. de Vreese, "The Effects of News Frames on Readers' Thoughts and Recall," *Communication Research* 26 (October 1999): 550–69, found that crime stories framed in terms of human interest prompted readers to emphasize emotions and implications for individuals more often, and to recall less information about an issue.

16. Matt Lait and Scott Glover, "Suspect in Cellmate's Death Was Termed Dangerous Before Killing," *Los Angeles Times*, November 26, 2001, B-1 (Home Ed.).

17. Matt Lait, interview by the author, October 4, 2004, Los Angeles.

18. Scott Glover, interview by the author, October 4, 2004, Los Angeles.

19. Leo C. Wolinsky, interview by the author, October 7, 2004, Los Angeles.

20. The goal of maximizing truth telling is included in "Doing Ethics: Ask Good Questions to Make Good Ethical Decisions," Poynter Online, www.poynter.org/content/content_view.asp?id=5600 (accessed May 24, 2006).

21. Vernon Loeb, interview by the author, October 5, 2004, Los Angeles.

22. Andy Dworkin, interview by the author, June 21, 2004, Portland, Oregon.

23. Robin Fields, Evelyn Larrubia, and Jack Leonard, "Guardians for Profit: When a Family Matter Turns into a Business," *Los Angeles Times*, Nov. 13, 2005, A1 (Home Ed.). infoweb.newsbank.com.

24. Vernon Loeb, e-mail message to author, February 27, 2006.

25. Loeb interview, October 5, 2004.

26. Vivian McInerny, "King of Hearts," *Oregonian*, March 28, 2004, L1 (Sunrise Ed.), infoweb.newsbank.com.

27. Vivian McInerny, interview by the author, June 23, 2004, Portland, Oregon.

28. Tom Hallman, Jr., "The Boy Behind the Mask Part One," *Oregonian*, October 1, 2000, A1, infoweb.newsbank.com.

29. Jack Hart, January 28, 2001, letter nominating "The Boy Behind the Mask" for the 2001 Pulitzer Prize in feature writing.

30. Jack Hart, interview by the author, June 21, 2004, Portland, Oregon.

31. Tom Hallman, Jr., interview by the author, June 21, 2004, Portland, Oregon.

32. Beatriz Terrazas, "Where the Tree Stands," *Dallas Morning News*, March 26, 2000, 1F (3rd ed.) and March 27, 2000, 1C (3rd ed.).

33. Beatriz Terrazas, interview by the author, July 20, 2004, Dallas.

34. Henry Fuhrmann, interview by the author, October 4, 2004, Los Angeles.

35. Sue Goetinck Ambrose, "Folic Acid: Who's Minding the Risks?" *Dallas Morning News*, April 18, 2004, 1A (2nd ed.). infoweb.newsbank.com.

36. Sue Goetinck Ambrose, interview by the author, July 21, 2004, Dallas.

37. Roy Peter Clark, quoted in Fred Brown, "Storytelling vs. Sticking to the Facts," *Quill* 90, no. 3 (April 2002): 22.

38. Matt Sabo, "Legal to Oregon, Illegal to Federal Agents," *Oregonian*, October 12, 2003, A1 (Sunrise Ed.).

39. Michael Arrieta-Walden, interview by the author, June 22, 2004, Portland, Oregon.

40. Michael Finnegan, "It's Party Time for Lobbyists," *Los Angeles Times*, May 27, 2003, A1 (Home Ed.).

41. Michael Finnegan, telephone interview by the author, November 26, 2004.

42. Steve Blow, interview by the author, September 14, 2004, Dallas.

43. Frank Christlieb, interview by the author, July 23, 2004, Dallas.

44. Jake Arnold, interview by the author, June 23, 2004, Portland, Oregon.

45. Brown, "Storytelling vs. Sticking to the Facts."

46. Sandra Mims Rowe, interview by the author, June 22, 2004, Portland, Oregon.

47. Brown, "Storytelling vs. Sticking to the Facts."

48. Martha Groves, "Living Wage Issue Put in Voters' Laps," *Los Angeles Times*, October 31, 2002, B1 (Home Ed.), infoweb.newsbank.com.

49. Arrieta-Walden interview.

50. Dworkin interview.

51. See Deni Elliott, "A Case of Need: Media Coverage of Organ Transplants," in *Risky Business: Communicating Issues of Science, Risk, and Public Policy*, ed. Lee Wilkins and Philip Patterson (New York: Greenwood Press, 1991), 151–58, a critique of news coverage of an organ transplant case in Maine.

52. Dworkin interview.

53. Kolata interview.

54. Kahneman and Tversky, "On the Psychology of Prediction"; Hammerton, "A Case of Radical Probability Estimation"; Lyon and Slovic, "Dominance of Accuracy Information and Neglect of Base Rates"; Hamill, Wilson, and Nisbett, "Insensitivity to Sample Bias."

55. Richard Nelson, interview by the author, October 5, 2004, Los Angeles.

56. Melissa McCoy became deputy managing editor for copy desks, design, and production in December 2005.

57. Melissa McCoy, interview by the author, October 8, 2004, Los Angeles.

58. Frank Smith, interview by the author, July 20, 2004, Dallas.

59. Don Frederick, interview by the author, October 5, 2004, Los Angeles.

60. Faye Fiore, "Political Passions Near a Fever Pitch," *Los Angeles Times*, October 5, 2004, A1 (Home Ed.).

61. Arnold interview.

62. Rowe interview.

63. Ted Sickinger, "A New Reality of Work, Wages," *Oregonian*, November 4, 2001, F1 (Sunrise Ed.), infoweb.newsbank.com.

64. Rowe interview.

65. Bryan Denson, interview by the author, June 21, 2004, Portland, Oregon.

66. Dworkin interview.

67. For recommendations on ways that anecdotes can be used to reflect the breadth of a topic, especially one involving ethical issues, see Craig, "The Promise and Peril of Anecdotes in News Coverage: An Ethical Analysis."

68. Dworkin interview.

69. Glover interview.

70. Lait interview.

71. Glover interview.

72. McCoy interview. See Janet Cooke, "Jimmy's World," *Washington Post*, September 28, 1980, A1 (Final Ed.), infoweb.newsbank.com. McCoy mentioned that William G. Connolly, a former senior editor at the *New York Times*, has done a seminar using "Jimmy's World" to show copy editors how they could have spotted and questioned problems in the story. See also Allan Reeder, "Beyond the Bounds: When to Speak Up, and Why," Poynter Online, www.poynter.org/dg.lts/id.41411/content.content_view.htm (accessed May 24, 2006). Reprinted from Copy Editor (June–July 2003): 1, 6–7.

73. Pat Mullarkey, interview by the author, June 24, 2004, Portland, Oregon.

CHAPTER THREE

Description and Attribution

Vivid, accurate description is at the core of good journalistic writing. News and feature stories without detailed description of people, events, and scenes are dry and distant. But in the quest for powerful and truthful description, journalists face many choices that have ethical implications. Along with these choices come decisions about whether and how to attribute pieces of description to the sources on which they are based. This chapter will explore several areas of ethical choice, particularly corroboration of the truthfulness of description, attribution to signal its truthfulness, and what to include and exclude in descriptions. Much of the focus will be on narrative writing because it raises especially sensitive issues related to corroboration and attribution, but the issues are relevant across journalistic genres. The perspectives of the reporters and editors interviewed will shape the discussion and, at the end of the chapter, will feed into suggestions for how description and attribution can be done ethically.

Truth is a central issue in evaluating the ethics of description. It comes into play in ways that are more complex than it might seem on the surface. Roy Peter Clark at the Poynter Institute for Media Studies has noted the complexity of finding truth amid the limitations of memory:

> To make things more complicated, scholars have demonstrated the essential fictive nature of all memory. The way we remember things is not necessarily the way they were. This makes memoir, by definition, a problematic form in which reality and imagination blur into what its proponents describe as a

"fourth genre." The problems of memory also infect journalism when re-porters—in describing the memories of sources and witnesses—wind up lend-ing authority to a kind of fiction.[1]

The discussion of truth becomes even more difficult when the work of jour-nalists is viewed from a postmodern perspective:

> The post-modernist might think all this irrelevant, arguing that there are no facts, only points of view, only "takes" on reality, influenced by our personal histories, our cultures, our race and gender, our social class. The best journal-ists can do in such a world is to offer multiple frames through which events and issues can be seen. Report the truth? they ask. Whose truth?[2]

Despite these complexities, Clark proposes two principles—"Do not add" and "Do not deceive"—to guide journalists in evaluating the line between fact and fiction.[3] But both the personal limitations of journalists and the philosophical backdrop against which they work make carrying out these principles difficult.

Journalism scholar Russell Frank has also pointed to the complexity of the ethics of describing events. He noted that narrative scholars have pointed out the problematic nature of the "relationship between 'events' and reports of those events"[4] and underlined the point by citing S. Elizabeth Bird and Robert W. Dardenne's statement that "While news is not fiction, it is a story about reality, not reality itself."[5] As Frank noted: "The reporter is locked into his own point of view, both physically and psychologically. He notices some things, misses others. Among the details he notices, he decides that some are relevant, others not, that some should be featured prominently, others sub-ordinately."[6] The writer, then, is inevitably crafting one version of events, not a full version of the truth about them.

A number of the journalists interviewed talked about issues of truth di-rectly, and related issues surfaced in many of the other conversations. The *Oregonian*'s managing editor and writing coach, Jack Hart, who has been ac-tive in discussions of narrative ethics both in his newsroom and nationally, said the biggest ethical challenge in narrative writing is: "Are you presenting an accurate version of the world? Is this truthful at some level?" Hart said truth applies both at the level of details of observation and reporting in set-ting a scene and "at the larger thematic level in which you're presenting facts and observations in a way that is a particular take on the world. Is it fair? Is it reasonable? Are you an honest broker?"[7] These issues are relevant beyond narrative because reporters across journalistic forms must observe and write about details, and—as narrative scholars would note—frame a particular version of events. The fact that writers are limited by their memories and perspectives makes it even more important that they carefully consider the ethical choices involved in description.

As Richard E. Meyer, a narrative editor at the *Los Angeles Times*, noted, attribution is closely connected with the truth telling involved in description.[8] Signaling to the reader how the reporter knows what he or she knows is vital in showing both the limits of the truth being told and the support for it. As Henry Fuhrmann, senior copy desk chief for business at the *Times* and later a deputy business editor, put it: "You have to tell the reader as clearly as you can, in most cases as soon as you can, how you know what you purport to know. How do you know the basic truth of what you're putting in the newspaper?"[9]

Although truth is the central issue in the choices about description and attribution, compassion also comes into play. Describing a scene powerfully or eliminating roadblocks to readability from overattribution can help make an account of a person or a situation more moving to readers—thereby simply building human connections or stirring them to help meet some need.

Corroboration and Attribution

Communicating accurately in a news story or feature depends on cross checking information as a reporter. Comprehensiveness—though impossible in full—also depends on careful corroboration. The journalists interviewed, though talking mostly about writing, had much to say about the importance of this strong foundation of reporting and about its companion issue, attribution.

Seeking Truth through Corroboration

The ethical choices involved in corroborating different information and accounts of events pose challenges that relate more directly to news gathering than writing, but careful corroboration is crucial as a foundation for truthful writing and is a central matter in the questions that editors raise about stories. Richard Read, senior writer for international affairs and special projects for the *Oregonian*, said cross checking information is important because it is tempting to go beyond what one knows in reconstructing scenes—an area of considerable discussion among narrative writers:

> That's the toughest thing to report and to write, and I think the ethical issues that that raises are probably the most troublesome because you're trying to put you and your sources and your readers back in time and yet make it so realistic

and make it sort of pop up to life so vividly that I think it's probably tempting to take shortcuts and just kind of imagine yourself being there and then make perhaps suppositions that aren't justified. So you constantly have to go back and check things against what people say and even read them passages and make sure that they remember it as you're portraying it. And if at all possible triangulate so that you have more than one source telling you the same thing. And make sure that it's accurate.[10]

Journalists cannot fully overcome the limitations of people's memories, but they can present a fuller version of a scene by painstakingly confirming accounts and details with different sources. Thomas T. Huang, Texas Living editor at the *Dallas Morning News* and a narrative writer himself, echoed Roy Peter Clark's concern about the limitations of sources' memories. He warned about the danger of relying on one source for reconstruction. "Even if the source is well intentioned and well meaning, we all know that people remember things differently. And so it's important to get as many viewpoints, people who witnessed something, to help you reconstruct it."[11]

It is clear from the interviews that strong and truthful storytelling requires painstaking cross checking of information. Sonia Nazario, who wrote the Pulitzer-winning "Enrique's Journey" series for the *Times* (see chapter 1), said the most challenging aspect of good description is "looking at the various versions of a scene and what happened and trying to find the points on which everyone agrees and the dialogue that they all agree upon that occurred at that moment. And sometimes people have slightly differing versions of what happened or what was said, and so you go to everyone who was present there and you try to find what areas overlap. And that requires a lot of work to try to really get at the truth of what happened in a circumstance and what was said in a given event."[12]

Barry Horn, a *Dallas Morning News* sportswriter, provided an example of the kind of corroboration a good reporter does for one descriptive segment. He wrote this lead on a story that was a finalist for an American Society of Newspaper Editors award for nondeadline writing in 2003, about an athlete son who killed his father after being driven ruthlessly toward success:

NORTH RICHLAND HILLS—It was a throwaway line at the end of a chance meeting in a faraway place involving a college football coach, a father and his 13-year-old son.

Just something nice to say to the father of just another kid whom the coach vaguely remembered from a Texas Christian University summer camp five months earlier.

Had the boy not worn a Horned Frogs football cap to lunch that day, the coach would not have struck up the conversation over Christmas vacation in 1991.

"If your boy keeps his head on straight, he's going to have a great future," the coach told the father in parting.

Some fathers might have taken the line as simple positive reinforcement for a skinny eighth-grader before returning to the business of the meal.

Others might have been content to thump their chests for a day or two before returning to reality.

And then there was Bill Butterfield, for whom the coach's words were an epiphany, a Rocky Mountain revelation right there in Brown's Country Store in the tiny Colorado resort town of South Fork.

This father saw it as the first step on his return to athletic glory.[13]

To confirm the details of what happened, Horn talked to the son, Lance; Bill Butterfield's wife; Bill Butterfield's best friend; and the university coach. He asked for recollections of the meeting. "And when things were different I'd go back again. There's a luxury here that I'd go back to the people numerous times. I'd say, 'OK, you said X. Kathy remembers it as X with a little Y in it. Do you remember the Y?' 'Oh yeah—I remember the Y and did she tell you about the Z?' Oh! OK. Now, call Kathy back and say, 'Yeah I talked to the coach and he remembers this also,' and she'd either say 'Yes' or 'No' and either she would 'Yes, OK,' and if she'd say 'No,' then I'd call up the best friend and I'd go, 'Here I know X, Y, or Z,' or 'I know X and Y but there's some question about Z. What's your recollection about Z?' And then it would become a consensus about it."[14]

For one anecdote, then—a crucial one to the story and a window on Bill Butterfield's life—Horn sought out a consensus on the details through interviews with several people.

Even a single detail may require time-consuming checking. Bryan Denson, a reporter who has done investigative and narrative writing for the *Oregonian*, referred to dark-purple carpet in Room 303 of the Holiday Inn Express in Grants Pass, Oregon, in a story about a detective's investigation of the desecration of a Native American grave site.[15] He described calling the Holiday Inn to ask about the color of the carpet, including checking whether any carpet had been changed since the day in question. Although that kind of checking may seem like a luxury for reporters or editors at small newspapers, it is an example of the kind of foundation of reporting needed to paint a picture that is not only vivid but also truthful. This kind of care contrasts starkly with the highly publicized fabrications of the *New York Times*'s Jayson Blair and *USA Today*'s Jack Kelley.

In features, it is sometimes important to talk about a person's thoughts. When the details that need corroboration are thoughts, special care is required. Steve Steinberg, a features copy editor at the *Dallas Morning News* who also writes features, did a story about Kay Burt, a woman who had once received a kidney from her father and, needing a second one, ended up with her daughter as the donor. He included this paragraph about her response to the news that her daughter was a good match:

> At first, Kay absolutely refused. Her 690 million-to-1 miracle baby? The child she had worried herself sick over, had hovered over? And now she was supposed to let her daughter lie down on an operating table and be "cut almost in two"? The donor's operation, "a very major strain," is longer and harder than the recipient's, Dr. Klintmalm says.[16]

Steinberg was comfortable going without attribution because he thought it would be clear to readers that these were Kay's thoughts—and because he questioned her closely.

> I asked her to tell me specifically: What were you thinking when your daughter offered you her kidney? What were your first thoughts? What went through your mind right then? And that's a question, I think, if writers are going to do this, if they're going to go without attribution, it's a question they have to be asking: What were you thinking right at that moment? What were you feeling right at that moment? Take yourself back, just re-create it and tell me exactly what was going through your mind, what you were feeling. Just paint the whole picture for me.[17]

Since no one else, strictly, can corroborate what a person thought, it is ethically more dangerous to use re-creations of thoughts. At a moment of great drama or stress in a person's life, it is more likely that he or she will remember exact thoughts. Still, at a minimum, close questioning is essential since true corroboration is impossible.

Kurt Streeter, who writes narratives for the *Los Angeles Times*, offered advice on evaluating sources: "I think it's important to get a sense for just who among your subjects would have a good memory and who's honest." Discussing a narrative on a girl from East Los Angeles who was a boxer,[18] he said that based on his experience with the girl's father, he determined he could trust him about details from the past—including details for flashback scenes of fights he got into years earlier. "His memory has checked out time and time again, even against public records."[19] Streeter's comments point not only to the importance of evaluating the trustworthiness of sources but also to the value, where possible, of cross checking their memories against documents.

Sometimes, too, simply spending time around the subject of a story—two years in the case of the girl in Streeter's narrative—enables greater accuracy in describing details, such as what expressions show she is happy or sad. "It's tough with her because she's a tough kid and she's learned to kind of protect herself by disguising things from the outside world, vulnerability. And so it really took a long time to kind of figure out where she's coming from."[20]

Investigative and crime stories pose particularly sensitive issues of corroboration. Scott Glover and Matt Lait of the *Los Angeles Times* face challenges regularly in covering corruption in law enforcement. Glover said he and Lait have to be aware that someone may have an ax to grind and may therefore offer a biased account. "It's your job to do enough digging that the elements that you do put in the story are supported by something other than contrary points of view."[21] Lait said that in many of the stories they do, views differ on what happened, and they have to try to document the sequence of events—and acknowledge where accounts conflict.[22]

Pam Maples, now the *Morning News*'s assistant managing editor for projects, offered an example of corroboration in a sensitive crime story—the Pulitzer-winning piece she wrote on violence against women in the United States. She talked about how she developed the lead about Sandy Henes, who "held her breath and waited to die."[23] (See chapter 1.)

> I really wanted to reconstruct that scene. She had a very clear memory. I back-checked the sort of factual parts of it through law enforcement. There was a police report on similar incidents. So I did the fact checking that made me feel confident of her story. The other thing I did before I invested any more time in her was I called my editor in Dallas and I said, "I have found this woman and here briefly is her story, and she's very compelling and very articulate and has a very vivid memory. It's supported by some documents, but I am absolutely not going to call her now ex-husband for his side of this story because he will kill her. So if you're not comfortable with that, then I'm not going to pursue her." . . . She had given me some information about him being arrested and stuff. And I went to police sources and I went to somebody who could look him up in NCIC[24] for me, and everything she had told me tracked. What I remembered, what struck me about her was she didn't overstate anything. And even somebody who's not trying to spin you, they've been through something dramatic, they will tend to overstate. "He shot me five times"; he shot you once. Everything, like she had told me about this barricading situation and stuff and this hostage. It all tracked. She said it was at the time of day roughly; I mean everything tracked. So before I went ahead and spent another 12 hours

with her or whatever I spent over about three days, I had that conversation with my editor and he said okay.[25]

Maples's careful evaluation of the truthfulness of this account—and her sensitivity to the problem of cross-checking with the woman's ex-husband in this case—reflects the difficult ethical balancing involved in corroborating information in stories about crime and violence. Although narratives present their own challenges, hard-news reporting on crime calls for persistence in checking matters with potentially life-and-death impact.

The difficulty of the task of corroboration that investigative journalists, as well as other journalists, face reflects an argument that James S. Ettema and Theodore L. Glasser made in their study of the work of investigative reporters: that in practice, pursuit of truth about what happened stays a step removed from what actually happened. Pointing to the work of historians, they wrote:

> The past, precisely because it is past, is accessible only indirectly through its traces: records, documents, artifacts, living memory. The standard for assessing the truth of statements about the past therefore cannot be the correspondence between the statement and what really happened. The standard can be only some acceptable degree of corroboration among the traces available—and that usually demands a great deal of hard work. So it is with journalists.[26]

Although seeking the full truth about events is an ethically praiseworthy standard, the difficult reality of reporting on people and events underlines the need to acknowledge the inherent limitations of the pursuit even as journalists strive to corroborate as fully as possible.

Signaling Truthfulness through Attribution

Attribution of the sources of descriptive details is basic to showing evidence for the truthfulness of what a reporter gathers—however short those details may fall from what philosopher Hilary Putnam called "a God's Eye point of view."[27] Traditional attribution calls for saying who said what early and often, but narrative features—and some investigative work—often streamline the writing through means such as umbrella attributions and accompanying story boxes noting the variety of sources used. This section will examine interviewees' perspectives on the ethics of attribution and evaluate several approaches to signaling how reporters know what they know.

Russell Frank has argued that narrative-style reconstructions, though powerfully written, leave readers without enough "signposts" and may cast doubt on the truthfulness of the writing.[28] Lisa Kresl, assistant managing editor for Lifestyles at the *Dallas Morning News*, noted the need for attribution to show truthfulness to readers. "I think sometimes it naturally falls into the story flow and it needs to be there—particularly now, after various things have happened in the industry and people are more wary. Readers are probably more wary and suspecting."[29]

Read, who wrote the Pulitzer-winning "French Fry Connection" series on the ties between the Pacific Northwest and the Asian economy (see chapter 1), said readers may be more inclined to be trusting with some kinds of description, so more attribution is needed in some cases than in others:

> If you're describing a scene and you say that . . . the Hutterite farmer got into the combine and the combine was green and he harvested this many acres of wheat, well, the reader will bear with you on that. They don't need to be told how do you know that it was green or how do you know how many acres. They'll believe you. But if you start talking about the swami being accused by a certain number of women of raping them, well, for the credibility of the piece let alone legally, you're obviously going to have to attribute that. And if it clutters the story, well, that's the price you pay. But we've found out as we get into this, if there are controversial details, even in just a regular, explanatory narrative, I've found that sticking in a short attribution . . . at key points really doesn't interrupt the story flow as much as I would have feared. So it's worth doing, I think.[30]

Attribution in sensitive matters such as criminal accusations is an essential signal from the standpoint of both fairness to the accused and credibility. It is important for readers to know when the details about a person or situation are in dispute. However, attribution can at times be a barrier to truth telling—through lack of clarity for readers—and even obscure whether what's being said is actually true. Huang of the *Morning News*, who was a Poynter Ethics Fellow, said:

> I think that if you're going to write large chunks of narrative without either an attribution or a footnote, simply because there's some aesthetic value to it, then I think that's not a good idea. But I do think that on the other end of that spectrum, you can clutter up the story with attribution to the point of it not being clear anymore. And also, you can almost depend on attribution so that you're no longer accountable for whether it's accurate or true or honest. I think sometimes reporters or editors will say well, let's at least, you know, we're not sure whether it's right or wrong, but it's in this report, so let's attribute it to the report. And then they feel like that's enough. . . . The attribution almost becomes the cover-yourself mode.[31]

At worst, then, attribution can ascribe the appearance of truth to something that is of questionable accuracy. This kind of attribution looks as if it were fulfilling one's ethical responsibility, but it does not in a deeper sense.

Avoiding overattribution and thinking of new ways to attribute may advance truth telling by engaging readers—perhaps stirring their compassion for the subjects of stories as well. Michael Merschel, an assistant features editor at the *Morning News*, said:

> I think the traditional way of thinking about it, of—we have to give attribution to every sentence and every line no matter what—I think it's rooted in a desire to be completely concrete and clear about who is saying what and what happened when. And I've got no problem with that. I also think that readers are more sophisticated than we give them credit for. And they haven't read all the old textbooks that say here's how you're supposed to write a story. They don't necessarily care about all those rules. They just want something that reads well. That's not a license to take liberty with facts, but I think we do have license to let somebody talk and reconstruct a scene without repeating attribution every time they say something. I think it comes back to that idea that a newspaper has got to give more than just news these days. A newspaper has got to give stories, and stories require proper flow. It goes back to a newspaper has to do more than deliver news; we've got to deliver good writing as well. Good writing sometimes bends the rules a little bit.[32]

Merschel's comments point to the challenge that newspapers face today in capturing the interest of readers, particularly young readers. He argues for keeping the "bigger-picture issue" in mind when evaluating attribution:

> I don't think there's an inherent conflict in how you attribute a story as long as it's true, as long as it's clear and the reader can tell who's doing the talking and where his thought came from, or if it's something that the reporter has witnessed with his or her own eyes. As long as that's in the story somehow, and a reader can reasonably deduce where it's coming from, I don't really care exactly how it's done.[33]

This bigger-picture concern about truth and clarity lays an ethical foundation that allows for flexibility in application—though Merschel was careful to stress that journalists have no license to manufacture details or thoughts.

John S. Carroll, editor of the *Los Angeles Times* until he retired in August 2005, expressed a concern about maintaining a high standard of factual truthfulness in narrative writing. He connected this standard to attribution:

> There are temptations in narrative writing to sacrifice literal truth for public yarn. And back in the '60s when the term "New Journalism" became current,

there was an awful lot of fudging, and I even heard one noted New Journalist laugh at people like me who were bound by facts and couldn't go beyond the facts. But I think for a newspaper, certainly for newspapers, we are what we are and we've got to have provable, largely attributed facts. And we're not artists; we're journalists. So sometimes that makes for a less stimulating story but it helps your credibility in the long run.[14]

Carroll's counterpart at the *Oregonian*, Sandra Mims Rowe, noted that it is possible to handle attribution in a deft way that preserves readability but also addresses the concerns of a skeptical audience. "A lot of people see this simplistically as the story's either smooth and narrative or it's cluttered, and attribution is either he said/she said or it's not. And what we've learned is that it can be deft and it doesn't have to be cluttered and it helps a story stand up to scrutiny from the most skeptical reader. And that's the person I want to satisfy."[35] Interviewees identified several approaches to attribution— some of which read more gracefully than others. Each sends a kind of signal about the truthfulness of story material.

In-Story Approaches to Attribution

Meyer, who has edited two Pulitzer-winning narratives at the *Los Angeles Times* and written two himself that were Pulitzer finalists in feature writing, pointed out three kinds of attribution that signal truthfulness differently but all do it within a story:[36]

- Attribution that stays in narrative, keeping the signal within the time and place of the scene being described. An example of this kind of attribution appears in a story by *Times* reporter Barry Siegel, part of a series called "The Secret of the B-29," about how the U.S. government lied to the Supreme Court about the cause of a plane crash in 1948—a lie that laid the foundation for the legal decision undergirding the USA Patriot Act. Judy Palya Loether, whose father was killed in the Air Force crash, was one of those petitioning the court to correct its mistake. Siegel wrote:

  > Judy Palya Loether typed e-mail messages and roamed the Internet. She fielded calls from reporters. She heard from her father's aging colleagues. She began to imagine that she might prevail. Here, she sensed, was a powerful way to right a wrong. More important, here was a powerful way to find her father. Judy began to feel like Dorothy in the "Wizard of Oz."
  >
  > "This whole journey of mine," she told those around her, "has changed my life."[37]

By saying "she told those around her," Siegel let readers know that others had heard her say this, but he does so in a way that maintains the flow of the narrative. He set up a similar signal later in the story in referring to a letter written by Judy's father: "Poking around, Judy found a letter he wrote that summer to a colleague: *All phases at present going smoothly and expect to complete Banshee sometime in October. I had some results on flight tests. . . . The plane [flies] in the right direction, but the run is by no means a straight line. We have not progressed far enough to determine exactly what the trouble is.*"[38] This attribution tells readers that the words come from a letter but keeps the signal in the place and time in which Judy found it.

- Attribution that comes what Meyer called a "half-step" out of the narrative. For example, in introducing the account of the B-29's fatal flight, Siegel wrote, "The survivors of that mission would never forget what happened."[39] "Would never forget"—or, further down in the story, "He'd later say"—stay connected to the time and place in the scene but signal that the survivors would be communicating their account in the future.

- Attribution that steps all the way out of narrative and looks back—providing an umbrella attribution for a scene. Chapter 2 of Nazario's "Enrique's Journey" takes place in Chiapas state, Mexico. It opens with people finding Enrique after he has been beaten. Later in the story, Enrique's own account of the beating is signaled with a full step out of narrative: "Here is what Enrique recalls."[40] This step makes clear that what follows is based on his memory of what happened—though the beating has already been confirmed earlier in the chapter through the accounts of people who found him afterward.

More frequent, conventional attributions—such as "he said"—would also step all the way out but are often used in narrative as little as possible.

What are the ethical implications of these approaches? All signal how the reporter knows what he or she has written—something Meyer says a reader "has the right to know." Whether one is ethically best depends on how one weighs the impact of interrupting the narrative versus signaling most obviously who is saying something.[41] Meyer, referring to John Gardner's notion that fiction narratives put people into a dreamlike state,[42] noted that stepping out of narrative interrupts this dream and may push the reader away from the story. On the other hand, stepping out of narrative leaves the reader with no doubt about the source of the information. He noted that the approaches can be mixed so that the reader gets the signal both subtlely and unsubtlely.

The approaches Meyer described could be used in nonnarrative stories as well. Investigative pieces often include a paragraph high in the story that provides a kind of umbrella attribution by noting the kinds of sources the reporter used to develop the findings of the story. However, investigative pieces are usually attributed relatively heavily as the story goes on, in light of the sensitivity of the topics and the likelihood that accounts will conflict. Because of narrative writers' tendency to seek minimum attribution for the sake of story flow, each attribution in a narrative carries, in a sense, greater ethical implications. The *Oregonian's* Hart raised a particularly important caution about responsibility, from a journalistic perspective, in talking about the power of a narrative to carry readers along:

> I think it does not relieve you of the obligation to be absolutely truthful, which memoirists would argue it does. I don't believe that. I think you always have that obligation if you are writing in a journalistic context. But be that as it may, I think that's true, you want people to suspend their disbelief and be carried along with the story in kind of a dream state. And anything that disrupts that is working against your role as a storyteller, which makes the ethical obligation even greater, because once you have them in that dream state you could really screw with their minds.[43]

Story Boxes or Editor's Notes

Numerous publications have signaled attribution through story boxes or editor's notes accompanying articles. They are a kind of umbrella attribution—placed outside the body of the story and often including more detail than an in-story umbrella attribution. They may be only a paragraph or two, or may run for several, but they provide an overview of what kinds of sources the reporter used to tell the story. For example, an *Oregonian* series by Tom Hallman, Jr., on life in a neonatal intensive care unit was accompanied by a four-paragraph note by Hart called "How We Reported the Story."

> Tom Hallman spent nine months visiting Level 3, getting to know nurses, parents and babies, and learning about the medical technology involved. He observed most of the scenes described in the story first-hand, and Bruce Ely was often there to record them with his camera.
>
> On the few occasions when Hallman found it necessary to reconstruct events, they are clearly attributed to the memory of a direct participant.
>
> No comment appears in direct quotes in this story unless Hallman heard it with his own ears. When he describes what nurses and parents were feeling or thinking as they performed their duties, he based his account on what they said in response to questions he asked during or immediately after the events depicted.

> Every nurse, doctor and parent who appears in this series gave permission to Tom Hallman or Bruce Ely to be present to record what they saw and heard.[44]

In addition to talking about how Hallman learned what he knew, the box provides a second signal about attribution—beyond the attribution in the story itself—by noting that reconstructions of events are attributed to participants' memories.

Normally a story box does not take the place of attribution in the article itself, but the writer may attribute less often. Russell Frank has criticized editor's notes, arguing that "footage that is labeled as a re-enactment is probably less deceptive than a story topped by a note saying parts of it were reconstructed from court records and interviews simply because the reader cannot tell from the way the story was written which parts were reconstructed and which observed."[45] He has also made an analogy between these notes and the designation "photo illustration," arguing that the specifics of attribution are left unclear, just as, for many readers, the meaning of the photo illustration label is vague.[46] However, in-story attribution that fleshes out what the editor's note says—such as the attribution of reconstructions in Hallman's story—mitigates this ethical difficulty. For details whose veracity is less open to question, it is less important to attribute beyond the box. Some balancing with the need to keep readers engaged in the story is warranted, though there is always the danger that readers will not look at the box.

Footnotes

In "Enrique's Journey," the *Times* showed how an extended version of a story box—a set of footnotes—could allow a detailed signaling of how the reporter gathered information. (See chapter 1.) The notes were so detailed that attribution was needed only in the most sensitive spots in the story—such as Enrique's account of a beating—and the writing moved forward with fewer interruptions. As Meyer put it: "It gives us the best of all worlds. We can write this very much like you would write a short story and at the same time we can have scene-by-scene attribution of every single thing in the story."[47] Carroll said he thought the notes were important to convince readers that the content was true.

> I think that this story was one that was very subject to second guessing because what we did, we met a kid down just south of the border and then he told us a whole lot of stories, and from his stories, we reconstructed something like seven trips through the length of Mexico. Now the reporter took his stories and checked them out every which way. She retraced his steps. She found people he had talked to. She found the farm worker who had found his beaten

body after he had fallen off the roof of a train. It was an amazing bunch of reporting, but we didn't witness any of the things that he said he did up to the point that he got to the Rio Grande. And so we knew people would say: "Well, hell, they just took this kid's word for it. He's a dope-smoking 16-year-old."[48]

Jamie Gold, the readers' representative for the *Times*, said audience reaction suggested that people appreciated the footnotes. Reaction to the stories, she said, "was overwhelmingly positive. And a lot of people did comment on the extensive footnotes, which is really unusual. But they appreciated that. And it might be as a result of that, that I didn't get a lot of questions about its veracity."[49]

Ethically the footnotes do provide the best of both worlds in that they enable a high level of disclosure about sourcing while also clearing the way for stories to be powerful and to engage readers. The main difficulty is the practical one of space when the story is something short of a large, long-term project.

Implied Attribution: First Person

First-person writing, although uncommon in newspapers outside columns, does appear occasionally. Meyer noted that the first-person voice represents a kind of attribution because it signals that the reporter was an eyewitness—though, in the worst ethical case, it is still possible to fabricate a scene. Streeter's piece on the girl boxer—a series edited by Meyer—was written in first person. Streeter said:

Part of the reason . . . , since I was there so much, was to signal to the reader, "You can trust this. I witnessed it." And then I think that helps the whole attribution problem. There was a fight that I witnessed between the father and a gang guy out on the street. I was actually next to the father, and the gang guy threw something at him. He was throwing something at me, too. I was right next to the dad. Gang ethics with a chair. He was throwing it at both of us actually, so I'm ducking out of the way. . . . So I think that's a powerful moment and a way to signal to the reader kind of with authority.[50]

Implied Attribution: Photographs

Even the presence of photographs can imply the source of information. *Oregonian* classical music critic David Stabler, who was a Pulitzer finalist at the *Oregonian* for a series about the troubled life of a teenage cello prodigy,[51] noted that running photos with a narrative—as the paper did with this series—can help enhance credibility by signaling that the reporter was there. "It's an indirect attribution," he said.[52] This kind of signaling helps to show the truthfulness of reported scenes in the story and also holds a reporter more accountable to be truthful in scenes because it is clear others observed them.

What to Include and Exclude in Description

Beyond the issues of corroboration and attribution, questions about handling of description emerge related to what to include and exclude—in both narratives and other stories. Leaving in and excluding particular details of description of people, events, and scenes can bias readers for or against a person or an issue in a story, raising concerns about fairness that overlap with considerations of truth telling. And, as Hart noted, choices about what to include and exclude in support of a theme also have implications for truthfulness. Even if one acknowledges, with media scholars and others, that all observers are biased by their perspectives and limited in their ability to overcome that bias, concern for fairness suggests that it is ethically important to consider the direction of the bias and minimize it. This concern is particularly significant when a skewed perspective may prove harmful to the subject of a story—by, for example, damaging someone's reputation or perpetuating stereotypes.

Carroll of the *Times* pointed to the goal of truth telling in saying that in "a complex story, one makes maybe 50, 100, 1,000 choices as to what goes in and what doesn't, and you have to be guided, I think, by a good-faith effort to include the things that reflect what you understand to be the truth—not your opinion but the factual truth—and to throw out things that are questionable or wrong."[53] A good-faith effort, as Ettema and Glasser would note,[54] will mean making choices that do not produce a perfect image of the outside world. But a writer's or editor's ethical commitment to truth telling as a standard is important as a motivator to do what one can.

This section explores a number of issues that writers and editors face in evaluating the ethics of inclusion and exclusion in both news and features— first, issues related to casting people in different lights through different details, then issues related to supporting a story's theme, stirring readers' emotions, and dealing with complexity.

Casting Different Light through Different Details

Description should convey the fullest possible picture, but it needs to be chosen fairly. Political writer Mark Z. Barabak of the *Los Angeles Times* has faced choices about description in an area in which reader sensitivities can run high: presidential campaign coverage. During the 2004 campaign, he and

Matea Gold did a story about the second debate between George Bush and John Kerry. The story included these paragraphs:

> Although Kerry mostly kept his composure, Bush seemed angry on occasion, especially when he accused the Massachusetts senator of disparaging the contribution allies had made to the U.S.-led war in Iraq.
>
> "You tell Tony Blair we're going alone!" Bush said of the British prime minister. "It denigrates an alliance to say we're going alone—to discount their sacrifices."[55]

Barabak said he thought it was important to say that Kerry mostly kept his composure and Bush seemed angry because these were part of portraying as fully as possible what happened.

> We run and the *New York Times* and other newspapers will run the verbatim transcript, so if the reader wants to just read what the words were that came out of their mouths, they can do that. I think part of what a political reporter should do, even a piece like mine which was not an analytical piece, is trying to convey the debate experience in its totality if you will. And part of that is giving that physical description, talking about mannerisms, talking about how they conduct themselves, how they comport themselves throughout the course of the debate.[56]

Barabak said that if Bush's anger about Kerry's comment about going it alone had been an isolated example at the debate, it might have been unfair to use it, but that it reflected something he saw throughout the debate. By pointing to his concern about fairness, he highlighted the ethical nature of the choices he had to make in covering the candidates.

Berta Delgado, a religion writer at the *Dallas Morning News* before she left the newspaper in January 2005, also noted the need to consider descriptions about people in proper context. For example, if a reporter is interviewing a leader and sees him or her chastising someone, that may be important as a reflection of how the leader treats people, but if—based on time spent around this person—the reporter sees this as "one incident out of a hundred," it may not represent a fair portrayal of who the person is.[57]

Talking more generally about the pitfalls of describing people, Jake Arnold, a copy editor at the *Oregonian*, said:

> When I come into a story that's got description, I've got to assume that description was put in there for a reason, and so I have to ask myself, What is this description saying about this person? And that, again, is a field with landmines

in it. Am I describing the desk as messy—am I saying this guy's a slob? Am I saying the walls were orange—am I saying he has no sense of fashion? What am I saying about this person with my choices of description? We fall into this with appearance all the time, describing how his hair was or what kind of clothes she was wearing or how she carried herself. Personal descriptions are just terrible as far as conveying bias.[58]

Arnold, though recognizing the importance of describing people and making stories interesting, highlighted the ethical challenges involved in trying to describe people and their surroundings fairly.

The difficulty in describing people and places is complicated by the fact that some descriptions are relative: they leave different impressions depending on the perspective of the observer. Bruce Tomaso, religion editor at the *Morning News*, said, for example, that a house that seems luxurious to one person may not appear so to another. "I think there are ways to be descriptive without being judgmental in ways that could be faulty. You can describe it as a 7,000-square-foot, nine-bedroom house. That gets the point across."[59] He also noted that physical descriptions such as "tall" or "stocky" might leave differing impressions. It is a basic of good reporting to describe specifics rather than slap on a label, but that choice has ethical implications, too.

Particular caution is warranted when descriptions connect with issues of stereotyping and the portrayal of minorities. Seth Prince, another *Oregonian* copy editor, offered a helpful perspective on sensitivities in description related to class and race:

I think on crime stories I notice some writers here will be more inclined to give me a tour of all the broken-down cars in the neighborhood around this house where there was a drug bust. Or they'll make reference to the fact that they lived in a mobile home or something like that. On other stories I think the copy editor has to ask, Is it that detail that we're providing that does cast some certain level of judgment on this source—the copy editor has to ask, Would we do that if someone up here in the West Hills, in the nicest part of town, if they were arrested for something, would we say, "And there were eight Lexuses down the block"? If we wouldn't say, "There were eight Chevys on blocks down the street," why would we say, "There are eight Lexuses in the circle drives of the million-dollar homes"? But I think it's just matters of fairness in the description. . . . How do we describe the lives of minorities? Do they only fit into the stereotypical framework of what people expect? And in a lot of the Indian stories, do we only ever talk about the frequency of drinking? Do we describe down to this type of beer or whatever the case may be?[60]

One area that raises ethical concerns about stereotyping and the portrayal of minorities is descriptions of crime suspects. Newspapers have to make daily choices about how to describe suspects, and writers and editors have to decide which details are relevant and how much detail is sufficient for readers to be able to identify someone. Race may be a relevant detail, but including race without a detailed description that points to an individual raises ethical questions because of the potential for stereotyping. Frank Christlieb, a senior editor on the news copy desk at the *Dallas Morning News*, stated the difficulty this way:

> The policy that we've arrived at is that you don't want to just say, "Okay, it's a black man who's about 6 foot 2 and weighs 180 pounds." You have to get some distinguishing feature physically about them into the story too, whether they have a cleft chin or they have a scar on their neck or whatever. You just have to get those kinds of descriptive things into those kinds of hard news briefs or stories. A 6-foot-2, 185-pound black man applies to an awful lot of people, or a 6-3, or a 200-pound white man.[61]

Christlieb sees problems in vague descriptions not only because of stereotyping, but also because readers do not get information useful in spotting a suspect.[62]

The choices about suspects and other issues of descriptive detail are part of the paragraph-by-paragraph ethical decisions that writers and editors face every day in newsrooms. Although each of these choices is a small one, cumulatively they contribute to the degree of truthfulness in portrayal of the social world in which both the journalists and their readers live.

Supporting a Theme

Difficult choices about inclusion and exclusion arise related to the broad theme or idea of a story. This issue comes up in both news and features. Whether the reporter is doing a 600-word breaking news story, a 1,200-word analysis, or an 8,000-word narrative, a central point makes the story clearer for readers—but also raises ethical questions.

Joshua Benton, who covers education for the *Morning News*, offered an example of a detail that implies criticism but fits with the point of a story. He wrote a story about a Dallas-area school district, Wilmer-Hutchins, that ran out of money and could not pay teachers.[63] "So teachers went to get their paychecks and all the checks bounced. It's a pretty big story for a school district. And I and some other people went to the headquarters to ask Dr. Matthews, the superintendent, about this and he refused to see us, and snuck out a back door, got into his Cadillac, and drove away. Now, the fact that he was in a Cadillac is a pretty telling detail on the day in which the district ran out of money. . . . If he was in a Geo Metro I don't know if I would've put Geo Metro in the paper."[64] Benton saw the Cadillac detail as reflecting the larger divide between district employees, not highly paid and now not getting paid, and the superintendent. Arguably, in light of the broader problems of the district, including this detail is more truthful than being what seems to be more objective and leaving it out. However, as Benton cautioned, it is important to monitor one's own thinking for fairness in light of the ethical dangers involved in different characterizations of events.

Nazario of the *Times* said that in writing "Enrique's Journey," one of the biggest ethical challenges she faced was the difficulty in trying to convey the "totality" of Enrique's life and experience:

> If you're writing about a person's experience or a person's life, or in this case 12 years of a person's life and a journey across thousands and thousands of miles, there are a lot of things that happen that are boring and uneventful but are part of the fabric of that person's life or that experience. And when we focus stories in terms of highlights and turning points and in a narrative, I sometimes worry about whether that really captures the reality of that situation or that person's life.[65]

Nazario said she and Meyer, her editor, planned out some chapters to be more positive or negative in tone than others. For example, chapter 3 on going through Chiapas was mostly negative. "And in a sense if something really positive happened in Chiapas, it might be in there in a sentence or two but not in a major way because the theme was this is hell." The negative theme was "truthful in that that's how both the boy I was writing about and other immigrants convey that place. But within that there are things that happened that are obviously positive." In contrast, chapter 4 in Veracruz later in his journey was positive, with a theme focused on getting gifts along the way. "And so if something negative happened to him there, then it was in there, but it might not have been in as large a way as it would have been in the Chiapas chapter; it might have been taken out altogether, just skipped over."

It would be too simplistic to condemn these choices in the name of narrative cohesiveness as distortions of the truth. As Nazario noted, "in a way you're always distorting the truth because you can't put everything." She strives for truth this way:

> I think you try to get at the heart of whatever part of a journey or segment of a journey that you're writing about. You try to write about the element that is

strongest or that is most evident both to you and to the person that you're writing about. And I think if you do that, then you're being truthful to your subject. But I think you're always weighing, should you put in these other elements in some limited form or in a sidebar form or in some other way?[66]

Being ethical, then, involves evaluating the importance of details from the vantage point of one's own observation about the context of the story but also from the perspective of the subject.

For narrative writers doing a series like Nazario's, the choices about description relate to themes at several levels: individual scenes, chapters or stories within a multiday narrative, and the overall series. The challenges of condensing reporting, which is sometimes done over a period of years, are great. The *Oregonian*'s Rowe, in discussing questions she asked about a series by Read on a Japanese businessman,[67] said writing that series meant boiling down "four years of interviews and actions into four stories." In the choices made, Rowe "wanted to make sure that we hadn't inadvertently, having known for a long time that was going to be the theme, picked out the pieces of the situation that just fit our theme."[68] She was satisfied with the answers she received, but her questions reflect ethical concerns that editors need to raise about many lengthy stories, both news and features. Even for writers who do not have the time available for extended reporting, questions about how description relates to broader points are important to raise.

Stirring Emotion Among Readers

From the standpoint of both truth and compassion, it is also important to weigh how details may make emotional connections with readers. Meyer linked the choice of descriptive details to truth and, by implication, to compassion because of the potential emotional impact of powerful details. He said a writer should choose the most telling detail—the detail that does the most to tell the truth that the writer wants to convey.[69] Sometimes that detail carries great emotional weight, as in an example Meyer cited from a Pulitzer-winning story by Siegel about a father haunted by the death of the son he left alone for too long during a trip in the wilderness to scout for deer. Siegel described the horrifying sight that a searcher, James Wilkes, came upon:

> It was the longest night Wilkes ever spent. He feared falling asleep, afraid he'd never wake up. Near 5 a.m., he rose and began to walk. Within minutes, Dino's nose went down. The schnauzer darted up a slope to the base of a pine tree. From below, Wilkes could see his dog licking a mound of snow. Then, as he approached, he saw two little feet.

By the time Wilkes reached the tree, Dino had cleaned off Gage's face. Six inches of snow covered the small body. Gage lay in a fetal position, his hands clenched, his eyes wide open. His pajama legs were up to his knees; his feet had worn through his thin booties. His throat was blue. In his eyes were frozen tears.[70]

By ending with the detail of frozen tears, Siegel brought home powerfully the tragedy of this little boy's death. This paragraph, especially in the context of the whole story, shows the power of a single set of details and the one most telling. It therefore underlines the ethical importance of careful choices about even one detail.

Nora Zamichow, a narrative writer for the *Times* until she left in January 2006, said it is important to pick the most poignant, evocative material for a scene to make a story as powerful as possible. In a narrative about Jeremy Strohmeyer, a former honor student accused of sexually assaulting and murdering a little girl, she included this paragraph in the opening, a scene at a casino:

Nearby, a 7-year-old girl named Sherrice Iverson was playing with a little boy. They pelted each other with paper wads. Jeremy picked up the fallen missile and tossed it at Sherrice. He chased her, and she sprinted away, her blue sailor dress swinging and her black cowboy boots padding along the carpet.[71]

Commenting on her choices of description, Zamichow said: "It's almost like in a Hitchcock movie where it's something very benign and this little girl is wearing what little girls wear. But there is almost a background tone that's much more ominous and also building." Her intent "was to pick out the details that would show you that this little girl doesn't have any idea what is about to happen, nor should she."[72]

This description, like the one in Siegel's story, may stir empathy among readers—and, in doing so, connect them more deeply with the truth of the lives of the story's subjects. It would be sensationalizing and might create undue pain to use this kind of detail excessively, but used judiciously, it may reach readers in ways that dry facts would not.

Simplifying Complexity

Some stories pose ethical choices in description not because of their emotional power but because of their intellectual complexity. Reporters and editors on many beats may encounter these decisions, but they are likely to surface most often in areas such as science, medicine, and technology where the subjects are technical and hard to explain simply.

Sue Goetinck Ambrose, a science writer for the *Morning News* who holds a Ph.D. in molecular genetics, often faces the challenge of how to conquer complexity. "I guess the biggest challenge is figuring out what to leave out," she said. "As I'm trying to write an explanation, I will think to myself, What is the absolute minimum I need to say to get this point across?" She said some science writers try to put too much in a story about research findings instead of focusing on only the most telling points.[73] The opening of a story she wrote about the abilities of the brain shows how she uses description simply:

Even the dumbest brain is a genius.

Unlike boring organs such as the stomach and liver, the brain can think and remember, see and smell. But one reason the brain has a higher IQ than other organs may be that it is a better editor. Its editing prowess may help it do many jobs with ease, despite working with a relatively small genetic blueprint, or genome. "People were a little surprised when the human genome was sequenced and it only contained 35,000 genes, which is not that different from a potato," says Dr. Eric Nestler, a neuroscientist at the University of Texas Southwestern Medical Center at Dallas. "On top of that, we were a little insulted to be so close to a potato."

New research is suggesting that brains come out smarter than potatoes partly by editing the very genetic instructions that make key portions of the brain's machinery. Rather than obeying each genetic instruction to the letter, scientists are learning that brains alter the instructions in many ways to create an array of parts, each capable of doing a slightly different job.[74]

The description in this opening emerged in the process of writing the story, trying to explain it to her editor, and writing a summary box that was to run with the story. This example points to the value of discussion between reporters and editors as a way of clarifying a complex explanation.

Andy Dworkin, who writes about medicine for the *Oregonian*, deals with similar challenges of making description simple. He said he is not a doctor but has developed his background through self-study with books, journal articles, and medical education websites, and through attending a seminar for science writers. He takes time to do thorough research to make sure he understands whatever he has to describe. For a story about how a doctor used a tiny wire net to treat a stroke threatening a girl's life,[75] he had the surgeon talk him through the operation and show him the tools he used, asked several doctors to describe blood clots, looked for a pencil eraser to compare to what he was told about the size of the clot, viewed scans showing the clot's location, and looked at *Gray's Anatomy* to make sure he understood how the device would be routed. He pointed out the importance of translating specialized jargon. "The longer you're on a beat the harder that gets in some ways. It's a Journalism 101 lesson to ask for those descriptions that everyone can understand, and then you end up being on a beat for years and years and you start talking the lingo of doctors or cops or whoever you're covering and you might forget to translate that back."[76]

Handling Description and Attribution Ethically

Handling the ethical challenges of description and attribution well involves a high standard of care[77] on the part of both reporters and editors. Thoughtful and thorough reporting is a key foundation for writing ethical description. Among the ideas that can strengthen this foundation:

- Whenever possible, be there rather than reconstructing. The *Oregonian*'s Hallman noted "the tools of narrative are very seductive." He said that when he began doing narratives, he saw the power in the ability to reconstruct the past. "But now more and more I try to, I want to be there and watch it unfold in front of me. So most of my stories now have little reconstruction of the past whereas if you looked at the stories 10, 15 years ago much more of that."[78] His comments are important for other stories, too, where it is possible to observe firsthand versus piece together after the fact.
- Do an extra layer of reporting, and look to a variety of sources for corroboration. Hallman and Read both used a term of scientific research—triangulation—to describe the kind of careful cross checking they do. As Read put it, "You just have to be relentless."[79] He said narrative reporting means not only doing reporting on the whole story but then, after looking at what you have and determining a scene is important to the story, going back and asking questions to flesh out that scene "in Technicolor detail." "That entails a whole other series of questions, not only to your main character, but to anybody else who was there or who had anything to do with it and any documentation that you can get." Again, the point is important not only for narrative writers but for anyone striving for a high standard of accuracy in reporting, particularly news reporters who may borrow narrative techniques for leads or descriptive segments of a story.
- Challenge your own perspective about what is important. Zamichow offered this illustration:

> I was just recently at the science museum and there's a wonderful exhibit where they have this film clip and it says to count how many times the

basketball bounces. And you focus on this bouncy basketball, and at the end of the segment it says, 'Did you get to twelve?' Some people got thirteen, some people got eleven. And then it says, 'Do you think you missed anything while you were counting? Watch the film clip again.' And it shows you the clip again. And this time you'll see that there's a gorilla that walks very slowly from one side of the court to the other side. And the vast majority of viewers are so preoccupied with getting that ball that they don't see the gorilla walking. Which I think is sort of a humbling reminder to all of us that in our endeavor to capture a scene or capture a news event, that we don't become so focused on this one thing that we may come to a story thinking this is the story, and miss the gorilla.[80]

Her caution is ethically important for reporters—and editors—trying to determine what description is relevant to include or exclude in a story, particularly in support of a theme. Similarly, Read said it is important to let the point of a scene come out of the details of the reporting rather than "marshaling details selectively to prove some sort of a partisan point."[81]

As noted in chapter 2, reading back material to sources—a practice supported by a number of the journalists interviewed—can provide a cross check beyond the reporter's own internal questions.

Aside from approaches that reporters can take, questions that editors raise about description—and about the companion issue of attribution—are vital to maintaining a high level of accuracy, as well as truthfulness in the broader senses of context and comprehensiveness. Editors need to be sensitive to writerly concerns about story flow, and they need to help foster an atmosphere of positive interaction and a level of trust appropriate to the experience and quality level of the reporters. But for the sake of truthfulness, as well as credibility with a highly skeptical public, editors also need to be persistent in their questions. As the concerns of the editors cited in this chapter make clear, this questioning role should involve all of the editors whose eyes see a story: assigning editors, copy editors, and—for sensitive stories—top-level newsroom editors.

Assigning editors are essential for what Hart calls "prosecutorial editing,"[82] which includes aggressive questioning about how a reporter knows what he or she knows in the details of a story. Copy editors, in particular, because they usually are not involved in story development, also play a critical role as a fresh set of eyes that may see what readers would see looking at a story. They can also act as fact-checkers—in a more extensive way in large newsrooms that have more editors. Particularly in stories heavy on description and scene-setting, fact-checking of the kind that magazines do may help to enhance accuracy and, in the worst case, head off more cases of fabrication.

Although it is unlikely that the term "epistemology" will pass the lips of an editor during questioning about a story, it is important for editors to question how reporters know what they know. In doing so, they are reflecting a philosophical commitment to communicating and signaling truth even though all stories will fall short of full, comprehensive truth.

Notes

1. Roy Peter Clark, "The Line Between Fact and Fiction," *Poynter Online*, www.poynter.org/content/content_view.asp?id=3491 (accessed May 24, 2006). For two discussions of problems of memory distortion from the viewpoint of psychologists, see Daniel L. Schacter, Kenneth A. Norman, and Wilma Koutstaal, "The Cognitive Neuroscience of Constructive Memory," *Annual Review of Psychology* 49 (1998): 289-318 and Asher Koriat, Morris Goldsmith, and Ainat Pansky, "Toward a Psychology of Memory Accuracy," *Annual Review of Psychology* 51 (2000): 481-537.

2. Clark, "The Line Between Fact and Fiction." In addition to the discussion of truth and postmodernism in chapter 1, see the discussion of the perspective of the "new journalists" in Norman K. Denzin, "Cultural Studies, the New Journalism, and the Narrative Turn in Ethnography," in *American Cultural Studies*, ed. Catherine A. Warren and Mary Douglas Vavrus (Urbana: University of Illinois Press, 2002), 134-49.

3. Clark, "The Line Between Fact and Fiction," notes that his essay "grew out of discussions at a 1998 conference involving 50 award-winning reporters, writers and editors from print and broadcast, as well as subsequent conversations with Tom Rosenstiel from the Pew Project for Excellence in Journalism, which cosponsored the conference." The principles "Do not add" and "Do not deceive" are also discussed in Bill Kovach and Tom Rosenstiel, *The Elements of Journalism: What Newspeople Should Know and the Public Should Expect* (New York: Crown, 2001), 79-80.

4. Russell Frank, "'You Had to Be There' (and They Weren't): The Problem with Reporter Reconstructions," *Journal of Mass Media Ethics* 14, no. 3 (1999): 149.

5. S. Elizabeth Bird and Robert W. Dardenne, "Myth, Chronicle, and Story: Exploring the Narrative Qualities of News," in *Media, Myths, and Narratives: Television and the Press*, ed. James W. Carey, Sage Annual Reviews of Communication Research vol. 15 (Newbury Park, Calif.: Sage, 1988), cited in Frank, "'You Had to Be There,'" 149.

6. Frank, "'You Had to Be There,'" 149.

7. Jack Hart, interview by the author, June 21, 2004, Portland, Oregon.

8. Richard E. Meyer, interview by the author, October 5, 2004, Los Angeles.

9. Henry Fuhrmann, interview by the author, October 4, 2004, Los Angeles. Philosophically, both corroboration of information and the signaling of the sources

of that information relate to epistemology, or the study of the nature of knowledge. Choices about what constitutes adequate knowledge and confirmation of that knowledge reflect epistemological assumptions.

10. Richard Read, interview by the author, June 25, 2004, Portland, Oregon.

11. Thomas T. Huang, interview by the author, July 22, 2004, Dallas.

12. Sonia Nazario, telephone interview by the author, March 11, 2005.

13. Barry Horn, "A Father Who Pushed Too Far," *Dallas Morning News*, September 15, 2002, 1A (2nd ed.).

14. Barry Horn, interview by the author, July 20, 2004, Dallas.

15. Bryan Denson, "Grave Injustice," *Oregonian*, December 30, 2003, A1 (Sunrise Ed.), infoweb.newsbank.com.

16. Steve Steinberg, "Twice in a Lifetime," *Dallas Morning News*, December 19, 1999, 1F (3rd ed.).

17. Steve Steinberg, interview by the author, July 20, 2004, Dallas.

18. Kurt Streeter, "The Girl," *Los Angeles Times*, July 10-14, 2005, A1 (Home Ed.).

19. Kurt Streeter, interview by the author, October 8, 2004, Los Angeles.

20. Streeter interview.

21. Scott Glover, interview by the author, October 4, 2004, Los Angeles.

22. Matt Lait, interview by the author, October 4, 2004, Los Angeles.

23. Pam Maples, "Bringing Fear Home: U.S. Women Face Pervasive Threat of Violence, Often at the Hands of Husbands, Boyfriends," *Dallas Morning News*, June 6, 1993, 1A (Home Final Ed.), infoweb.newsbank.com.

24. National Crime Information Center, an FBI-maintained criminal justice database.

25. Pam Maples, interview by the author, September 14, 2004, Dallas.

26. James S. Ettema and Theodore L. Glasser, *Custodians of Conscience: Investigative Journalism and Public Virtue* (New York: Columbia University Press, 1998), 132.

27. Hilary Putnam, *Reason, Truth, and History* (New York: Cambridge University Press, 1981), 49. Cited in Ettema and Glasser, *Custodians of Conscience*, 134.

28. Frank, "'You Had to Be There,'" 147. See also Russell Frank, "Wait Before You Narrate," Poynter Online, www.poynter.org/content/content_view.asp?id=4151 (accessed May 24, 2006).

29. Lisa Kresl, interview by the author, July 21, 2004, Dallas.

30. Richard Read, interview by the author, June 25, 2004, Portland, Oregon. For the series on the swami to whom Read referred, see Richard Read, "In the Grip of the Guru," *Oregonian*, July 15-18, 2001, A1 (Sunrise Ed.), infoweb.newsbank.com.

31. Huang interview.

32. Michael Merschel, interview by the author, September 13, 2004, Dallas.

33. Merschel interview.

34. John S. Carroll, interview by the author, October 6, 2004, Los Angeles.

35. Sandra Mims Rowe, interview by the author, June 22, 2004, Portland, Oregon.

36. Meyer interview.

37. Barry Siegel, "How the Death of Judy's Father Made America More Secretive," *Los Angeles Times*, April 18, 2004, A-1 (Home Ed.).

38. Siegel, "How the Death of Judy's Father Made America More Secretive" (italics in the original).

39. Siegel, "How the Death of Judy's Father Made America More Secretive."

40. Sonia Nazario, "Badly Beaten, a Boy Seeks Mercy in a Rail-Side Town," *Los Angeles Times*, September 30, 2002, A1 (Home Ed.), infoweb.newsbank.com.

41. Meyer interview.

42. John Gardner, *On Becoming a Novelist* (New York: W. H. Norton, 1999): esp 5–6.

43. Hart interview.

44. Jack Hart, "How We Reported the Story," *Oregonian*, September 24, 2003, A6 (Sunrise Ed.).

45. Frank, "'You Had to Be There,'" 153.

46. Russell Frank, "'About This Story': Newspapers Work to Make Narrative Journalism Be Accountable to Readers," *Nieman Reports* (Fall 2002): 49–52.

47. Meyer interview.

48. Carroll interview.

49. Jamie Gold, interview by the author, October 7, 2004, Los Angeles.

50. Streeter interview.

51. David Stabler, "Lost in the Music," *Oregonian*, June 23–25, 2002, A1 (Sunrise Ed.), infoweb.newsbank.com.

52. David Stabler, interview by the author, June 22, 2004, Portland, Oregon.

53. Carroll interview.

54. Ettema and Glasser, "Custodians of Conscience."

55. Mark Z. Barabak and Matea Gold, "Differences Sharpened in Debate," *Los Angeles Times*, October 9, 2004, A-1 (Home Ed.), infoweb.newsbank.com.

56. Mark Z. Barabak, telephone interview by the author, November 24, 2004.

57. Berta Delgado, interview by the author, July 19, 2004, Dallas.

58. Jake Arnold, interview by the author, June 23, 2004, Portland, Oregon.

59. Bruce Tomaso, interview by the author, July 19, 2004, Dallas.

60. Seth Prince, interview by the author, June 23, 2004, Portland, Oregon. For an example of the different impressions left by different sets of facts about a place, see Daniel Okrent, "What Do You Know, and How Do You Know It?" *New York Times*, February 29, 2004, 4-2 (Late Ed.-Final).

61. Frank Christlieb, interview by the author, July 23, 2004, Dallas.

62. Frank Christlieb, e-mail message to author, June 25, 2005.

63. Joshua Benton, "Payroll Not Met in W-H," *Dallas Morning News*, August 26, 2004, 1A (2nd ed.), infoweb.newsbank.com.

64. Joshua Benton, interview by the author, September 13, 2004, Dallas.

65. Nazario interview.

66. Nazario interview.

67. Richard Read, "Racing the World," *Oregonian*, March 7–9, 2004, A1 (Sunrise Ed.), infoweb.newsbank.com.

68. Rowe interview.

69. Meyer interview.

70. Barry Siegel, "A Father's Pain, a Judge's Duty," *Los Angeles Times*, December 30, 2001, A1 (Home Ed.).

71. Nora Zamichow, "The Fractured Life of Jeremy Strohmeyer," *Los Angeles Times*, July 19, 1998, A1 (Home Ed.).

72. Nora Zamichow, interview by the author, October 6, 2004, Los Angeles.

73. Sue Goetinck Ambrose, interview by the author, July 21, 2004, Dallas.

74. Sue Goetinck Ambrose, "Letter-Rewriting Campaign," *Dallas Morning News*, December 22, 2003, E1 (2nd ed.), infoweb.newsbank.com.

75. Andy Dworkin, "Snagging a Stroke," *Oregonian*, April 24, 2002, A20 (Sunrise Ed.), infoweb.newsbank.com.

76. Andy Dworkin, interview by the author, June 21, 2004, Portland, Oregon.

77. Ethicist Kenneth Goodman has discussed the notion of "standard of care," a term from medicine, in relation to journalism. Telephone interview by the author, September 19, 1996. Quoted in David A. Craig, "Covering the Ethics Angle: Toward a Method to Evaluate and Improve How Journalists Portray the Ethical Dimension of Professions and Society" (Ph.D. diss., University of Missouri–Columbia, 1997).

78. Tom Hallman, Jr., interview by the author, June 21, 2004, Portland, Oregon.

79. Read interview.

80. Zamichow interview.

81. Read interview.

82. Hart said he first heard the phrase "prosecutorial editing" from Amanda Bennett, the former managing editor for enterprise at the *Oregonian* who became editor of the *Philadelphia Inquirer*. E-mail message to author, June 26, 2005.

CHAPTER FOUR

Quotes and Paraphrasing

Kevin McManus dropped his readers into the sticky world of quotation ethics in a 1990 *Columbia Journalism Review* article when he decided to give purists what they ask for: the exact words of the speaker. He quoted his sources talking about quotes—with all of the "ums," filler words, and redirections. "What I'm trying to do here is, of course, simply to demonstrate the power each writer wields when placing words (and sometimes ellipses) inside quotation marks," he said.[1]

Quotes may convey exactness to a reader, but for a journalist they imply small but important ethical choices about whether to edit for hesitation words, grammar, or clarity. But the ethical decisions involving quotes—and the related issue of paraphrasing—extend well beyond choices about whether and how to clean up wording. For narrative writers, they include how to confirm and represent dialogue that is reconstructed from other sources. For investigative writers, they include how to handle emotional or inflammatory quotes, and whether to quote anonymously. For all kinds of journalists, they include concerns about clarity, context, and diversity. This chapter explores the ethical landscape of journalists' everyday choices about quoting and paraphrasing by looking at both the benefits and challenges connected with these practices. Truth is again a central issue in the mix for ethical discussion—but again the issues are more complex than they might appear on the surface. Compassion enters the discussion because of the power of words to hurt people or to grab their hearts.

Benefits of Using Quotes

Quotes can reveal the voices and lives of people. They also have the potential to enhance journalists' credibility with their audience and to hold officials accountable for their statements.

Showing People's Voices and Lives

Quotes can enhance the insight that readers gain about the people they see described in ink on a page or pixels on a screen. They can highlight people's distinctive voices and opinions and enhance readers' understanding of who they are. Thomas T. Huang, the *Dallas Morning News*'s Texas Living editor, said this about what a quote can contribute:

> It can back up and reinforce certain things that you're saying in the story. It can reveal the personality of a person that you're talking to—the way they think, the way they express themselves. I think in general, a story without quotes would be pretty flat, so you add some quotes so that you actually hear. I think when you read you're listening internally, and so when you read a quote you're almost listening to a person say it. And so it helps bring the story alive and make it more human.[2]

Quotes, then, enliven stories and give readers reason to stick with them. For those whose interest they capture, quotes can reveal some truth about a person that a bare recitation of facts would not.

Henry Fuhrmann, senior copy desk chief for business at the *Los Angeles Times* and later a deputy business editor, said it is important for journalism "to try to talk to real people through real people. I think that's where empathy develops naturally. And by extension, that's where your authority is enhanced because you have managed to reach people using their neighbors, their peers, their colleagues, the archetypes that they represent."[3] His comment suggests that when readers see ordinary people, not officials, being quoted, their compassion may be stirred and their sense of connection enhanced.

The language used in a quote can provide insight about a person. Vivian McInerny, a feature writer for the *Oregonian*, used a short quote in this passage from her story about a couple coming to terms with having a child with Down syndrome:

> A cold front silenced the city, closing shops and offices. Jackson's surgery was scheduled to take place in 11 days. The Webbs' appointment to meet the surgeon was canceled because of weather. Normally busy streets looked bleak and

white and bitter cold. Ice and snow crunched beneath the tires as Heath drove the car slowly through the desolate January landscape.

They crested the hill. Nothing but white. In the distance, a lone figure waited at a bus stop. A teenage boy, wearing a black leather jacket and a blue bandanna tied over his head, flung both arms in the air. He stomped both feet. Tacee and Heath inched closer on the snow-packed street. The boy held a CD player in one hand and wore headphones beneath his bandanna. He danced on the snowy sidewalk, swaying and bopping with complete abandon, oblivious to the car rolling past.

"He was busting a move," Tacee says.

Then, as they drew nearer, they realized something else: The boy had Down syndrome.[4]

McInerny said Tacee Webb's comment about his "busting a move" revealed something distinctive about who she was—"very young and hip" and "full of life."[5]

Good quotes also help to bring home people's opinions powerfully and distinctively. Crayton Harrison, a business writer for the *Dallas Morning News*, said quotes can help a writer to step outside the blandness of conventional journalistic language:

We're all about mincing words and kind of honing things down to their grayest, most neutral stance, and a quote allows you to let somebody make an argument on one side or the other using more colorful language and kind of being a real person about it and not so surgical.[6]

In narrative writing, quotes often appear most powerfully in dialogue between figures in the story. This kind of quoting can be particularly important as a vehicle for revealing truth about a person. Jack Hart, managing editor and writing coach at the *Oregonian*, said:

Most journalists don't understand the difference between quotes and dialogue. And if you're going to write good narrative you have to write dialogue, which is you're describing action, you're describing people within the context of the scene talking to one another—whereas a quote is something that somebody says to the journalist that you kind of capture, put in a bag, and bring back home to the office and then use as a tool in building a story.[7]

Hart said good dialogue both reveals insight about characters by showing how they relate to one another and carries the storyline forward. This section of dialogue from Tom Hallman, Jr.'s, "Boy Behind the Mask" series provides an example. Sam Lightner's mother, Debbie, and father, David, along with his brother and sister, are discussing the decision to allow surgery for Sam's facial deformity:

Debbie touched Sam's arm. "Sam, do you still want to do this?"

Sam nodded.

"I want to hear it."

"Yes," Sam said, firmly.

"It's your decision," his father said. "That's the deal. If I felt something was wrong, I'd intervene. I don't sense that. But I have to be honest, it scares me a little bit."

"Me, too," Nathan said.

"Me, too," Emily said.

"I worry about the potential damage to him," said David. "As it stands, he's Sam. He is who he is."

"He'll look different," Emily said. "Sam is Sam."

"He is who he is," said David. "We don't think anything's wrong with him."

David leaned forward, arms on the table, and stared across at his son. "Any doubts, Sam?" he asked. "If you say 'no,' we call and cancel right now, date or no date."

"I'm a little nervous," Sam said. "But I like the doctors."

"Well, it scares me," his father said. "It's the unknown. Here we have the situation that Sam deals with. It's the known. It's not ideal for him because of his face. His face freaks people out. But it's a known property. And it's a little bit scary to risk everything because the world doesn't accept his face."

"Dad, I'm sure," Sam said. "Look what happened at Grant."

His father bowed his head.

"That's what people think about him," Debbie said. "They think he's mentally defective."

Sam leaned forward and mustered all his strength.

"I want to do this," he said.

David placed both hands on the table.

"We are fearfully and wonderfully made," he told his family. "And very fragile."

He sighed.

"All right," he said. "It's a go."[8]

This dialogue, which closes the second day of the series, reveals insight about the family's sensitivity and care for Sam, as well as their fears about the surgery, and brings the reader forward to the point of decision to go ahead with it. This approach provides a particularly detailed and compelling window on the voices and lives of people.[9]

Enhancing Credibility

Along with allowing readers to hear and understand the subjects of a story, quoting helps to establish the credibility of the reporting. Although it is still possible to make up quotes and even sources, citing people's words still goes further to establish truthfulness than writing entirely in the reporter's own voice. Pam Maples, assistant managing editor for projects at the *Dallas Morning News*, said, "If you have a story in which everything is paraphrased, the reader begins to wonder if you really talked to them."[10] Doug Swanson, a reporter who does investigative projects at the paper, said: "I think it gives it some credibility if you have actual people talking with their actual names attached. Then you convey that you've talked to these people and they feel strongly enough about it to have their point of view put in the story."[11]

Michael Arrieta-Walden, as public editor of the *Oregonian*, learned that readers welcome hearing people's own words: "One thing that we've found that is consistent is that people like to hear subjects in their own voice. And I think that may be an outgrowth of some skepticism about us as journalists in terms of being filters."[12]

Holding Sources Accountable

Not only can quotes help establish the truthfulness of journalists; they can also help hold public officials to a standard of truth by supplying a record of their words. Dean P. Baquet, managing editor and more recently editor of the *Los Angeles Times*, commented on how quotes can serve readers in this way:

> It's very helpful to be able to look back. Quotations are more important in this day and age when everything is on computers than they were even 25 to 30 years ago. . . . It would have been a major research project 10 years ago to find out everything the president said about the events leading up to a decision. I can do it in an hour now. They can even—the library can do it in an hour. It's really important to have quotes—full, meaty, undisputable quotes from the president about how he makes decisions. It just lets us go back in and three years from now, whoever is president, we will be able to look at what they said during the debate and hold them to a certain standard.[13]

Quotes, then, have long-range ethical implications related to truth because they can preserve truthfully what an official said and enable journalists to accurately evaluate the extent to which promises have been kept.

Challenges of Using Quotes

The ethical challenges related to quotes emerge on three fronts: corroborating their accuracy, particularly in reconstructions; choosing which quotes to use and how, including decisions to paraphrase; and rendering them properly. The choices about how to render quotes raise issues such as whether to change them and how to signal that they were reconstructed. This section will explore interviewees' insights on many of these everyday choices.

Challenges in Corroborating Quotes

Corroborating quotes is a key facet of journalists' efforts to "seek truth and report it," as the Society of Professional Journalists Code of Ethics puts it.[14] But just as confirming the accuracy of description presents practical and ethical challenges, so does corroborating quotes. Even when the reporter is present, it is difficult—sometimes impossible—to get quotes verbatim when a person is talking quickly or at length. When a reporter was not present and tries to reconstruct quotes or whole streams of dialogue, the difficulties multiply. Here the journalist again enters the realm of the historian, doing what James S. Ettema and Theodore L. Glasser referred to as seeking "some acceptable degree of corroboration among the traces available."[15] And again the journalist encounters the challenge of what Roy Peter Clark called the "essential fictive nature of all memory,"[16] the recognition that people do not always remember things with complete accuracy. Thoughtful narrative journalists step carefully when they are trying to reconstruct quotations.

Sonia Nazario of the *Los Angeles Times* offered an example of careful cross checking from her work on "Enrique's Journey." She pointed to the vagaries of memory in saying that "if you're not there to hear the quote, and sometimes even if you are there to hear the quote, your or people's recollections of it can be different." She found that different people in the same room could all remember "the core or a snippet" of what a person said in the same way. That corroborated recollection usually produced short quotes—such as when Enrique was on the phone in Honduras and said to his mother, "When are you coming home?" She warned of the danger of reconstructing long statements:

> I think when you're getting into quoting people in really long quotes, then you might be getting into trouble in terms of people's recollections of exactly how they said something. So my sense is that what everyone could agree upon were quotes that kind of were, I guess in a sense, fairly obvious and at the core of what the person would have been trying to convey in that given moment. So I think you have to be really careful about reconstructing quotes, and as a re-

sult a lot of quotes were stripped out of the story toward the end, especially if they were based on one person recalling them versus two or three people recalling the quote.[17]

Nazario's approach meant that quotes that fail to meet what Ettema and Glasser called an "acceptable degree of corroboration" were discarded. In some instances, a quote based on one person's memory of a short segment was acceptable, but the trustworthiness of the person was crucial. "With Enrique, everything he told me checked out, and so I found him to be very believable," Nazario said. She also considered how easy a quote would have been to remember and how obvious it might have been to say in the circumstance—as well as how dangerous the situation was. She used a few quotes based on Enrique's account of what people said when he was being beaten on top of a freight train because she has found that in dangerous situations, "your senses are very heightened in terms of what you remember of an experience like that."

Similarly, Hallman of the *Oregonian* assumed in "The Boy Behind the Mask" that Sam Lightner's parents were likely to recall the conversation that took place before he was born when they learned the gravity of his birth defect:

> They led the Lightners down the hall to a prenatal specialist. Their unborn child, he said, appeared to have a birth defect. The ultrasound indicated that the child's brain was floating outside the body.
> He had to be blunt. This child will die.
> Some parents, he said, would choose to terminate.[18]

This whole passage came from the parents, Hallman said. "Every parent would remember being told that. So I felt confident that they remembered that accurately."[19] However, even though he could be reasonably sure of the substance of the dialogue, he did not use quotation marks because he could not be absolutely sure the dialogue was verbatim.

As these reporters' work suggests, evaluating what is enough in corroboration of reconstructed quotes—especially dialogue—takes careful judgment that recognizes the difficulties of memory and the circumstances in which people speak.

Challenges in Choosing Quotes

Beyond deciding how to corroborate quotes, journalists face a large range of decisions about what quotes to use and how and whether to paraphrase. The issues include matters of story advancement, clarity, context and representativeness, balance and bias, and diversity. Difficult choices also arise in handling emotional or inflammatory quotes and being sensitive to sources, especially those who are not used to working with the media. Decisions about anonymous quotes present another set of challenges.

Advancing the Story

Quotes may be conventional in journalistic writing, but they are not ethically mandatory in the context of the goal of telling truth about people and situations. Spencer Heinz, another reporter who has done narrative work for the *Oregonian*, said, "Some stories I'll interview somebody and I won't use a quotation through the whole story, just because they don't seem to add anything to telling the story."[20] Across forms of journalistic writing, quotes are a tool to carry the story forward, but they should be discarded when they do not. Bob Yates, assistant managing editor for sports at the *Dallas Morning News*, pointed to the overuse of useless quotes: "I think quotes should be like good music in a Broadway show. They need to add something and keep it moving. If quotes stop the story like the old-fashioned musical where all of a sudden they'll stop and sing a song . . . then they're not very useful. And I think you see a lot of quotes like that."[21] Others noted the too-common practice of paraphrasing a quote to introduce it, then saying essentially the same thing by using the quote itself.

Quotes can provide insight about people, reveal their distinctive voices, and bring home their opinions powerfully. In the interest of maximizing truth telling in a story,[22] writers and editors need to evaluate whether they do these things or just take up space.

Clarity

Writers and editors also need to evaluate quotes carefully to decide which are the clearest and when to rework or boil down quotes as paraphrases. Lack of clarity keeps readers from more fully understanding an issue or a person, so it, too, has ethical implications.

If writers use quotes too freely and uncritically, readers may become confused. Leo C. Wolinsky, the *Times's* deputy managing editor and more recently managing editor, said:

> Some writers go overboard with quotes and are afraid to put themselves in the story, ultimately making those choices of what you use and what you don't. It becomes, and they can become, as obfuscating as they can be clarifying if you put too many of them together and just string them on, because then there's no clarity as to what's going on at all. It's just a bunch of talking heads. And if

you can get that from just getting a transcript, which is different than writing a story—so you have to be selective.[23]

Jargon poses a challenge to clarity on beats as different as science, business, religion, sports, and police. It is natural for people to adopt specialized language in their fields as they develop expertise, but the language that is familiar to them may pose a barrier to readers. Sue Goetinck Ambrose at the *Morning News* said, "In science stories, we probably have fewer quotes per column inch than a lot of other types of stories do just because the scientists tend to talk in their laboratory language and that's not usually understandable to the reader."[24] *Times* investigative reporters Scott Glover and Matt Lait pointed out the jargon in police language—for example, alighting from a vehicle instead of getting out of a car, and setting up a perimeter instead of surrounding a building. "Sometimes you slip into it because you're around it so much and you've really got to guard against it," Lait said. "We go back in our stories sometimes and critique them and say how did we do this, why did we do that."[25]

Paraphrasing is a staple of journalistic practice because it enables writers and editors to get around unclear quotes or condense them to their essential points. But paraphrasing also is an ethical issue because it presents opportunities to communicate elements of truth in a story more clearly—and dangers that accuracy and completeness will be diminished.

Huang of the *Morning News* pointed to the virtues of paraphrasing in saying: "I think overall, whenever you can, you should paraphrase. I think more often than not you should paraphrase so that there's clarity and conciseness, so you can move the story along."[26] But Arrieta-Walden of the *Oregonian* warned that a paraphrase, while clearer and more efficient for the reader, may look less authentic to the source and may actually be less accurate or complete.[27]

Context and Representativeness

The ethical challenges become even more complex in the areas of context and representativeness. G. Michael Killenberg and Rob Anderson, in an article analyzing ethical and rhetorical issues in quoting, made this provocative statement: "Each quote, no matter how literally accurate in a self-contained sense, is necessarily inaccurate in a contextual sense. Ultimately, readers or listeners of a journalistic account will hear only selected quotes and will themselves have to depend on the journalist to try to reconstruct the context of the quote."[28] Here, the ethical ideal of truth telling runs up against the reality that a journalist's choices about what to communicate shape and inevitably limit what readers take away—not only about one snippet of information but also about its larger backdrop. However, even with these constraints in mind, journalists retain an ethical obligation to use quotes to represent as best they can the broader context of a person's life or arguments. Patt Morrison, an opinion-page columnist for the *Times* who shared in two team Pulitzer Prizes as a reporter, put it this way:

> We have to truncate. We have to cut. We have to select. We also have an ethical responsibility to make sure that if we extract two or three words or 10 words to put in quotes, that we aren't doing it just because they're the most inflammatory. We're doing it because they are the most representative of what it was the entire quote or the entire sentence or paragraph or speech represents.[29]

Other journalists pointed out several areas where context and representativeness become issues. Steve Blow, a Metro columnist for the *Morning News*, said context is important in communicating the tone of a quote's delivery.[30] He cited a column about a Dallas-area Muslim couple, Hujefa and Insiyah Vora, who were booed at a Dallas Cowboys football game when they appeared on stadium video screens during a "fan of the game" contest. Talking about the couple's Cowboy fan clothing, Blow mentioned Insiyah's *rida*, a long skirt and hooded shawl that, in this case, was in Cowboy colors with stars on it. He quoted the couple this way:

> "Hujefa bought this material, and I made it just for Cowboys games," Insiyah said. "He even bought these stars," she said, showing off the star-shaped buttons on the skirt.
> "I was *really* in touch with my feminine side," Hujefa clowned.[31]

Blow said it was important to capture Hujefa's humor this way—even though "clowned" is not a traditional attributing verb in journalism—because part of his intent in the column "was undercutting the stereotypes that are attached to the word Muslim now."

In a similar way, Hallman talked about the importance of providing context in narrative scenes. "You have to be alert that the quote is not king. Just because they say it and then you stick it in there doesn't mean that you're accurately representing how it was said or the context of what is being said. So I think that again gets back to the reporting, putting the reader there."[32] For example, in a series on life in a neonatal intensive care unit, Hallman recounted dialogue between a doctor and a couple whose child was likely to die. But he described how she set up a circle of chairs, how she sat forward and put her hand on the husband's knee, and other details that showed the heart behind what she was saying.[33]

More broadly, quotes should fit the whole picture of who people are—though this kind of context is much easier to provide in features than in brief news stories. As noted in chapter 2, Beatriz Terrazas, a feature writer at the *Dallas Morning News*, said it would have been easy to do a quick-hit story focused on drinking instead of the in-depth two-part narrative she wrote on two teenagers who died in a car accident.[34] She recalled that a member of one of the teens' families had told her about a local television story that quoted a young person at a memorial service about what happens when people drink and drive. But there was a much broader context for the lives of these teens, and the quote implied they had been drinking without any evidence to back that up. Terrazas said toxicology reports later showed that the alcohol level of Ryan Jones, the driver, was well below the legal limit for intoxication.

> Was he careless in his driving? Maybe. Was he drunk? The evidence says he wasn't, but the story let people assume he was. Had our paper done a daily story about it, we might have done the same thing—quoted another kid saying the same thing. It's that easy to let something like that go in a story while we are on deadline and scrambling for information, and in the process let readers make assumptions because of our lack of clarity.[35]

Mark Z. Barabak, who covered the 2004 presidential election for the *Times*, talked about the value of quotes in reflecting broader points in a story about a candidate. His story with Michael Finnegan on the first debate between George Bush and John Kerry included this passage:

> Citing Kerry's recent depiction of the invasion of Iraq as "the wrong war in the wrong place at the wrong time," Bush said such comments not only demoralized U.S. troops but gave other countries reason to question Kerry's conviction. "You can't expect to build an alliance when you denigrate the contributions of those who are serving side-by-side with American troops in Iraq," Bush said.
> To drive home his point, he used the words "mixed message" or "mixed signals" half a dozen times to characterize Kerry's position on Iraq.[36]

Barabak said he thought it was important to cite Bush's repeated use of "mixed message" or "mixed signals" because "one of the things that a good politician knows is if you want to get a message across you've got to repeat it several times," so it showed readers what Bush wanted people to take away from the debate.[37]

Many news stories—political, investigative, and others—call for using quotes that might make the people quoted look foolish, not because of reporters' spitefulness but because the quotes honestly reflect the sources' viewpoints. Here, too, context is an important issue. Victoria Loe Hicks, one of the authors of a *Morning News* series that evaluated the health of the city of Dallas compared with other large cities, included this passage about the former mayor and his views toward the consultant's report that supplied key elements of the series' findings:

> Ms. Miller's predecessor, Ron Kirk, said Booz Allen's work will only complicate the leaders' job, which is to sell the city—if necessary, by drawing attention away from its defects just as a home seller does in dealing with potential buyers.
> "You put vanilla on the light bulb," he said.[38]

It is ethically important to double check that a sensitive comment such as this is in proper context. Hicks said she went back through the interview several times to "double check that this wasn't just a random, off-the-cuff remark that was totally divorced from the rest of his commentary but that it was, in fact, the heart of his commentary."[39]

Balance and Bias

It would be too simplistic to say that a fifty-fifty balance in quoting sources equates with ethical use of quotes. Even if that represented the most ethical approach, it would be impossible to achieve because all journalists operate within the filters of their educational, cultural, and sometimes spiritual backgrounds and the values they have developed, explicitly or implicitly, that shape what they see as important or noteworthy. No one is free of bias. But journalists act in an ethically questionable way if their implied promise to the audience is fairness and they are intentionally unfair or are careless about fairness. They then risk skewing their quote choices so that an individual or a position is poorly represented.

Wolinsky, who did early evaluations of front-page stories as deputy managing editor at the *Times*, said he occasionally spotted evidence of bias when he read stories either unedited or not fully edited.

> One of the interesting things when you do that is, you tend to see the reporter's thinking process a lot more because it hasn't been through the edit yet, and you'll get red flags for things, particularly things like bias. Because sometimes editors can be pretty good at covering that stuff up. And that's fine, because that's what they're supposed to do, they're supposed to balance it all. But it's important for you to know, because then you can look for other details that might be problematic in the story. It's just a kind of extra check. I mean, you don't find that much that's like that, but occasionally you do. You'll see when a story is really troubled early on.

He said one of the problems he sees in some stories is use of quotes that make one side look bad.

> You'll get stories that are pointed and don't have response from the subject un-til way down low in the story, for example, in which the reporter very clearly is laying out a case against somebody or something, but allows for no opportu-nity for response. And I think that can show bias. . . . Sometimes it's not just that it's low down in the story; sometimes it's just completely dismissive. They'll have a huge case built up and then the subject will be given one sen-tence, and sometimes it's a sentence that's actually, it's like getting a quote from somebody. It's like the worst quote that they could possibly give you, where they are completely inarticulate, weren't even on the point. And then later on you see other material down in the story which actually explains their position more but doesn't give them a real chance to explain, because it's a good quote that makes them sound more foolish, in effect. And you can see those things when the copy is raw a lot easier.[40]

Wolinsky's experience underlines how easy it is to choose quotes in a story in a way that leaves the impression of bias. Even if the writer does not intend to bias the reader against that side, that may be the result.

Diversity

Another ethical challenge in quote choice is reflecting a diverse array of voices. Truth telling that goes deeper than factual accuracy means commu-nicating about the lives and views of the full range of people in a community, particularly those who have little power or influence and have often been underrepresented in the news media.[41] At its heart, this is an issue of report-ing, but it also relates to the choices that writers make about quotes and sources—and the questions that editors ask.

Seth Prince, a copy editor at the *Oregonian* who is Choctaw and Chero-kee, commented on his concerns about sourcing and quotes when he handles stories about Native Americans and other minorities:

> One of the things that I watch for on attribution on stories about minorities in general, but Native Americans in particular, is who we have say certain things. And the tendency historically on Indian stories if you look back over decades and then some, it seems to be that a lot of people could talk about Indians but Indians themselves were never quoted about their own lives. And you'd have anthropologists, you'd have historians, and it all kind of characterized Indians as though they were people of the past who didn't exist anymore, they were relics for museums. . . . If you're only quoting historians and anthropologists who deal with things dead and buried, then what does that say about the

people you're writing about? And why should anyone care about that today necessarily? But also, there are a lot of experts who are of those minority groups who can have even more credible things to say on those issues because they have a deeper level of understanding some of it.[42]

Prince copyedited a five-part series about high death rates among children on the Warm Springs Reservation in Oregon.[43] The Warm Springs project said the reservation was the deadliest place for children in Oregon. Prince said it was important to have Indians from the reservation backing up that point and not just non-Indian sources—not only for the sake of credibility but also for fairness. "I think you've got to look at the historical ties between sources, and if you quote one who's traditionally wielded a great amount of authority over the lives of another, and then you're quoting him saying, 'These people have it really bad, and it's all their fault,' then you sort of feed into the historical unfairness that has gone on over the years."

When writers and editors strive to include diverse voices in choosing quotes, they help to tell truth about peoples and issues in a more nuanced way. In doing so, they also show compassion toward groups that have often been marginalized.

Emotional or Inflammatory Quotes

Quotes that convey strong emotions and can inflame the feelings of those who hear them create difficult ethical choices. They can also stir the opposite of compassion—outrage. By stirring outrage, they can obscure the truth that readers might otherwise gain. Or they might bring the truth home more powerfully, and even prompt readers to harness their outrage and try to help change an unjust situation.[44]

Choices about emotional quotes often become an issue in investigative stories. Strong statements from people who have been wronged or allegedly wronged can be ethically justifiable—though legal concerns about libel also need to be considered. Swanson of the *Morning News* used strongly worded quotes in a story about the Texas State Board of Medical Examiners' lax handling of cases in which doctors' negligence killed their patients. For example, he quoted Debby Stanley, whose son died after Dr. Charles C. Bittle, Jr., failed to diagnose his cancer:

> Mrs. Stanley said her lawyer told her the matter would be taken to the state board. No investigator ever contacted her, she said. The board took no action on the case.
> When she found that Dr. Bittle was still in practice, she said, she bought a .38-caliber handgun.

"I was going to kill him," she said. "He destroyed me. I was going to walk into his office and shoot him. And then I thought, who's going to take care of Meha?"

Meha was her son's horse.[45]

Pam Maples, Swanson's editor, said this quote brought home the human impact of the doctor's mistake:

In each case we talked about bringing the real human impact of these bad doctors to life. And it is one thing to tell a reader that a guy missed a diagnosis. You know, he missed a diagnosis—a kid dies. It's another thing to talk about what all that then continues to bring to the family. One of the things I always like to tell my reporters is kind of a cliché, but "You're telling me; I want you to show me." Her quote shows the depths of her despair over this—all brought on by this error—in a very sort of human, personal one-person way.[46]

In another investigative story—about Clay Dean Hill, the founder of a foster care center for emotionally troubled children—strong evidence from Swanson's reporting provided justification for another strong quote:

While Mr. Hill collects his millions, some Daystar children live in isolated trailers in this semi-rural town south of Houston.

"The kids stay all doped up, stuck in a house somewhere in the country with baby sitters who are unqualified," said Kristine Hopkins, mother of a child who resided at Daystar.[47]

Commenting on this quote, Swanson said:

While it may have been at the far end, it was not dishonest. It was not illegitimate. There was not anything in there that was untrue. It was simply a matter of degree, or of force of emotion and viewpoint and all of that. But it wasn't patently false. It was simply one side of the argument, strongly put. And that's exactly what I needed, I thought. If there hadn't been anything to back it up, then I think its use would have been questionable. There were dead kids to back it up, so that's why I felt justified in using it. And I went to them and said, hey, this mother says you keep them all doped up in trailers. What do you have to say about that? And let them answer it.[48]

Swanson, then, had strong factual support for using the quote and fairly sought out comment from the other side. He worked for months on the story and had, as Maples put it, "overwhelming evidence that there were multiple problems at this facility."[49]

Swanson's work provides a good example of ethical handling of inflammatory quotes because of the care he has brought to his reporting. He also enhances the power of the quotes by keeping them brief.[50]

Choices about inflammatory quotes also arise occasionally when people in the news use racial epithets. Thoughtful newspapers avoid quoting racial slurs unless they have compelling relevance to a story—and even then they might paraphrase to minimize the pain or offense they could cause. The *Oregonian* chose to use the word "nigger" in a story based on an interview with basketball player Rasheed Wallace, then of the Portland Trail Blazers:

> Wallace thinks that the white establishment of the league is exploiting young black athletes to enrich itself, and he doesn't mince words in talking about it.
>
> "I ain't no dumb-ass nigger out here. I'm not like a whole bunch of these young boys out here who get caught up and captivated into the league," Wallace, 29, said. "No. I see behind the lines. I see behind the false screens. I know what this business is all about. I know the commissioner of this league makes more than three-quarters of the players in this league.
>
> "There's a whole lot of crunching numbers that, quote-unquote, me as an athlete and me as an NBA player should know. In my opinion, they just want to draft niggers who are dumb and dumber—straight out of high school. That's why they're drafting all these high school cats, because they come into the league and they don't know no better. They don't know no better, and they don't know the real business, and they don't see behind the charade.
>
> "They look at black athletes like we're dumb-ass niggers. It's as if we're just going to shut up, sign for the money and do what they tell us."[51]

The paper ran an editor's note telling readers that during the interview, "Wallace was direct and emphatic in his opinions and occasionally graphic in his language. Although we understand some readers will find his use of a racial epithet offensive, we chose to leave it in the story to convey the strength of the opinion and the manner in which he expressed it."[52] Arrieta-Walden said the newspaper "did get some reaction, but I think the editor's note helped mute some of that."[53]

The newspaper's choice to use Wallace's quotes is ethically defensible not only because it underlined his opinion and his manner, but also because he was reflecting as an African American on the justice of the NBA's treatment of players, not throwing the word out gratuitously or hurtfully.

Sensitivity to Sources

Several writers talked about the importance of being sensitive to people who are not savvy about how journalists work and may not realize how their statements or lives will look in print. The point is not to give sources veto power over what goes into print, but to be fair and compassionate in dealing with them. Nora Zamichow, who wrote narratives for the *Times* before leaving the paper in 2006, reflected on the way she related to people who are not used to being in the media spotlight:

> When you're writing about people on the street, it's different from writing about politicians or political figures. They're media savvy. They know the rules; they know what they're up against. But if you're reaching into a community and you're reaching out to a person who may never have met a reporter or read this paper, you have a different threshold of how you're going to deal with this person. There are things where you think, well, did she really understand what she was saying? If I were to quote her literally, it would be a very harsh spotlight.[54]

Compassion does not mean cleaning up quotes, but it means being sensitive to the context of people's remarks. Commenting on her story about Jeremy Strohmeyer, who was accused of sexually assaulting and murdering an African American girl, Zamichow said:

> If Sherrice Iverson's mother goes into a tirade about white people, I understand that she's a grieving woman and that she's angry, and that while she may be saying a lot of stuff, A, it may not be necessarily relevant to what I'm writing, and, B, she may not really mean it—if you were to come back the next day, she'd be embarrassed. But that you don't capture the steam that somebody's blowing off.[55]

Reporters who show this kind of sensitivity in their choices about quotes are not only acting compassionately but also providing a picture of people that is, in the context of their lives, more truthful.

Anonymous Quotes

From the standpoint of truth telling, the stakes are ethically high when journalists evaluate whether to use anonymous quotes. Great caution was evident among interviewees who discussed the practice.

George Rodrigue, managing editor of the *Morning News* and a two-time Pulitzer winner as a reporter, warned that anonymous quotes allow for back stabbing and may cost a newspaper in credibility. "We lose the public's confidence, I think, when we do unattributed stuff to excess—or even in fact, if I want to do it day to day under normal circumstances. You leave people kind of blind in terms of judging the veracity of what you're saying."[56] Glenn F.

Bunting, a national correspondent for the *Times*, said anonymous quotes raise a red flag with readers about accuracy and authenticity, as well as the bias of the speaker. He thinks placing them high in a story raises particular problems because it may grab readers' attention but raises questions about the source.[57]

Baquet, the *Times*'s managing editor and later editor, argues for avoiding anonymous quotes for statements of opinion—with some exceptions. "Anonymous sources can state facts. They shouldn't hide behind their anonymity to state opinions. On occasion, though, you bend the rule. I mean, if you have a great reporter, if your most senior reporter, says I got somebody really high up in the White House is starting to be critical of the president, that to me might warrant using the quotation."[58] Baquet said avoiding anonymous opinions is a matter of both fairness and communication of truthful information to the reader.

Reporters and sources in Washington have taken anonymous sourcing to excess.[59] But sometimes there are strong ethical arguments for using them when they can help in uncovering truth about wrongdoing or abuses. Vernon Loeb, California investigations editor for the *Times*, who has also covered the CIA and the Pentagon for the *Washington Post*, said anonymous sources can be critically important in investigations of social abuses:

> The sources we deal with here in the real world in Los Angeles where we're investigating police violence, municipal corruption, health care fraud, these are people who work in a government agency. They see how the public is being ripped off and they do something about it very heroically. They call us up and they say, hey, we need your help. There's this ripoff going on. Here it is. Let me describe it for you. But you've got to promise me my name's not going to appear because if it does, I'm fired. I'm gone. I'm gonna lose my job. That's a very real fear they have. And if you didn't use anonymous sources, you'd never get at many of the most egregious abuses in our society. The anonymous sources are critical.[60]

The *Times*'s Glover said anonymous sources can help in investigations such as those he and Lait do of law enforcement corruption and can be hard to avoid with breaking criminal investigations because of police unwillingness to be quoted by name. But it is important to corroborate what a source offers anonymously. "You try to talk them into coming on the record, you try to talk them into giving you some documentation to support what they're saying. You take their information and before putting it in the paper try to knock it down through other sources and see if it withstands scrutiny."[61] However, Lait noted that there is a danger of being misled.[62]

Even in political stories, anonymous sources can provide perspective for readers. Don Frederick, national political editor for the *Times*, said: "It's impossible to cover politics, it's impossible to cover Washington and do a thorough, in-depth assessment to a story that's at all hard-edged without anonymous quotes. It's just too often people have too much on the line that if they're honestly critiquing somebody on their team—on their side of the aisle—it would be career suicide in some cases for them to put names to quote."[63] However, he said *Times* political editors push reporters to quote at least one named source—more if possible—before using an anonymous one.

Anonymous sources, then, may help in revealing social problems, providing deeper knowledge about law enforcement, and supplying perspective on political activity. But they carry a potential cost in reader credibility.

Challenges in Rendering Quotes

Writers and editors must wrestle with another area of decision on quoting besides corroboration and choice of quotes. They must also decide how to render them in print. In this realm they must evaluate how to condense them accurately, whether to change or edit, and how to signal reconstructions.

Preserving Accuracy in Paraphrasing and Tightening

The challenge that journalists face with accuracy in quoting most obviously relates to getting the words right in direct quotations—though, as will be discussed more below, that in itself is complicated. But other challenges arise in the choices about how to paraphrase and tighten quotes. These kinds of reworking can serve to get the people and ideas of a story across to readers more quickly or cleanly, but they require care to retain nuances of meaning as fully as possible.

Berta Delgado, a religion writer at the *Morning News* until she left in 2005, talked about the danger of losing accuracy in paraphrasing during the editing process:

> And sometimes your editor will read something and he thinks that he's interpreting a quote that you have in a story one way when that wasn't the way it was intended. And in trying to edit things down for space and trying to paraphrase something they'll get it all wrong. So it's really on you. It's on the reporter to be the subject's defense mechanism really. Because that happens a lot. I realize that more and more. You have to be real careful because we all make mistakes, and the editor wasn't there. He doesn't know exactly what this person meant. So when you're trying on deadline to edit things down and squeeze

things a little bit and you think, Well, maybe we can paraphrase this; they paraphrase it incorrectly.[64]

Because editors are a step removed from the reporting, it is always a danger that they will lose nuances—though they may also bring a fresh perspective on how to condense a passage.

Bunting of the *Times*, who has been both a reporter and an editor, also sees dangers in tightening involving quotes. Although being an editor helped him appreciate the challenges of condensing, he said he has found that some editors, "in the sincere attempt to make a quote a better quote for the reader and to make it make more sense," will not exactly represent what the person said. Sometimes the tightening comes through paraphrasing, other times through a combination of paraphrasing and partial quotes, or through cutting a quote of several sentences down to the equivalent of a sound bite.[65]

The challenges of tightening that these journalists note echo Killenberg and Anderson's analysis in their study of ethical and rhetorical issues in quoting.[66] Any effort to paraphrase or condense, no matter how conscientiously and skillfully done, only underlines the fact that each quote falls short of full accuracy in the broader context of a story since the full story in every nuance can never be told. Even without additional tightening, many selections have already been made.

Changing and Editing

Within individual quotes, journalists run up against decisions about whether and how to change or edit. They must also decide how to reflect deletions of intervening quoted material. These kinds of choices are unavoidable. Even the U.S. Supreme Court, in *Masson v. New Yorker Magazine* (1991), assumed that some editing of quotes is inevitable. Justice Anthony Kennedy's opinion said, "Writers and reporters by necessity alter what people say, at the very least to eliminate grammatical and syntactical infelicities." He also pointed to the "practical necessity to edit and make intelligible a speaker's perhaps rambling comments."[67]

Despite the recognition among both professionals and scholars[68] that decisions about changing quotes must be made, journalists vary in their opinions on what is acceptable. As McManus wrote in his *Columbia Journalism Review* article, "It is an area in which, oddly, there are no hard-and-fast rules for us to go by."[69] But these small judgments that journalists easily take for granted are ethically important. Bryan Denson, a reporter who has done investigative and narrative writing for the *Oregonian*, argued that being loose on changing quotes helps create a newsroom culture that supports "taking liberties with the truth."[70] Steve Steinberg, a features copy editor and writer at the *Morning News*, said he thinks "readers still have that perception that if it's in quotes, this is exactly what came out of that person's mouth," so cleaning up people's language violates readers' trust.[71]

Daily choices about editing quotes include:

- Cutting the end (or the beginning) off a longer comment. "When we speak, we ramble," Blow of the *Morning News* noted. "And I don't think it's our duty as journalists to include all the rambling. I think we do favors neither to the speaker nor the reader." He wrestles with how far to go in truncating, but feels comfortable if he has not left out anything that alters the truth of what he keeps in.[72]
- Using an ellipsis for deleted material in the middle of a quote. Bunting of the *Times* said he has argued with editors who have wanted to take out ellipses.[73] His concern is that if an ellipsis is cut, it will appear the quote was said verbatim when it was not.[74] Ethically those three dots are important to clearly signal that something is missing—at least for material beyond hesitation or filler words like "um." Ellipses may confuse readers or make them suspicious, though, so it is sometimes best to paraphrase.
- Deleting restarts in sentences. John S. Carroll, the editor of the *Times* until he retired in 2005, said: "If you really listen to tapes of how people speak, I think a lot of reporters clean up their grammar without even thinking about it. For example, some people will start a sentence, then back up and start it again or back up three or four words and start again. You'll never see that reflected in the quote. People will sort of stitch the thing together for that."[75] Carroll argues for rendering quotes literally, but he said it might be acceptable to remove restarts depending on the instance.[76]
- Adding minor words such as articles when words were omitted in notes. Andy Dworkin, a medical writer for the *Oregonian*, throws out quotes if they are missing words that might significantly affect meaning. "I'm not going to invent the driving verb of a sentence or something important like that," he said. But if the dropped word is clearly a minor one like "a" or "the," he will add it.[77]
- Putting together quotes that were not continuous and adding attribution between them. It is common journalistic practice to collapse quotes this way without an ellipsis signaling a gap. But Bunting said the context of the quotes is important to consider—for example, whether the two quotes are merely the beginnings of two different thoughts set

alongside each other, or appear to be one powerful statement when they were not in the original.[78] It is debatable whether readers realize that quotes separated this way were not continuous.

One of the most significant areas for ethical choice in quote editing is when, if ever, to change grammar. Minor changes in grammar may not materially alter the meaning of a sentence, but even people's grammar says something about who they are—so choices about grammar raise issues about truth telling. They even connect with compassion because, particularly for people who are not used to being in the news or are poorly educated, communicating their grammar in a literal way can cause embarrassment.

Frank Smith, the deputy copy desk chief on the news copy desk at the *Morning News*, said the paper handles choices about grammar in quotes case by case, taking into account the writer's perspective and the views of editors. "If it's someone in power who misspeaks and it's an important issue, I think you're more likely to see then this statement in quotes," he said.[79] Melissa McCoy, assistant managing editor for copy desks at the *Times* and later deputy managing editor, said the paper has faced choices about how to handle quotes from a prominent official, President Bush, who has himself acknowledged that he does not always speak cleanly and articulately—and in fact has laughed at his own stumbles. Since the main goal of the newspaper is to communicate clearly with readers, paraphrasing may help—but McCoy said editors would not edit inarticulate quotes and leave them in quotation marks.[80]

When the speaker is not in a position of power or in the media spotlight, more ethical sensitivity is needed on how to render quotes. McCoy cited the example of a PTA meeting where parents may be present to represent their children's interests but may not be very articulate: "I think what I would do is simply not use a lot of quoted matter from those people. I would paraphrase what they said because it's the information that's important, not the way they said it. But that's an ethical issue."[81] Some journalists would probably make minor grammatical changes in that case, but the choice to paraphrase better preserves truthfulness while showing compassion for the people.

In some stories about ordinary people, the importance of preserving the distinctiveness of communication style or dialect calls for quoting, not paraphrasing, and leaving the grammar alone. "Clearly," McCoy said, "when it's a personality profile or it's a story with flavor about a neighborhood or something, if you didn't write it the way they said it, it would look as if you hadn't been there."[82] Kurt Streeter of the *Times* showed he had been there in a profile of Arthur Winston, a ninety-seven-year-old man who had worked for seventy years cleaning vehicles for the Los Angeles transit agency—with one day's absence. He opened the story this way (quotes in italics):

> Strong and sharp and bearing down on 100 years of living, Arthur Winston has drawn a bead on what it takes to age well.
> Cut up the credit cards.
> *They don't do nothing more than bring about worry. Worry will kill you.*
> Get off the couch.
> *Stop in one place too long, you freeze up. Freeze up, you're done for.*
> Work as long and hard as you possibly can.
> *Folks retire, they end up on the front porch watching the street go by. Despair sets in, you're good as gone.*[83]

Streeter said he set the story up this way to take readers quickly "into his unique character, his unique way of talking."[84] By providing this window, he brought Winston to life in a way that he would not have by paraphrasing his statements or editing his grammar.

No matter what writers and editors decide about grammar in quotes, their choices run up against issues of fairness. Both McCoy and Smith pointed to situations that bring these issues to light. "If you have a death row inmate, his final words," Smith said, "you can be pretty sure that if they're not profane, that they'll probably go in as they're said even if they're used wrong. Now are we implicitly making some sort of moral judgment? I don't know. I mean that's a fair question."[85] McCoy, reflecting on what to do if a school official used bad grammar, said: "I would probably use it, but then maybe I'm setting a double standard by saying that. But if a person gets paid to do that for a living and that person is there to represent the school and education in the wider frame, then I think you have to. But maybe that's not fair."[86] Fairness issues become particularly sensitive when politicians are involved. Carroll said the late Alabama governor George Wallace "used to complain that every bad construction he used ended up in the paper but other politicians who were liberal politicians who spoke pretty poorly didn't get their bad language in the paper—which I think there is an issue of fairness there."[87]

Signaling Reconstructions

As discussed earlier, journalists—in particular, narrative writers—have to weigh what constitutes sufficient confirmation of the accuracy of quotes and extended dialogue. They also must decide how to signal for readers what they know.

The choices again point to what Ettema and Glasser called an "acceptable degree of corroboration."[88] The *Oregonian's* approach provides an example of careful thought on signaling reconstructions. Different degrees of corroboration are handled in different ways. If the reporter cannot confirm the speaker's exact words but is confident of their substance, they stay out of quotation marks. If the reporter can reasonably confirm the exact words, they are quoted. In addition, in both cases, writers will use "remembers" or a similar word to attribute the material to the memory of one or more people. Hallman used both approaches, with "remembers" as attribution, in this passage from "The Boy Behind the Mask":

> Years later she still wonders if it was something she missed, some sign that things weren't right. But it wasn't until her seventh month that Debbie Lightner learned something had gone terribly awry.
>
> She struggled to sit up on the examination table. The baby, her doctor said, was larger than it should be. Debbie watched him wheel up a machine to measure the fetus. She felt his hands on her stomach.
>
> "Something's wrong," the doctor said again.
>
> He told Debbie he would call ahead to the hospital and schedule an ultrasound. He laughed and told Debbie he just wanted to be sure she wasn't having twins.
>
> The next morning, at the ultrasound lab, the technician got right to work. He immediately ruled out twins.
>
> Then, a few minutes into the test, the technician fell silent. He repeatedly pressed a button to take pictures of the images on the monitor. After 30 minutes, he turned off the machine, left the room and returned with his boss. The two studied the photographs.
>
> They led the Lightners down the hall to a prenatal specialist. Their unborn child, he said, appeared to have a birth defect. The ultrasound indicated that the child's brain was floating outside the body.
>
> He had to be blunt. This child will die.
>
> Some parents, he said, would choose to terminate.
>
> No, Debbie remembers telling him. She and her husband were adamant that they would not kill this baby.[89]

Hallman used a short direct quote, "Something's wrong," because it was a brief statement that Debbie would easily have remembered verbatim. He rendered the rest without quotation marks.

David Stabler, a classical music critic for the *Oregonian* who was a 2003 Pulitzer finalist in feature writing for a narrative on a teen cello prodigy, brought readers compelling dialogue, too, while being careful not to signal certainty on exact wording when he was not present. The first day of the three-part series ended with this passage about a wild car ride that included the teen, Sam Johnson:

Sam was itching to see what Levy Mahoney's new car could do. His best friend's Acura 3.2 TL is midnight blue with black leather seats, 18-inch wheels and a Bose sound system. After a football game last fall, they found out.

They picked up Jake, then 14, and his cousin, Caleb, 16, then headed for the curves west of Sam's house. Levy, a slight, dark-haired boy, drove with Sam sitting next to him and Jake and Caleb in the back seat. It was a windows-down night, and Sam cranked up "Guilty Until Proven Innocent" by rap star Jay-Z.

The boys remember the night going like this. They took the first curve at 80 mph and straightened out. Levy accelerated into the next one when Jake spotted lights in the mirror.

Cop!

Levy took his foot off the gas.

No! Speed up! Sam yelled. The police car was maybe half a mile back, and Sam knew the roads. Levy pushed his foot down.

Slow down! Slow down! Jake yelled, shaking Levy's seat.

No! Don't listen to him! Just go!

Oh, man, Jake moaned. We're in trouble! We're in trouble!

Oh my, Caleb said. Oh my.

Levy gripped both hands on the wheel, and the needle climbed: 90 . . . 100 . . . 110. . . .

The police lights faded.

Sam told Levy where to turn off the road and double back to Sam's house. They crept into the driveway and parked out of sight beyond the Johnsons' Suburban van. Minutes later, a police car cruised by without stopping.[90]

Stabler said the boys' words were as they remembered them, but he avoided quotation marks because he was not present. "We could have put them in italics, which is sometimes a signal that it's a quote but you weren't there. But no, we couldn't put it in quotes because I didn't hear it."[91]

Handling Quotes Ethically

Ethical use of quotes rests on basics of good reporting. It starts with good listening, note taking, and, if needed, tape recording to preserve what a speaker said as accurately as possible. It involves double-checking notes and tapes, preferably soon after an interview. As with description, the highest level of accuracy is likely to come when the reporter is present in a scene rather than interviewing participants later. Good reporting also makes it possible to have diverse sources from whom to draw comments. When reporters have to corroborate comments they did not hear, careful questioning and cross-checking are essential, just as they are with reconstruction of description.

Many of the journalists interviewed support reading back quotes to sources. Read backs can not only help ensure accuracy in wording but can also help writers to cross-check their understanding of the context in which the person spoke. They can also be valuable for confirming the clarity and accuracy of paraphrases. Reporters have to stand firm to avoid giving sources free rein to edit or withdraw quotes, but read backs can lead to ethically stronger stories if they are done carefully.

Careful reading and questioning by editors—not only about accuracy and clarity but also about context, bias, and diversity—can also strengthen what readers see. Jake Arnold, a copy editor at the *Oregonian*, pointed to some of the kinds of questions editors—including copy editors—need to ask beyond individual words: "Is this quote taking me in a different direction than the rest of the story has taken me? Is this quote taking me in a different direction than other stories I've read about this person? Does this quote fit in the character?"[92] As Arnold noted—echoing scholars in media studies—being truly unbiased is impossible. But these kinds of questions can help to ensure fairness. It is also important for editors to double check meaning and context with reporters when they tighten passages by cutting some quotes or paraphrasing.

Open newsroom discussion—involving reporters, top editors, assigning editors, and copy editors—is important to clarify and develop more thoughtful approaches to sensitive choices such as how to handle racial slurs and other inflammatory quotes and how to handle anonymous quotes.

Accurate and thoughtful rendering of quotes calls for newsroom discussion of the taken-for-granted little choices involved in editing and smoothing out quotes. These are not likely to be high on the list of topics for an in-house ethics workshop, but they are serious ethical matters. Discussion and critique of how reporters and editors actually handle these choices would raise awareness of the possible approaches.

Notes

1. Kevin McManus, "The, Uh, Quotation Quandary," *Columbia Journalism Review* (May–June 1990): 54.

2. Thomas T. Huang, interview by the author, July 22, 2004, Dallas.

3. Henry Fuhrmann, interview by the author, October 4, 2004, Los Angeles.

4. Vivian McInerny, "King of Hearts," *Oregonian*, March 28, 2004, L-01 (Sunrise Ed.), infoweb.newsbank.com.

5. Vivian McInerny, interview by the author, June 23, 2004, Portland, Oregon.

6. Crayton Harrison, interview by the author, July 19, 2004, Dallas.

7. Jack Hart, interview by the author, June 21, 2004, Portland, Oregon.

8. Tom Hallman, Jr., "The Boy Behind the Mask Part Two," *Oregonian*, October 2, 2000, A1 (Sunrise Ed.), infoweb.newsbank.com.

9. For an interesting example of a different kind of dialogue—between a reporter and the subjects of a story—see Nora Zamichow, "The Fractured Life of Jeremy Strohmeyer," *Los Angeles Times*, July 19, 1998, A-1 (Home Ed.).

10. Pam Maples, interview by the author, September 14, 2004, Dallas.

11. Doug Swanson, interview by the author, July 22, 2004, Dallas.

12. Michael Arrieta-Walden, interview by the author, June 22, 2004, Portland, Oregon.

13. Dean P. Baquet, interview by the author, October 5, 2004, Los Angeles.

14. Society of Professional Journalists Code of Ethics, www.spj.org/ethics_code .asp (accessed May 24, 2006).

15. James S. Ettema and Theodore L. Glasser, *Custodians of Conscience: Investigative Journalism and Public Virtue* (New York: Columbia University Press, 1998), 132.

16. Roy Peter Clark, "The Line Between Fact and Fiction," Poynter Institute for Media Studies, www.poynter.org/content/content_view.asp?id=3491 (accessed May 24, 2006).

17. Sonia Nazario, telephone interview by the author, March 11, 2005.

18. Tom Hallman, Jr., "The Boy Behind the Mask Part One," *Oregonian*, October 1, 2000, A1 (Sunrise Ed.), infoweb.newsbank.com.

19. Tom Hallman, Jr., interview by the author, June 21, 2004, Portland, Oregon.

20. Spencer Heinz, interview by the author, June 22, 2004, Portland, Oregon.

21. Bob Yates, interview by the author, July 19, 2004, Dallas.

22. "Doing Ethics: Ask Good Questions to Make Good Ethical Decisions," Poynter Online, www.poynter.org/content/content_view.asp?id=5600 (accessed May 24, 2006).

23. Leo C. Wolinsky, interview by the author, October 7, 2004, Los Angeles.

24. Sue Goetinck Ambrose, interview by the author, July 21, 2004, Dallas.

25. Matt Lait, interview by the author, October 4, 2004, Los Angeles.

26. Huang interview.

27. Arrieta-Walden interview.

28. G. Michael Killenberg and Rob Anderson, "What Is a Quote? Practical, Rhetorical, and Ethical Concerns for Journalists," *Journal of Mass Media Ethics* 8, no. 1 (1993): 50.

29. Patt Morrison, interview by the author, October 7, 2004, Los Angeles.

30. Steve Blow, interview by the author, September 14, 2004, Dallas.

31. Steve Blow, "Cowboys Fans Reeling from Sting of Jeers," *Dallas Morning News*, September 10, 2004, 1B (Collin County Ed.).

32. Hallman interview.

33. Tom Hallman, Jr., "Fighting for Life on Level 3," *Oregonian*, September 24, 2003, A1 (Sunrise Ed.).

34. Beatriz Terrazas, interview by the author, July 20, 2004, Dallas. Discussing Beatriz Terrazas, "Where the Tree Stands," *Dallas Morning News*, March 26, 2000, 1F (3rd ed.) and March 27, 2000, 1C (3rd ed.).

35. Beatriz Terrazas, e-mail message to author, June 24, 2005.

36. Mark Z. Barabak and Michael Finnegan, "Bush, Kerry Trade Barbs on Iraq War," *Los Angeles Times*, October 1, 2004, A-1 (Home Ed.).

37. Mark Z. Barabak, telephone interview by the author, November 24, 2004.

38. Victoria Loe Hicks, ["Dallas at the Tipping Point"] "Dallas. 'A can-do city,' that's how Dallas loves to see itself—and with good reason. Energy, ambition, vision and hard work have made it the centerpiece of the fastest-growing region in the country. The trouble is, Dallas itself isn't nearly as healthy as the region. And a lack of self-analysis blinds it to that fact," *Dallas Morning News*, April 18, 2004, 3W (2nd ed.), infoweb.newsbank.com.

39. Victoria Loe Hicks, interview by the author, September 14, 2004, Dallas.

40. Wolinsky interview.

41. Clifford G. Christians, John P. Ferré, and P. Mark Fackler, arguing from a communitarian ethical perspective, contend that just portrayal of the marginalized is at the core of the mission of the news media. See Christians, Ferré, and Fackler, *Good News: Social Ethics and the Press* (New York: Oxford University Press, 1993).

42. Seth Prince, interview by the author, June 23, 2004, Portland, Oregon.

43. *Oregonian* staff, "A Place Where Children Die," *Oregonian*, December 7–11, 2003, infoweb.newsbank.com.

44. The title of David L. Protess et al., *The Journalism of Outrage: Investigative Reporting and Agenda Building in America* (New York: Guilford Press, 1991) aptly sums up the kind of feelings that investigative stories often convey.

45. Doug J. Swanson, "Patients' Deaths Haven't Moved State Board to Act," *Dallas Morning News*, July 28, 2002, 1A (2nd ed.), infoweb.newsbank.com.

46. Pam Maples, interview by the author, September 14, 2004, Dallas.

47. Doug J. Swanson, "Owner Reaps Millions through Foster Homes," *Dallas Morning News*, October 19, 2003, 1A (2nd ed.), infoweb.newsbank.com.

48. Swanson interview.

49. Maples interview.

50. Huang of the *Morning News*, discussing use of emotional quotes in general, pointed out the power that can come from being brief rather than quoting at length and being "heavy-handed."

51. Geoffrey C. Arnold, "Raw'sheed: Rasheed Wallace Cares, Just Not About Fans' Feelings or the NBA," *Oregonian*, December 11, 2003, D1 (Sunrise Ed.), infoweb.newsbank.com.

52. Dennis Peck, "Editor's Note," *Oregonian*, December 11, 2003, D1 (Sunrise Ed.), infoweb.newsbank.com.

53. Arrieta-Walden interview.

54. Nora Zamichow, interview by the author, October 6, 2004, Los Angeles.

55. Zamichow interview.

56. George Rodrigue, interview by the author, September 14, 2004, Dallas.

57. Glenn F. Bunting, interview by the author, October 7, 2004, Los Angeles.

58. Baquet interview.

59. Some news organizations have tightened their policies on anonymous sources. See Rachel Smolkin, "A Source of Encouragement," *American Journalism Review* (August–September 2005), www.ajr.org/article.asp?id=3909 (accessed June 4, 2006). For the *Washington Post's* revised policy, see "The *Washington Post's* Policies on Sources, Quotations, Attribution, and Datelines," Poynter Online, www.poynter.org/content/content_print.asp?id=61244&custom= (accessed June 1, 2006). See also "Editors' Letter to the *Washington Post* Staff about Style Book Revisions," Poynter Online, www.poynter.org/content/content_print.asp?id=61247&custom= (accessed June 1, 2006).

60. Vernon Loeb, interview by the author, October 5, 2004, Los Angeles.

61. Scott Glover, interview by the author, October 4, 2004, Los Angeles.

62. Lait interview.

63. Don Frederick, interview by the author, October 5, 2004, Los Angeles.

64. Berta Delgado, interview by the author, July 19, 2004, Dallas.

65. Bunting interview.

66. Killenberg and Anderson, "What Is a Quote?"

67. *Masson v. New Yorker Magazine*, 501 U.S. 396 (1991).

68. Killenberg and Anderson in "What Is a Quote?" explore several areas of choice about quote editing.

69. McManus, "The, Uh, Quotation Quandary." A later article in another professional publication made a similar argument. See Fawn Germer, "Are Quotes Sacred?" *American Journalism Review* (September 1995): 34–37.

70. Bryan Denson, interview by the author, June 21, 2004, Portland, Oregon.

71. Steve Steinberg, interview by the author, July 20, 2004, Dallas.

72. Blow interview.

73. Bunting interview.

74. Glenn Bunting, telephone interview by the author, June 23, 2005.

75. John S. Carroll, interview by the author, October 6, 2004, Los Angeles.

76. John S. Carroll, e-mail message to author, June 24, 2005.

77. Andy Dworkin, interview by the author, June 21, 2004, Portland, Oregon.

78. Bunting interview, October 7, 2004.

79. Frank Smith, interview by the author, July 20, 2004, Dallas.

80. Melissa McCoy, interview by the author, October 8, 2004, Los Angeles.

81. McCoy interview.

82. McCoy interview.

83. Kurt Streeter, "A Working Knowledge of Life," *Los Angeles Times*, February 13, 2004, A-1 (Home Ed.), infoweb.newsbank.com.

84. Kurt Streeter, interview by the author, October 8, 2004, Los Angeles.

85. Smith interview.

86. McCoy interview.

87. Carroll interview.

88. Ettema and Glasser, *Custodians of Conscience*.

89. Hallman, "The Boy Behind the Mask Part One."

90. David Stabler, "Day One: Lost in the Music," June 23, 2002, A1 (Sunrise Ed.), infoweb.newsbank.com.

91. David Stabler, interview by the author, June 22, 2004, Portland, Oregon.

92. Jake Arnold, interview by the author, June 23, 2004, Portland, Oregon.

∽✕∾

CHAPTER FIVE

Word Choice, Labeling, and Bias

Bias in the news media is a hot topic. On radio and television talk shows, in popular books, and on the Internet, strong words fuel a debate grounded in sharply different political and ideological perspectives. On the right, for example, former CBS News reporter Bernard Goldberg argues that the network is rife with liberal bias,[1] and Bob Kohn accuses the New York Times of turning its back on a tradition of objectivity.[2] The Media Research Center's website talks about the organization's mission "to bring balance to the news media" and describes a tracking system to provide evidence of liberal media bias.[3] On the left, Eric Alterman argues that the real bias is conservative, rooted in media ownership.[4] Fairness and Accuracy in Reporting's website talks about that group's work to advocate press diversity and communication of dissenting views, and its support for structural reform "to break up the dominant media conglomerates."[5] Al Franken, host of the The Al Franken Show, criticizes what he calls "the right-wing media" such as Fox News, the Wall Street Journal editorial pages, and talk radio, saying they are not interested in seeking truth.[6]

Scholarly studies have shown that journalists tend to lean to the left politically, but this research has not clearly demonstrated a link between their leanings and their reporting.[7] Still, many members of the public are skeptical about balance in news media. Michael Arrieta-Walden of the Oregonian said bias was the biggest issue he heard about from readers as public editor. And the complaints ranged from seeing wording in coverage of Ronald Reagan's death as too friendly to saying gay marriage was covered too favorably.

Jamie Gold, readers' representative at the *Los Angeles Times*, said bias has been the most common complaint there, too. She gets regular complaints that the paper is too liberal—mostly broad statements but also some specifics.[8] But probably one-fourth of the bias charges "are from those saying the paper is too conservative. As with the liberal charges, the bulk of them don't include specifics, or give specifics that are repeated almost verbatim in each e-mail or phone call and seem to be based on a broadcaster's or blogger's opinion."[9] She said jumps in charges of bias are linked to times "when local or national broadcasts put their spin on a story in the *Times* and tell folks to write or call."

In reality, it is impossible for any journalist to become free of bias—however little or much one's individual biases affect writing and editing. Personal perspective is too deeply rooted, and the limits of language are too great. But as an ethical matter, journalists striving to be truthful and fair must weigh carefully the implications of their words. Descriptive phrases and shorthand labels for social, political, and religious issues and the people involved in them present difficult ethical challenges for writers and editors. Other ethical choices come with many other descriptors for people and situations including superlatives, as well as qualifiers and transition words, that have implications related to bias. (For discussion of physical description and observation of people and places, see chapter 3.)

This chapter examines areas of word choice and labeling that surfaced in the interviews with journalists, then reflects more generally on the difficulties involved in making ethical choices about words within the limitations of people and language. Again, ideas to foster ethical choices are also presented.

Difficult Areas of Word Choice

Single words and phrases are inexact instruments for communicating about complex issues. Sensitive readers will view them in different ways depending on the lens of their worldview. Poor choices of words can hurt people or distort the picture of an issue. This section explores several sensitive areas of word choice: war and terrorism, other social and political matters including abortion and ideological labeling, religion, and descriptors and qualifiers in various other areas. The discussion is based on what stood out to the journalists interviewed as sensitive and important issues—some that are ongoing and some that were particularly significant at the time of the interviews. Some comments from readers are also included from *Times* readers' representative reports.

War and Terrorism

Words describing armed conflicts and the people involved in them are among the most ethically sensitive matters of word choice that publications face. Differences of viewpoint are sharply evident in how readers evaluate language decisions, and the life-and-death nature of war and terrorism makes it easy for them to be sensitive about these choices.

Terrorism

Gold and several *Times* editors brought up the use of the word "terrorist" or substitutes as a key challenge for the newspaper in word choice. The differences in reader vantage points make choices in this area challenging. The complaints about terrorism-related terms extend beyond coverage of the Middle East—though that is the most common area of criticism.

The sensitivities of some readers are evident in this summary from the *Times* readers' representative report, which Gold compiles and distributes weekly:

> "Terrorist"—Three dozen readers have sent e-mails in an apparently orchestrated effort to ask why the word "terrorist" has been applied to those who carried out the attacks in Madrid, but isn't used as often in stories about suicide bombings in Israel: "Why is it that when The Times had reports on the terrorism in Iraq and Spain, the words 'terrorists' and 'terrorism' were used regularly, but when The Times reports on incidents in Israel, such as the terrorist attack in Ashdod on March 15, the reference is to 'militant organizations'? Hamas and the Al Aqsa Martyrs Brigade are recognized on everyone's lists as terrorist organizations. Why don't you use that term in referencing them?"[10]

For readers who strongly oppose attacks on Israel, the terrorist label is important. They want the more rhetorically powerful label applied, and they want it applied evenhandedly to different groups. Dean P. Baquet, the *Times's* managing editor and more recently editor, said the paper also hears from readers when a Palestinian suicide bomber blows up a bus and kills Israeli schoolchildren and the newspaper calls him a "suicide bomber" instead of a terrorist.

Another set of complaints noted in the readers' representative report criticized the use of "separatists":

> ETA—In an apparent campaign, 13 readers wrote or called to criticize references to Basque "separatists" in stories out of Spain. Sample: "Call the ETA by its real name, 'terrorists' . . . That's what they are. The same kind of people as Al Qaeda. A 'separatist' exercises his voice and freedom and doesn't go out

killing innocents, kids, students, regular people. Be more careful with your language, and consider the victims."[11]

The point this reader made about victims underlines the fact that whatever they are called, the activities of these groups kill people. That reality means important ethical judgments are unavoidable because any label for "terrorist" will represent a choice that might imply condemnation or support of the activity. And which it implies will depend a great deal on the perspective of the reader. As Baquet noted, "One country's terrorist is another country's freedom fighter."[12]

If the word "terrorist" is ethically loaded, is there an alternative that is not? Tim Lynch, senior copy chief of the foreign and national desks at the *Times*, said the newspaper has not developed an official policy or banned the word, but has leaned toward describing what a person or group does rather than supplying a label:

> Right now the thinking is that we will let the description of the event define for the reader what the activity is. If a bomb blows up on a bus in Jerusalem and kills a lot of women and children, that description enough will lead probably most readers to discern that that was a terrorist attack. However, if we don't use the word and someone wants to consider that a legitimate political reprisal, if the reader wants to imbue the story with that, then that's the reader's choice. So what we're leaning more toward now is describing the events as clearly as possible and letting the reader conclude what that is. The word is not banned by any stretch. We're just really thoughtful, we're really stepping back and saying, Should we characterize this as a terrorist attack or this as a terrorist group? And there are times when we will, but that's one of those hot-button words.[13]

Melissa McCoy, the *Times*'s assistant managing editor for copy desks and more recently deputy managing editor, said caution in using the word "terrorist" means describing "what it is the person has done or is accused of doing"—for example, in some cases using a noun such as "gunman" or "hijacker."[14]

Avoiding both the label "terrorist" and other labels enables a publication to provide truthful details without taking sides—though not taking sides is itself an ethical position and one that not all readers will accept.

Israeli-Palestinian Conflict

Interviewees at both the *Times* and the *Dallas Morning News* brought up the Israeli-Palestinian conflict as a sensitive area. The choices here relate to headlines and photos and to balance and context in coverage beyond word choice—and beyond use of the word "terrorist." But decisions about words and phrases are a key concern.

Gold said the Israeli-Palestinian conflict is a common area of reader complaint at the *Times*. The newspaper hears about both context and wording. She characterized the complaints—about that conflict and other Middle Eastern conflicts—this way:

> Side A did such and such to side B and then side A will write and say, why didn't you say what side B did to side A first? So it's the context that people don't think is there, so it's often more subtle than just, that word was the wrong word. But it might be something less subtle, like so and so attacked, when they'll say, no, they were defending themselves, just because it's out of context.[15]

Robert W. Mong, Jr., editor of the *Morning News*, also pointed to the importance of context—including the whole package of the story.

> It's really not uncommon for me, a couple times a month, to on the same day get a call from somebody in the Muslim community about a story and maybe the same day or a day later on the same report you hear from one of the interest groups in the pro-Israeli community—same story, same headline, same photos—and they both claim bias. And it's hard often to believe when I say, "You might not believe me, but so and so felt that the story was biased in favor of, say, Israel."[16]

Mong's comments also show how different the same event can look through the lenses of perspective of readers with different backgrounds.

At the *Times*, a few readers questioned wording describing the barrier that Israel was building along the West Bank. Gold said readers made at least two arguments: "When it was called a security barrier, we had a few complaints by those who said we were using their [Israel's] euphemism for what was a land grab by Israel." Some also questioned the use of "wall," saying it was not a wall in most places but rather a fence.[17] One, for example, complained about a headline using "wall":

> The Sunday article repeatedly refers to the security barrier being built to protect Israeli civilians from mass murderous terrorist attacks as a "wall." In fact, the barrier is planned to be about 94% fence, 6% wall. The wall locations are where Palestinians have shot Israeli civilians driving on nearby highways and also where adjacent towns are located. Why are you inaccurately referring to it in the sub-headline as a "wall" which is part of the Palestinian Propaganda

campaign (e.g. Berlin Wall) rather than a "fence," which many countries have along their borders?[18]

Lynch said the *Times* has developed this approach: "We avoid 'wall' in virtually all cases because, in fact, there isn't much wall there. We typically go with 'fence' or 'barrier.' We also tend to avoid 'security' as a modifier. If we do use a modifying word, we tend to go with 'separation.'"[19] It might be impossible to find language everyone would find acceptable, but this approach avoids some language likely to appear loaded.

For clarity of communication, it is important to be aware of the vantage points from which readers will evaluate details of wording. Laura Dominick, a copy editor on the *Times*'s foreign desk, pointed out another sensitive passage related to Israel. The story referred to the late Egyptian President Anwar Sadat's signing of a peace treaty with Israel and to the Islamic militants who "shot him dead for his crime." Dominick said she changed this wording to "assassinated him." "Obviously," she said, "the reporter wasn't agreeing with the militants that it was a crime, but there were bound to be readers who would've thought so."[20]

Truthful communication in word choice can be difficult because of the influence of the different political, social, and religious vantage points of readers, but the goal of truth telling makes it important for journalists to try to communicate in ways that are sensitive to these different vantage points. Sensitivity in word choice also amounts to compassion for the audience when the issues are this deeply felt and controversial.

Iraq War

The seriousness of war and its consequences makes word choice about war particularly sensitive. *Times* editors described two issues related to the Iraq war where they have made calls about word choice.

One issue involved what to call those who fought U.S. and other countries' troops through various attacks in Iraq after the initial phase of the war. Initially the *Times* used the term "resistance fighters" to describe them. However, Baquet said, "I came to believe that it was one of those phrases that had been romanticized from World War II with these romantic French guys smoking cigarettes and plotting attacks against the Nazis." The term seemed loaded.[21] In a memo—which was picked up and posted on L.A. Observed, a blog about Los Angeles media—McCoy said, "Although this term is not inaccurate on its face, it conveys unintended meaning. To many, it romanticizes the work and goals of those killing GIs. We should avoid using it outside of quoted material."[22] "Insurgents" and "guerrillas" became the preferred terms.

The other issue was how to handle euphemisms used by the U.S. military and the Bush administration in talking about the war—terms such as "collateral damage," "softening up," and "shock and awe." McCoy said that before the war, she and her chief deputy at the time, Clark P. Stevens, put together a list of terms to watch for to counter government efforts to put a positive spin on the war. "To me," she said, "those issues are right at the heart of a paper delivering accurate and as close to unbiased information as you can—not just sort of like taking a direct feed from the Defense Department and just spilling it, just pouring it right on to the page."[23] In contrast to these vague terms, description provides clarity on what is really happening. For example, instead of saying troops softened up an area, "What you want to say is they decided to take Apache helicopters in and drop bombs on this neighborhood. Just say that. What are they going to do exactly? They're going to take tanks in and they're going to clear the area by setting houses on fire."[24]

Government efforts to use language that puts the best face possible on the military effort in this way amount to a distortion of the truth about war. But again the issue of readers' vantage point complicates decisions about what amounts to the most truthful wording because some readers may question whether the newspaper is telling the truth or doing its own spin. In the case of use of "resistance," the *Times* made a call that looked supportive of the Bush administration's position; in the case of war-related description, the decision appeared to be opposed. A decision in either direction in these cases not only changes the truth content of the statement but also alters some readers' willingness to believe the statements are true. And no decision in either direction could lead to completely unbiased language because of the value-ladenness of language.

Other Social and Political Matters

The value-ladenness of language and the inescapability of bias, as well as the impact of reader perspectives, are strongly evident in word choice about abortion; about political leanings such as "conservative" and "liberal"; and about issues related to tax, government, and budgets.

Abortion

An item in the *Times* readers' representative report highlights the sensitivity of language use related to this topic:

> "Unborn child"—The front-page headline said "Senate Passes Bill on Unborn" (3/26), and a reader wrote: "The word 'unborn' has political implications and is used by those who wish to deny the choice of abortion to women. I know

that the word is in the dictionary but it is only used by those with the afore-mentioned agenda. I have worked in the healthcare field for 28 years, fre-quently with pregnant women, and that term is never used. 'Unborn' is not used in educational literature for women of childbearing age, except by these groups. . . . Please show journalistic neutrality and use the acceptable word 'fe-tus(es).'"[25]

Although this reader urged "journalistic neutrality," neutrality is itself an ethical stance, and it is unlikely to satisfy some readers. As with "terrorist," terms related to abortion and the fetuses or children aborted are all freighted with ethical implications for this debate. The word "fetus," for example, will imply to some a mistaken judgment that a child is not at issue, while for oth-ers it will imply justified support for that position. All of this does not sug-gest that it is necessary to abandon the quest for fairness to all sides' positions in wording, but it underlines the difficulty of that effort.

The *Times, Oregonian,* and *Morning News* have all established styles that avoid pro-life and pro-choice—the preferred terms of the two sides in the de-bate. The *Morning News* says those on one side "oppose abortion or oppose abortion rights"; other acceptable phrasings include "anti-abortion" and "abortion opponents." For the other side, the newspaper says "those who fa-vor abortion rights" or "abortion rights proponents." "Pro-life" and "pro-choice" are used only in direct quotes or in names of groups. Joel P. Thorn-ton, chief of the *Morning News*'s news copy desk, said editors think both "pro-choice" and "pro-life" are "more political slogans than accurate descrip-tions of the people's viewpoints."[26] This approach avoids the most politically and emotionally charged terms.

The *Los Angeles Times* Style and Usage Guide follows a similar approach. Its entry under "abortion" states:

> Those who favor maintaining legal access to abortion are *abortion rights advo-cates, supporters of legal abortion* or *those who favor abortion rights.* They should not be called abortion advocates or be characterized as being pro-abortion or pro-choice. Those opposed to abortion may be called *opponents of abortion* or *abortion foes* or may be characterized as being *anti-abortion.* Do not use the term pro-life.[27]

An entry under "pro-abortion, pro-life" makes an additional comment: "These terms can so easily be misunderstood or misapplied that they should not be used except in commentary, quotes and letters." *Times* style, too, strives for language most likely to be taken as neutral. Stevens—the newspa-per's senior editor, copy desks, and more recently chief of copy desks—said:

"The *Times*' intent is to remain neutral on the abortion issue, avoiding language that may be perceived as sympathetic to or casting negative light on either side in the debate."[28]

The *Oregonian*'s style points to the problem of shorthand by saying:

> Reporters should avoid routine use of the labels pro-choice and pro-life as shorthand in stories about the abortion debate. Ideally, stories should briefly describe the views held by each group in the debate without resorting to labels. Where labels improve the clarity of the story, however, we should use some form of the phrase abortion-rights advocates (or activists) to replace the pro-choice label and some form of the phrase anti-abortion to replace pro-life.[29]

This approach is commendable for pointing to the alternative of describing a group's views rather than using labels. Labels always make it difficult or impossible to fully represent a position. As Doug Swanson, an investigative projects writer for the *Morning News*, put it: "People who are in favor of abortion rights are not necessarily pro-abortion, and it just gets very complicated and we're all reduced to its shorthand."[30]

Bruce Tomaso, religion editor at the *Morning News*, pointed to the significance of wording nuances in this terminology: "There is a not-so-fine distinction between being somebody who favors abortion and being someone who favors a woman's right to an abortion."[31] The rights language avoids implying that supporters of abortion rights favor abortion themselves in every—or even any—instance. But Mark Z. Barabak, the *Times* political writer who covered the 2004 presidential election, noted that even rights language has values implications. "To me pro-choice is a loaded term, as is pro-life. So I prefer to say 'supports legal abortion' or 'opposes legalized abortion,'" he said. Barabak said he is "not comfortable writing 'opposes a woman's right to choose.'" He drew a parallel to use of "gay rights," saying he prefers to say "recognizing the legal status of gay and lesbian relationships." "There are certain words that for me have a value attached to them. You know, who can be opposed to rights?"[32]

Using rights language, then, provides greater accuracy than saying that a "pro-choice" person or group is "pro-abortion." However, journalists remain in the wording values maze.

Political Leanings

Word choices about the political perspectives of people and groups—such as conservative and liberal, right wing and left wing—are another form of shorthand that stirs reader sensitivities and raises ethical questions.

Arrieta-Walden of the *Oregonian* noted that readers see political issues through the prisms of their own perspectives and that those prisms make them sensitive about coverage.[33] Don Frederick, national political editor for the *Times*, said the biggest ethical challenge in political writing is "trying to keep an obvious bias out of the copy, to really be careful with loaded words." For example, it is important to label evenly: "Make sure that if you talk about a conservative think tank that you then identify a think tank as liberal."[34]

Barabak said some readers argue that he has been biased in his wording.

> There's a guy who regularly e-mails me and I write something and I know I'm going to be hearing from this guy. He has this thing about the use of the word conservative and that we never identify people as liberal or left-leaning—that we always use right wing and we never use left wing. And of course I'll e-mail back, here's a Nexis Lexis search and here's all the times I've used left wing and on and on and on. But I am very sensitive to word choice. And when I write I do have those voices in the back of my mind.[35]

Liberal and conservative labels are unclear and may oversimplify or distort positions. As with the language of war and terrorism, specifics have the ethical advantage of clarity. Barabak, who has covered six presidential campaigns including 2004, said this about the dangers of political labeling:

> To me, covering politics in particular, I think you need to be very, very careful. I'm very mindful of labels. I hate using them. I plead guilty to having done so, but I really try to avoid words like liberal and conservative because I'm not sure what exactly they mean anymore. I think by most measures you would argue Barbara Boxer is a liberal senator. That said, she supports the death penalty. Well, what does that mean? So to me, it seems like it's very facile sometimes; we'll just fix on, well, this person supports abortion rights or opposes them so they're liberal or they're conservative.[36]

Barabak applies the idea of showing, not telling, to labeling. "When you've got the opportunity, I'd rather say this is a candidate that believes this, this, that and that as opposed to saying he's a liberal or she's a conservative."

McCoy also pointed out the vagueness of labels and argued for specifics. For example, she said, the Sierra Club "is about conserving something that was there, so in the truest sense of the word it is a conservative organization. Of course it's not. What we know, it's a liberal organization. But we've just turned that whole word on its head so that it doesn't mean anything anymore."[37] She thinks it would be better not to label political figures, as a rule, but rather to state their stances and votes. If a label is used, it should be as precise as possible—for example, stating where a person stands on the political spectrum in his or her own party.

As with war and terrorism terms, labels such as liberal, conservative, and moderate are slippery because they depend on one's perspective. Labeling is challenging even within one political party. Michael Finnegan, a state politics reporter who also covered the 2004 election for the *Times*, said conservative leaders sometimes object to the label "moderate Republican" and would instead like to see "liberal" used:

> The typical template of a moderate Republican in California is one who is a fiscal conservative—supports lower taxes, for example—but takes positions on social issues such as supports abortion rights and gun control and gay rights in some measure. For example, Schwarzenegger—we describe him as a moderate Republican and we get complaints from conservatives sometimes that a Republican who takes those positions on the social issues ought to be described as a liberal.[38]

Finnegan thinks the phrasing is appropriate because "moderate" Republicans are, on balance, moderate in their positions. He noted that judgments must be made. Given the values embedded in the language of politics, these judgments are ethically difficult but unavoidable.

The ethics of labeling involves not only weighing the problems of vagueness and relativity of labels, but also monitoring for equity in the use of labels across the political spectrum. McCoy said the *Times* has been inconsistent in its use of political labels—but that any effort to label is going to fall short.

> If we're going to use these labels, we need to apply them fairly. Teddy Kennedy is an extremely liberal member of Congress. I'm not sure how often we've put any kind of label before liberal. Should we call him ultraliberal? Should we call him an archliberal? Maybe we have, maybe we've done that, but it's that fair application of things. And that's why I think once you get into the labeling game, you can't win. You're not going to win it.[19]

Labeling political leanings, then, becomes difficult because many readers are sensitive about political matters—sensitive in divergent ways because of the differing prisms through which they see the world and issues. This kind of labeling carries ethical dangers of lack of clarity and oversimplification as well as inequity in application. Giving descriptive specifics provides an alternative that can enhance clarity and provide greater nuance.

Tax, Government, and Budget Terms

The *Oregonian* has grappled with how to handle terms related to taxes, the size of government, and budget cuts or shortfalls. Arrieta-Walden said government stories often draw complaints from readers who say the newspaper is promoting government and its ability to solve problems. "There's a huge readership out there that says, 'No government, it's too big, it's shown it can't solve problems, and your perspective is still so stuck in the New Deal'" with the notion "that government can work and does work and makes a difference." To readers sensitive about government size and taxes, a label such as "anti-tax" can jump out and prompt objections. "People say, well, no, we're not necessarily anti-tax; we are for smaller government. In their minds there's very much a distinction."[40]

Arrieta-Walden said describing government cutbacks has proven difficult.

It's very complicated because on the one hand, some state spending has increased. Now within that state spending you're paying for extra salaries, you're paying for your light bills, you're paying for all these expenses, so it has not increased at the rate where, though, to keep the level of services that you're providing to people up at the same level. So how do you characterize that? Is that a shortfall? Are they budget cutbacks? Or is it expenses not meeting, revenue not meeting expenses—how do you characterize that in an easy, understandable way? Are they budget cuts? Well, yes and no. On the one hand you're cutting services because your budget doesn't meet all the expenses you have, but from a conservative standpoint it's like, what are you talking about budget cuts? Their budget is bigger than it was last year.[41]

Viewpoints, then, again depend on vantage point. Reader sensitivity over budget and tax language shows that, as Arrieta-Walden put it, "even the language of math is complicated and can convey bias in terms of how you perceive that and how you describe that."

Lynch at the *Times* pointed out another government-related term that raises ethical questions: reform. It is important to use the term carefully because, as he noted, "one person's reform is another person's change for the worse."[42]

Wording about government might seem a less value-laden realm than abortion-related terms or descriptions of political perspective. But they pose the same issues of clarity and relativity as the other terms.

Religion

For many people, religious convictions run even deeper than political beliefs. Nuances of language are sensitive matters, and truthful representation through shorthand labels is particularly difficult because of the complexity of religious faiths.

The *Morning News* has one of the most thorough religion sections in the country, and its reporters are sensitive to the nuances of religious language. Berta Delgado, who covered evangelical Christians, talked about the importance of being sensitive about religious terms.

> Faith is the most important thing in people's lives—or should be, I guess, if you're a true believer in your particular faith—and so you have to treat it as such. It's real easy to upset people, and I've been covering the Southern Baptists for a long time and one of the things that I've found is that when I cover an issue, that if I get e-mails from both sides, conservatives and moderates, then I know I've done my job.[43]

Delgado, then, strives for objectivity, and she said Southern Baptists from different theological perspectives have thanked her for that.

Still, for anyone covering religion, seeking neutrality is an elusive goal because—as with politics—no terms are truly neutral. Delgado said the *Morning News* avoids loaded terms such as fundamentalist for people of any faith, except in quotes. The newspaper uses conservative and moderate, and sometimes liberal, in writing about people from Christian denominations, such as Baptists, Methodists, and Episcopalians. These terms present the same problems as their political counterparts because their acceptability varies depending on one's perspective. A case that highlights the problem is the leadership fight within the Southern Baptist denomination from 1979 through the late 1980s between more and less theologically conservative people. Bruce Tomaso, the *Morning News* religion editor, said:

> Neither side really agrees on what the other side should be called. The people who wound up winning the fight were the people who called themselves the conservatives, and they would say what they did is threw the liberals out of positions of leadership, while the liberals would say they were the moderates and the Southern Baptist Convention has been hijacked by these ultra-conservatives.[44]

The overlap between religious and political terminology also creates problems of clarity. Labels such as conservative and liberal are often used for theological positions—such as beliefs about the nature and role of the Bible. Sometimes those who fit these labels hold political positions that are likewise conservative or liberal, but that is not always the case. Pam Maples, the assistant managing editor for projects at the *Morning News* and a former national editor, talked about the problems with another label, "religious right."

> We went through a period where we were using, the wires were using, religious right. And we got away from that. Because I personally know a lot of people who are religiously conservative. They are not necessarily right-wing voters. So, to me I sound like I'm a broken record just because I've been so fixated on this with my staff, but a lot of that kind of stuff comes down to precision.[45]

A clear message to the reader may again mean spelling out the specifics of what a person believes rather than using the label.

Lack of precision in religious terms can be a problem even for terms that may seem innocuous. Tomaso cited the use of the term "Christian music":

> Christian music is a very commonly used phrase. In fact it really doesn't describe Christian music. It describes music that is listened to by evangelical Christians. There's a much narrower slice of people who would call themselves Christian music or Christian books or the Christian publishing industry. And they really don't reflect the views of all Christianity by any means. You're really talking about the evangelical Protestant Christians. And that's a difficult distinction to draw sometimes when you're writing.[46]

Subtleties of language, then, are important in writing about religion even apart from theological controversy or the overlap of religion and politics. Given the continuing influence of religion in American society, it is an important ethical matter for journalists to consider these subtleties.

Other Descriptors for People and Situations

Ethical decisions about other issues of word choice and labeling can come up in many kinds of stories—on war, politics, and religion but also on other topics. The writers and editors interviewed pointed out many trouble spots including:

- *Superlatives.* John S. Carroll, the *Times*'s editor until he retired in 2005, said journalists tend to make exaggerated claims about people and events without doing their homework—claims such as Paul Newman being "the best-known actor in the world" or the September 11, 2001, attack being "the worst terrorist attack in history."

  > You know, history runs a lot of centuries, a lot of millennia, and nobody's checked out whether it is or not. They just say it. People make it up.

What's the difference ethically between that and making up a quote? We fire people for making up a quote. Why shouldn't a person be fired for making up a fact? I tell you, if you put people to a lie detector, they will admit that they are much more tolerant of making up a fact than making up a quote. But I don't see the difference. So I've hammered people on that.[47]

- *Business terms.* Crayton Harrison, a *Morning News* business writer, has dealt with corporate sensitivities in, for example, saying a company's stock had "plummeted" rather than declined and describing Dell as "mocking" Hewlett Packard's business model.[48]
- *Sports language.* Bob Yates, the *Morning News*'s assistant managing editor for sports, said even seemingly innocent phrasing that would be acceptable for professional athletes can be sensitive when it is used for high school athletes. For example, a story about two teams that finished second in the state baseball tournament said both "settled for second." "Well, you know, that's ridiculous," Yates said. "If any of us were on a team that finished second in the state in some sport, we would have nothing but great memories about it; that's a major achievement. But you sort of get that pro mentality where if you don't win the Super Bowl, you're a loser."[49]
- *Disability terms.* As a matter of compassion, it is important to be sensitive to avoid terms that imply judgment or limitations or perpetuate stereotypes—such as "wheelchair-bound,"[50] "afflicted with," or "retarded."[51] An entry in the *Times* readers' representative report illustrates the point:

  > "Afflicted"—Two readers made comments along these lines: "Your story about how Bree Walker is challenging the boundaries of her disability and the perceptions of TV viewers (7/27, E1) falls into the same trap as those Walker criticizes when it says, 'Aaron James Lampley, afflicted with ectrodactylism, was born in August 1991.' Later the piece describes Walker's daughter: '16-year-old Andrea also has ectrodactylism.' The first description is judgmental and negative due to the use of the word 'afflicted.' The second description is neutral; it gives the information without the negativity. All of us, and newspaper writers in particular, need to be sensitive to the words we use to describe people."[52]

- *Controversy.* Although this is a popular word for journalists, it is vague and needs to be used thoughtfully. As Maples stated the problem, "That's the word you throw on anything you don't know what to do with."[53]

- *Expert.* Whether someone is an expert is a matter of opinion. Dominick of the *Times* foreign copy desk said, "I think that has a bias and it's never really been discussed that much."[54] Like controversy, it is an easy word to throw into a story.

- *Victim.* Patt Morrison, a *Times* opinion columnist and longtime reporter, recalled a conference at which a journalist from a smaller paper complained that editors, when handling stories about women whose husbands had tried to kill them, would change the wording from "survivors of domestic violence"—the women's term for themselves—to "domestic abuse victim" or "domestic violence victim." The women "no longer thought of themselves as victims."[55] It would have been an exercise of compassion to use the phrase the women applied to themselves.

- *Beloved or well respected.* Jake Arnold, a copy editor at the *Oregonian*, pointed out that beloved—a term used in coverage of the death of Ronald Reagan—was not a term that everyone would apply to him. Similarly, well respected may or may not be justified as a label for someone.[56]

Qualifiers and Transition Words

Even routine words of qualification or transition can carry ethical implications. For example, Dominick said, "We often take out 'just' and 'only' . . . as in 'just four "enemy combatants" have been charged.'" That leaves it to the reader to "decide whether it's enough or too few."[57] A transition word like "however" can imply that the writer is taking a side on an issue.[58]

Assessing the Ethics of Word Choice

The ethics of word choice encompasses intriguing issues related to bias and the limitations of both journalists and their audience, and of language itself. In the interviews, some journalists talked about their efforts to keep bias out of stories. Vernon Loeb, California investigations editor for the *Times*, talked about how he tries to do that—and about the skepticism in the public about what journalists are really doing:

> Just because a fact or a part of a way you can describe somebody or characterize somebody is true, doesn't always make it either fair or relevant or worthy of inclusion, even though it's true. Because you . . . want to try to engineer biases out of your reporting. And I think we journalists are sort of trained to do that and we're good at that. And I think a lot of people outside of journalism don't

even understand how that's possible. But it really is. I personally believe it's possible for conservatives to write dispassionately about liberals and liberals to write dispassionately and fairly about conservatives. But again, that takes a lot of sort of engineering. Your own bias is out of the equation all the time. And so, you're always trying to do that, I think, in almost everything you write. And some people might say, well, there's a subtle sleight of hand going on in all of these things where you're trying to hide your biases, but they're still there. I tend to think of it as trying to acknowledge them and then deal with and engineer them out. Or I often found myself when I was writing about somebody I disagreed with going out of my way to try to, even more fully than I otherwise would, draw his argument or put his argument into a piece, knowing that I disagreed with him, really going out of my way to sort of fully and dispassionately capture this person's argument, more so than I would have had I been writing about somebody with whom I agreed.[59]

Loeb's comments reflect the kind of commitment to fairness that many journalists bring to their work—a commitment that would probably shock many members of the public. But Loeb rightly acknowledges that personal biases do exist. With the limitations of both people and language, it is impossible to fully engineer bias out—even for the journalist who is earnestly striving to be neutral.

As noted in chapter 4, all journalists operate within the filters of their educational, cultural, and sometimes spiritual backgrounds and the values they have developed. Even values about what constitutes fair wording are shaped by journalists' own worldviews.[60] People can step back very well, as Loeb noted, but they may still have blind spots on what is fair wording. Even when journalists try to step back, their audiences have their own biases that color their reading of wording—and some tend to be very sensitive about these matters today.

Apart from the inescapable biases of even the most conscientious journalists, biases stay intertwined with word choice decisions because of the limitations of language. All of the word choices in the areas discussed in this chapter have ethical implications based on the language itself. Wording that implies taking a side suggests lack of representation of the truth of another position, but even neutral wording can be weighted with ethical liabilities because it implies rejection of the truth of any position or stance represented by the word—rejection that amounts to a kind of bias against the truth of all positions. For example, saying someone is "anti-abortion" may imply to some a rejection of the notion that abortion involves a life (as implied in "pro-life") and to others a failure to frame the argument in terms of choice or rights. Taking a position on an issue amounts to journalistic heresy if one

views the role of journalists as "honest brokers" of information, but not taking a position still entails a position of its own. Just as a fifty-fifty balance in
quoting sources does not equate with ethical use of quotes, neutral wording
does not equate with ethical wording.

Still, the ethical limitations of seeking neutral wording do not imply that
journalists should stop striving to be fair in wording about issues. Seeking
neutrality, even though it is impossible to do fully, does have ethical merit,
too. Coupled with wording in the voices of people on different sides of an issue, it may provide a fuller portrayal of the issue than partisan wording alone.
"Neutral" terms may also help keep the lines of communication with some
readers open by showing an effort to be fair and thereby enhancing the credibility of a story. As with quotes, journalists act in an ethically questionable
way—violating both truthfulness and compassion—if their implied promise
to the audience is fairness and they are intentionally unfair or are careless
about fairness in their word choice. They then risk skewing audience perspectives toward an individual or a position without providing as full a portrayal of an issue as possible.

Even apart from the issue of bias in wording, the use of shorthand labeling presents complex ethical issues. On the positive side, a well-chosen label
may enable people to grasp some truth about a person or position quickly. On
the negative side, aside from labeling that is careless and leaves unfair perceptions, even carefully chosen shorthand wording necessarily cannot portray all of the nuances of a person or issue. It is inherently inadequate in its
truth-telling ability in terms of the depth and breadth of its representation.
It also may amount to uncaring treatment of a person or issue if the wording
sharply narrows the reader's ability to understand a person and his or her
views as they are.

Taken together, the ethical issues connected with word choice call for
journalists to think carefully about the inherent biases implied in any word
choice and about the limitations of brief labels for complex matters.

Handling Word Choice Ethically

Any suggestion about making word choices more ethically runs up against
the ethical difficulties embedded in word choice. But the interviews with
journalists, and the foregoing discussion of ethics, point to several recommendations:

- Carefully evaluate the ways in which values are implied in a particular
  word or phrase. In the words of Morrison, the *Times* columnist: "What

is the word value of this? How loaded, how freighted is it? Is it neutral? Is it tilted? Do I want it to be tilted? Do I want to make a point?"[61] Seeing the word from different reader vantage points may help answer these questions more fully.

- Strive for maximum clarity and minimum distortion or bias by being specific where possible rather than labeling. Maples, the *Morning News* projects editor, said: "What are you really trying to tell the reader? And it's kind of lazy writing to grab the label or the adjective, and it doesn't really convey anything that could really help the reader."[62]
- Be aware of your own biases and work to counter them. Even though it is impossible to spring all the way loose from one's biases, evaluating them is important for the sake of fairness. Lynch, the senior copy chief of the *Times*'s foreign and national desks, said: "Obviously I check my views at the door when I come in as best I can, and then I'm hyper aware of them so I don't infuse anything that I do with that. I try very hard. It's a very conscious effort."[63] Even being "hyper aware" may not uncover every bias, but may do much to enhance fairness in word choice.
- Hire a diverse staff. One way to address the limitations of people's worldviews in evaluating word choice is to hire people from a variety of backgrounds. Lynch sees diversity in the newsroom as a counter to bias because it helps to ensure fairness and to foster evaluation of nuances of meaning. For example, a practicing Muslim on the foreign desk has provided valuable insight.
- Develop background in a subject to allow better understanding of the implications of word choices—especially in sensitive and complex areas such as religion. Tomaso, the *Morning News* religion editor, noted, for example, that Susan Hogan/Albach, another religion reporter at the newspaper at the time of the interview, brought master's degrees in journalism, theology, and religious studies to her coverage of Catholicism.[64]
- Work to avoid an "orthodoxy" in the newsroom about contentious issues, in the words of Sandra Mims Rowe, the *Oregonian*'s editor: "I do find that both people in the public and journalists certainly, too, have a hard time recognizing that reasonable people can disagree. I mean, again the more political or polarized something is the more they want to assume, my position is the only reasonable position. And that's a position that I find troubling and offensive, whether it's in public and certainly if it's in the newsroom."[65] An acknowledgment of other people's arguments—if not agreement—may help to minimize unfairness in wording.

If journalists put these recommendations into practice, the result will not be word choices free of bias, but it may be word choices that more truthfully and fully reflect the nuances of people's life and opinions.

Notes

1. Bernard Goldberg, *Bias: A CBS Insider Exposes How the Media Distort the News* (Washington, D.C.: Regnery, 2001).

2. Bob Kohn, *Journalistic Fraud: How The New York Times Distorts the News and Why It Can No Longer Be Trusted* (Nashville, Tenn.: WND Books, 2003).

3. Media Research Center, www.mediaresearch.org (accessed May 24, 2006).

4. Eric Alterman, What *Liberal Media? The Truth about* Bias and the News (New York: Basic Books, 2003).

5. Fairness and Accuracy in Reporting, www.fair.org (accessed May 24, 2006).

6. Al Franken, *Lies and the Lying Liars Who Tell Them: A Fair and Balanced Look at the Right* (New York: Dutton, 2003).

7. For two recent and thorough reviews of scholarly studies on media bias, see David Niven, "Objective Evidence on Media Bias: Newspaper Coverage of Congressional Party Switchers," *Journalism and Mass Communication Quarterly* 80, no. 2 (Summer 2003): 311–26, and Tien-Tsung Lee, "The Liberal Media Myth Revisited: An Examination of Factors Influencing Perceptions of Media Bias," *Journal of Broadcasting and Electronic Media* 49, no. 1 (March 2005): 43–64.

8. Jamie Gold, interview by the author, October 7, 2004, Los Angeles.

9. Jamie Gold, e-mail message to author, June 23, 2005.

10. "Readers' Rep Report," March 29, 2004.

11. "Readers' Rep Report," March 15, 2004.

12. Dean P. Baquet, interview by the author, October 5, 2004, Los Angeles.

13. Tim Lynch, interview by the author, October 6, 2004, Los Angeles.

14. Melissa McCoy, interview by the author, October 8, 2004, Los Angeles.

15. Gold interview.

16. Robert W. Mong, Jr., interview by the author, September 14, 2004, Dallas.

17. Jamie Gold, e-mail message to author, June 29, 2005.

18. E-mail message to the *Los Angeles Times* from a reader, November 30, 2003.

19. Tim Lynch, e-mail message to author, June 24, 2005.

20. Laura Dominick, e-mail message to author, October 12, 2004.

21. Baquet interview.

22. Melissa McCoy memo, www.laobserved.com (accessed May 2, 2005).

23. McCoy interview.

24. McCoy interview.

25. "Readers' Rep Report," March 29, 2004.

26. Joel P. Thornton, e-mail message to author, June 21, 2005.

27. The *Los Angeles Times* Style and Usage Guide (in-house style guide used at the newspaper). Italics in the original.

28. Clark P. Stevens, e-mail message to author, June 30, 2005.

29. "Abortion" entry, the *Oregonian* Style Guide (in-house style guide used at the newspaper).

30. Doug Swanson, interview by the author, July 22, 2004, Dallas.

31. Bruce Tomaso, interview by the author, July 19, 2004, Dallas.

32. Mark Z. Barabak, telephone interview by the author, November 24, 2004.

33. Michael Arrieta-Walden, interview by the author, June 22, 2004, Portland, Oregon.

34. Don Frederick, interview by the author, October 5, 2004, Los Angeles.

35. Barabak interview.

36. Barabak interview.

37. McCoy interview.

38. Michael Finnegan, telephone interview by the author, November 26, 2004.

39. McCoy interview.

40. Arrieta-Walden interview.

41. Arrieta-Walden interview.

42. Lynch interview.

43. Berta Delgado, interview by the author, July 19, 2004, Dallas.

44. Bruce Tomaso, interview by the author, July 19, 2004, Dallas.

45. Pam Maples, interview by the author, September 14, 2004, Dallas.

46. Tomaso interview.

47. John S. Carroll, interview by the author, October 6, 2004, Los Angeles.

48. Crayton Harrison, interview by the author, July 19, 2004, Dallas.

49. Bob Yates, interview by the author, July 19, 2004, Dallas.

50. Gold and Lynch interviews.

51. Seth Prince, interview by the author, June 23, 2004, Portland, Oregon.

52. "Readers' Rep Report," August 2, 2004.

53. Maples interview.

54. Laura Dominick, interview by the author, October 8, 2004, Los Angeles.

55. Patt Morrison, interview by the author, October 7, 2004, Los Angeles.

56. Jake Arnold, interview by the author, June 23, 2004, Portland, Oregon.

57. Dominick e-mail.

58. Dominick interview.

59. Vernon Loeb, interview by the author, October 5, 2004, Los Angeles.

60. Writing about religion coverage, Terry Mattingly talks about the bias of worldview—among other possible biases of journalists—in "Religion in the News," *Quill* (July–August 1993): 12–13.

61. Morrison interview.

62. Maples interview.

63. Lynch interview.

64. Tomaso interview.

65. Sandra Mims Rowe, interview by the author, June 22, 2004, Portland, Oregon.

CHAPTER SIX

Interpretation and Analysis

Across media, interpretation and analysis are at the heart of the best journalism of the early twenty-first century. Writers with in-depth knowledge of science and business explain complex topics to their audiences in newspapers, on television, and on the Internet. Investigative reporters sum up abuses of power unearthed through months of interviews and document searches. Political writers cut through spin to evaluate the implications of decisions by officials and candidates. Feature writers who immerse themselves in the lives of people provide insight into their lives and difficulties. Columnists draw on their knowledge of issues and make arguments to challenge their audiences' thinking.

Interpretation and analysis go well beyond the opinion pages. Sometimes that is a sore point for critics of mainstream journalism, who see it as evidence of bias. But all journalistic writing, even "straight" news, involves interpretation and analysis. Doing them well takes careful thought and raises ethical challenges. This chapter explores a range of writing approaches that involve interpretation and analysis and the ethical issues they create.

Forms of Interpretation and Analysis

A variety of terms and writing approaches are wrapped up with analysis and interpretation. The term "analysis" has a broad sense, but in professional discussion in newsrooms it often represents a name and literally a label for a kind of story. An "analysis" or "news analysis"—labeled as such—offers a reporter's perspective on the meaning and significance of a news event or development in the reporter's area of expertise. The writer's judgments about meaning and significance imply opinion, but he or she typically does not take a side on an issue or overtly criticize a position or a person. Mike Drago, who has worked extensively with education stories as an editor at the *Dallas Morning News*, commented on an analytical piece by Joshua Benton assessing the tenure of Dallas Independent School District Superintendent Mike Moses:[1]

> The challenges here were for Josh to be able to analyze for himself what were the pluses and minuses here without injecting his point of view. He was just sort of coldly, we hope, looking at the facts and interpreting them for the reader, and the challenge is to keep that objective distance without the crutch that we reporters can have to pin the attribution on Professor X up at O.U.[2]

Drago's comment sums up the conventional wisdom on labeled analysis as a form that interprets without offering overt opinion. Interpretation, however, may also appear in stories that are not labeled analysis. Drago and a few others referred in interviews to "writing with authority," which he summed up this way:

> It means that you are backgrounded enough in a story to give an intelligent analysis, even through a conventional news story, and you're able to write without attribution a lot of things. You don't need Professor X to tell you because you know what the research says and you can just say it. You don't need so many people to tell you the sky is blue. You're authoritative enough on the subject to know that the sky is blue.

The authority of "writing with authority" comes from developing a strong background and doing careful reporting on a topic. This authority plays out in the freedom to depart from conventional journalistic attribution and speak in one's own voice based on accumulated knowledge—even without the umbrella of the analysis label.

Along with labeled analysis and other writing that includes the reporter's statements, writing that offers overt opinion also represents a kind of analysis. This kind of writing may appear on a news or opinion page as a column that presents a position and provides commentary about an issue.

In the writing itself, interpretive and analytical elements may be prominent—appearing in the lead or in a "nut graf," a paragraph that frames the key point of the story. Or they may surface later in the article. They may appear only once or twice, or run throughout. The writing elements fall into several categories (with some overlap):

- unattributed factual statements,
- summation of broad findings—especially investigative reporting,
- explanation of complex matters—including explanatory narrative,
- assessment of meaning or significance—through a nut graf or other statements,
- statement of opinion.

Only the last of these involves explicit commentary that voices the writer's own views and takes sides, but all involve interpretation and assessment—and all imply opinion to the extent of reflecting evaluative judgments. All of these approaches have ethical implications. The following section explores these implications, drawing on the perspectives of writers and editors.

The Ethics of Interpretation and Analysis

Interpretation can be a sensitive issue for readers. Jamie Gold, readers' representative for the *Los Angeles Times*, said some readers complain about stories that provide analysis and interpretation.

> And it's usually for a sentence that many people would not find questionable, but I would say the reporter is talking with authority. He's using his knowledge of the issue and of what happened to interpret. And yeah, we get a lot of complaints, but I think in many cases they're ill-founded, and yet I also understand why readers resent it because, in a way, by doing that the reporter and the editors are saying: "Trust me. You have to trust me. This is an impartial perspective on what happened." It's interpretation and readers will say: "I don't want an interpretation; just say what happened."[3]

Despite these readers' skepticism about the newspaper's use of interpretation, in reality interpretation is impossible to avoid. No journalist just says what happened. Value choices are inevitable in all forms of interpretive writing. James S. Ettema and Theodore L. Glasser point to the inseparability of fact and value in their analysis of investigative journalism:

> We maintain that any attempt to gain truly important knowledge of human affairs—knowledge of individual innocence and guilt or institutional malfeasance and responsibility, for example—is built on a foundation of facts that

have been called into existence, given structure, and made meaningful by values. The separation of fact and value is inevitably breached by all but the most elementary and isolated bits of information about the social world.[4]

Whether a journalist is summing up investigative findings of wrongdoing or offering outright opinion, the use of facts is wrapped up with the values being stated.

The concept of framing, which has received a great deal of attention from media researchers in the past two decades, underlines the presence of value choices in interpretive writing. Robert M. Entman defines framing this way: "Framing essentially involves *selection* and *salience*. To frame is to *select some aspects of a perceived reality and make them more salient in a communicating text, in such a way as to promote a particular problem definition, causal interpretation, moral evaluation, and/or treatment recommendation* for the term described."[5] Journalists make value choices when they choose ways to portray problems and causes, assess some approaches as better or worse, or offer opinions about solutions. All of these choices underlie the various kinds of interpretive writing discussed here. For example, the nut graf "contains the 'kernel,' or essential theme, of the story,"[6] in the words of Chip Scanlan, a senior writing instructor at the Poynter Institute for Media Studies. By choosing a nut graf, a reporter inevitably narrows the focus of the story and puts particular aspects of it in the foreground. In doing so, he or she sheds light on particular aspects of the truth of the issue being covered and ignores others. Leo C. Wolinsky, deputy managing editor of the *Times* and later managing editor, also highlighted the inevitability of framing in noting that "there's never a story that's done that isn't subjected to the background and the viewpoint of the writer. By nature, all of those things are being filtered when you're selecting certain information to be used and certain information not to be used."[7]

In terms of truth, in one sense it is more honest to be open about the analysis that a story provides than to hide it. Victoria Loe Hicks, who did analytical writing as a reporter for the *Morning News* and then wrote editorials until she left the newspaper in 2006, said: "I think we're always analyzing and we're always applying analysis even when we're writing in a format that suggests that we're not. And so I think, again it's a matter of transparency to be openly analytical."[8]

Barry Johnson, arts editor for the *Oregonian*, discussing David Stabler's narrative about a teen cello prodigy, noted Stabler's honesty in his reflection in a paragraph about Sam Johnson's decision to give back a valuable cello. Stabler wrote:

What is it like, exactly, to walk away from yourself? To decide on your own to return the instrument that symbolized your identity? Luciano Pavarotti can't do it. Michael Jordan can't do it. What they do defines who they are. For almost his entire life, the cello has told Sam who he is. It gave him a voice more articulate and powerful than his own.[9]

Johnson said Stabler showed his feelings in this reflective passage. "A lot of the time we don't acknowledge that, as reporters, we're out there trying to make sense of it and this is basically our account. And as we're watching, we're as prone to normal human feelings—some say we have none—but normal human feelings and questions as anybody else, and I think this was David's honest response."[10] By expressing his reaction through this passage, Stabler made explicit the kind of reflection that thoughtful journalists do whether they state it in print or not.

A number of facets of ethical choice are evident in interviewees' comments on the various forms of interpretation and analysis: unattributed factual statements, summation of findings, explanation of complex matters, assessment of meaning or significance, and opinion.

Unattributed Factual Statements

Even attributed information involves interpretation about what facts and whose perspectives to include and exclude. However, a first step toward what is more obviously interpretive writing comes when reporters state information without attribution based on their accumulated knowledge or their reporting for a story. Unattributed assertions of fact are ethically troublesome if they are based on reporters' guesswork or thin research based on single sources. But the best practices of reporting—evidenced in the interviews—include making unattributed factual statements when they are well researched. For example, Sue Goetinck Ambrose, in her science coverage for the *Morning News*, went without attribution in the second paragraph of her story on possible unintended results of the addition of folic acid to food: "Since folic acid was added to breads, flours and other grain products in 1998, rates of neural tube defects—which affect the brain or spinal cord—have dropped."[11] This sentence is interpretive in that Ambrose wrote it without attribution after assessing what scientists told her in interviews. "I could have said, 'studies have shown that rates of neural tube defects have dropped.' But every scientist I talked to was so in agreement with the interpretations of those studies I didn't feel I had to attribute it."[12] In this case, then, what Ambrose's research showed to be a consensus led to a statement in her voice, not the voices of sources.

Similarly, Sonia Nazario, in the "Enrique's Journey" series for the *Times*, had no qualms about saying without attribution that police in Chiapas state, Mexico, shake down migrants.

> If you interview a hundred people and you read twenty studies and you know that the cops are corrupt in Mexico and they shake down immigrants for their money, and you've talked to 300 immigrants who tell you the exact same story, then I can say with authority that a large percentage of cops in Chiapas are shaking down migrants, and I have no doubt in making that statement and I did make it, and statements like that, in the story.[13]

She noted that it takes in-depth reporting to make this kind of statement, but pointed out that a definitive statement—when well grounded in reporting—helps readers more than conflicting views of different sources "because you're sorting through the evidence and you're telling them what the reality is."

Readers, then, gain greater insight into the truth of the issue. They may also get at some truth about the issue more easily because dropping the attribution streamlines the writing. As Drago put it, "If you write with authority, you can remove some of that clutter and help the reader get more to the point—help the reader connect the dots."[14] Given the limitedness of all journalists' perspectives—as observers bound by limitations of background and worldview—there is always the possibility that different reporters may present different sets of dots. But if reporters do their jobs thoroughly, particular pieces of information will be well enough grounded to stand up to the critical scrutiny of sources and of skeptical readers.

Aside from the danger of limited perspective, though, reporters making unattributed statements of fact run the risk of losing credibility with readers. Drago noted that some attribution is necessary for credibility. Henry Fuhrmann, senior copy desk chief for business at the *Times* and later a deputy business editor, said that if writers go too far without saying how they know what they know, they may appear condescending as the only voice in the story. "You're saying, 'I know this, and you're going to have to just trust me on this.'"[15] From a philosophical standpoint, journalists may not be providing enough epistemological warrant—leaving unclear the source of their knowledge. In ethical terms, this lack of an epistemological signal can call into question the truthfulness of the story—even though, when used carefully, unattributed statements can bring truthful elements across more strongly.

Summation of Findings

Investigative reporters use their knowledge and reporting to create another interpretive element in writing: sentences or paragraphs that provide a broad summary of their findings. These statements may include direct or indirect signals about the sources of the information, but they are interpretive in that they characterize patterns of problems or wrongdoing in broad and often dramatic terms.

For example, a story by *Morning News* projects reporter Doug Swanson about the Texas State Board of Medical Examiners opened this way:

> The Texas State Board of Medical Examiners, the agency that pledges to protect the public, has shown routine mercy to doctors whose negligence killed the people they were treating.
>
> It has granted second and third chances to surgeons who were thrown out of hospitals because they botched operations. It has forgiven physicians who overlooked cancerous tumors, who maimed infants or whose mistakes left women sterilized.
>
> It has refused, in the last five years, to revoke the license of a single doctor for committing medical errors, a *Dallas Morning News* analysis of board records has found.
>
> And it has, since January of last year [2001], failed to investigate the deaths of more than 1,000 patients. Thousands more may have been ignored over the last decade.[16]

Further down, the story made this additional statement about the pattern Swanson uncovered:

> The *News* reviewed thousands of pages of medical board disciplinary orders, as well as more than 100 malpractice case files in 18 county courthouses across Texas. The pattern evident over the last decade was one of state-sanctioned tolerance for serious medical mistakes.

The story delayed attribution until the third paragraph but clearly stated that it was based on the newspaper's analysis of board records, and the later paragraph provides more detail about the investigation. However, the broad and dramatic framing of the findings—in statements such as "routine mercy to doctors whose negligence killed the people they were treating" and "state-sanctioned tolerance for serious medical mistakes"—reflects Swanson's interpretation of the records and their significance. His interpretation, though, was well grounded because of the depth of his reporting and gained authority because of that depth. Commenting on his statement about tolerance of medical mistakes, Swanson said:

> Eventually, I went down to Austin, to the state medical board headquarters, and they had every disciplinary record, every record of a doctor they had taken action against, in chronological order going back to 1988, in these binders. There were 30-something binders down there. And I thought it would take me a couple hours and it ended up taking me four days. And I read every one of them, and these patterns started jumping out at me. . . . It was just undeniable. This wasn't a case of some advocate group calling me and saying, "Hey we figured this out," and then me running with the story. I mean this was all original research. So that, combined with later reporting that I did, I thought gave me the knowledge and the credibility to write that sentence.[17]

By stating the case this strongly, Swanson brought the truth of the situation more strongly to readers and may have done more to stir outrage about the board's problems. The story did help to spur change in the system: Swanson said the legislature threatened to dismantle the board, then gave it more money and power. The board changed its conduct and started doing its job.

A story by *Times* investigative reporter Ted Rohrlich provides another example of wording that packs more punch than the typical news lead. Its opening paragraphs said:

> Los Angeles parks Commissioner Christopher Hammond is no ordinary deadbeat.
> He's bounced a campaign check to the mayor. He's bounced campaign checks to six members of the City Council. Hammond, a leading developer of subsidized housing, has even bounced checks to the city attorney, the official responsible for prosecuting people who bounce checks.
> Remarkably, this has done little if anything to harm his relations with the elected officials he relies on to approve subsidies for his projects.
> Despite the bounced checks, a trail of angry business creditors and the more than $500,000 he owes in back federal and state taxes, Hammond's business entities have received substantial government subsidies over the last few years and stand to receive, in partnerships with other firms, an additional $31 million for redevelopment of Santa Barbara Plaza, a decrepit shopping center in South Los Angeles.[18]

The lead uses strong language in calling Hammond a deadbeat. California investigations editor Vernon Loeb, who edited Rohrlich's story, said the word was defensible because Hammond was receiving public subsidies, benefiting from political ties, and bouncing checks repeatedly.[19] Rohrlich said he thought carefully about the term and consulted a copy desk manager to get an opinion on the word from an expert on nuances of language. Rohrlich recognized the ethical stakes in even the choice of this single word:

> It's a weighty responsibility that you're taking upon yourself. It's like well, you're essentially judging a fellow human being and put a label on his behavior that's pejorative, very pejorative, so yeah, it's a weighty ethical thing. But again what are you trying to be? You're not trying to make friends with this fellow. You're trying to be a mirror. And would you be a good mirror if you pretended he wasn't a deadbeat? No, not in my opinion.[20]

For Rohrlich, then, stating his findings with this strong term reflects the truth about Hammond's conduct. As Loeb noted, his lead provides "a provocative, compelling opening to the story that will make people want to read it in a way that they wouldn't want to read a hard news lead about 'Christopher Hammond, a leading developer, has bounced 36 checks over the past 29 months.'"

From the standpoint of truth telling, provocative wording—if justified by the reporting—can get the reporter's findings across to readers more effectively by motivating them to read the story and by underlining the seriousness of those findings. As Pam Maples, assistant managing editor for projects at the *Morning News*, put it, "Readers are busy. I'm asking them to read sixty-five or seventy inches or two blanks on a Sunday. I need to punch them in the gut if I think the story can carry it."[21] As an example, she pointed to this lead on a story that was part of the paper's investigative work on priests accused of sexual abuse:

> Frank! Frank!
>
> About a dozen children circle around the Rev. Frank Klep after Mass one sun-kissed Sunday. They chirp his name, trying to catch his eye as he begins handing out foil-wrapped candy. He calls them by name, too, beams and hugs some of them.
>
> Few, if any, locals are aware that the friendly priest is a convicted child molester who has admitted abusing one boy and is wanted on more charges in Australia. In 1998, his religious order placed him here in the South Pacific, where Australian police can't touch him because their country has no extradition treaty with Samoa.
>
> Neither he nor the church feels an obligation to tell anyone about all that.[22]

Commenting on the approach to the lead, Maples said: "We're going to ask the reader to bite into a topic that's not particularly pleasant, that a lot has been written about. We've got a different hook on it, but is the reader going to make the distinction and invest a lot of time? We've got to grab them. We've got to grab them, we've got to hold them and carry them. But be ethical."[23]

For investigative reporters and editors, being ethical includes nailing down findings through in-depth reporting and presenting them both powerfully and carefully. Loeb said the biggest ethical challenge in investigative writing is to "walk the fine line between writing something in a way that's powerful and provocative and dramatic but not unfair and hyped."[24] The facts—the "superstructure" of the house—have to be right, but if "you use a lot of judgmental words or loaded words and adjectives and pile on in such a way, you can actually almost distort the factual picture and create impressions that you don't want to create." The interplay of facts and values, then, comes to the forefront in the decisions made about word choice—decisions that are difficult to make because it is impossible to discern perfectly whether readers will see the story's characterizations as crossing the ethical line.

Explanation of Complex Matters

Outside the realm of investigative reporting, some other stories use extensive analytical passages to frame and explain complex topics. Explanatory narratives such as the Pulitzer-winning "French Fry Connection" series by the *Oregonian's* Richard Read (introduced in chapter 1) combine engaging storytelling with clear writing.[25]

In Read's series, the french fry provided the centerpiece for telling the story of the Asian economic crisis and its effect on the Pacific Northwest. He explained how the story developed:

> I was over in Asia in '97 covering the Hong Kong handover and after that I was in Bangkok doing some unrelated stories, and essentially that was when that whole Asian currency crisis began. And so I came back from that trip having some sense of how huge that story was going to be and how big the effect was conceivably on Americans. And yet people back here just had no idea, and to them it was just some sort of esoteric currency exchange story. And so I was trying to figure out how do I bring this to life for Americans and make it meaningful? I mean, I could write a long treatise on Asian economics; nobody would ever read it. But I thought if I could find one product that would kind of exemplify what was happening and document the effect on that one product, then it would come to life and mean something to people here. And so I picked the french fries really for three reasons. One is that I had no idea when I was initially doing the research but, as I said in the story, it was a $2 billion industry in the Northwest, so a lot of money's at stake. The other reason is that those products are sold to members of the middle class in Asia, and during the time

that I was reporting, living out there, the emergence of this middle class was politically and economically really important. And so this was an ideal product that kind of allowed me the chance to explain that whole development and its significance, both the rise of the middle class and then the Asian economic crises' gutting of that middle class and what that meant. And then the third reason was just that french fries are not a widget. Everybody can identify with a fry and there's some whimsy to it, and so it would be an entertaining story.[26]

Read was thus able to grab readers' attention about a daunting and seemingly distant topic by pegging it to the french fry, a product that was economically significant to his readership and to Asians and something with which people connect. The stories in the series showed readers a diverse cast of characters linked to the passage of french fries from the Northwest to Asian markets.

Read brought considerable expertise to the series based on eight years of reporting experience in Asia and his observation of developments there, as well as a yearlong Nieman Fellowship he had just completed at Harvard University in which he took courses on international economics. He also interviewed a variety of experts, but his background enabled him to write more analysis in his own voice without attribution to them—as he put it, not showing readers the "plumbing." This kind of analysis explaining a complex topic was evident in passages such as the opening from the third day of the series. The setup of the story weaves together the storyline of the passage of a load of fries to Asia with commentary about the broader meaning of the story:

Randy Thueson helped fire rockets at North Vietnam when Nixon administration hawks warned that Southeast Asian countries could topple like dominoes to communism.

In April, Thueson launched a load of potatoes at the Far East as Southeast Asia succumbed to economic contagion that proved more virulent than political ideology.

Thueson, a wiry man with a trim brown mustache and frizzy gray hair, loaded 20 tons of frozen french fries at a warehouse next to the J. R. Simplot Co. potato-processing plant in Hermiston. Among them were potatoes grown the summer before in Circle 6 of an Eastern Washington farm run by members of the Hutterite religious sect.

He pulled out of the Eastern Oregon city and drove north, crossing the Columbia River on the Interstate 82 bridge. Watching sunlight shimmer on the water below, Thueson's thoughts drifted to the USS Clarion River, a 201-foot warship that he rode from Cam Ranh Bay, South Vietnam. He likes sending spuds to Asia a whole lot better than rockets.

"Nothing wrong with a little business," Thueson said, grinning as his Kenworth truck roared.

More than two decades after Vietnam, the United States wages trade, not war, in Asia. Vietnam wants to turn Cam Ranh Bay into a commercial port. The old domino theory has been consigned to the Cold War history books.

But a new domino effect, more widespread and damaging than the imagined syndrome of old, is sweeping Asia. When stocks and currencies plunged in Southeast Asia in the summer of 1997, financial chaos spread throughout the Far East, reversing Asia's stunning economic rise.

In the summer of 1998, the panic leaped unexpectedly from Asia to Russia and Latin America, as spooked investors withdrew money. It left the United States an oasis of prosperity as the world struggled to stave off a global recession.

"I see it as almost the equivalent of the destruction a war would do," says Desmond O'Rourke, director of Washington State University's international marketing program for agricultural commodities and trade.

Economists continue to debate how the contagion spreads and where it will head next. Farmers, processors, truck drivers and sailors live with the fallout.

The Hutterite potatoes—enough to produce about 113,000 large servings of McDonald's fries—were headed into the Asian economic storm.[27]

Read quoted an analyst from Washington State, but the paragraphs before and after that stated the assessment of the situation and its significance in Read's voice. As with the more streamlined statements of investigative findings, this approach brought some aspect of the truth of the issue more directly to readers. The clarity of Read's communication based on his knowledge and without constant attribution—combined with the thread of the french fry story line—enabled him to provide insight and perspective about a complicated matter with global implications.

Assessment of Meaning or Significance

Through a variety of passages, including nut grafs, journalists reflect on the meaning or significance of events, issues, and people. This kind of reflection overlaps with summation of investigative findings and explanation of complex topics, but it encompasses a wide range of evaluation across journalistic beats and genres—including political writing, business news, and feature writing. Four examples illustrate the kinds of passages that do this kind of assessment:

- Mark Z. Barabak, in his coverage of the 2004 presidential campaign for the *Times*, used this lead on a story about the third night of the Republican convention, a night of strong speeches by Vice President Dick Cheney and Democratic Senator Zell Miller of Georgia: "Turning from compassion to aggression, Republicans launched a withering assault Wednesday on John F. Kerry, using the third night of their national convention to attack his character, credibility and nearly 20 years in Congress."[28] Barabak said his experience covering six presidential campaigns gave him the appropriate background to say that the Republicans turned "from compassion to aggression." "I think it's my job to provide the fullest accounting that I can. And I suppose necessarily you're going to make some subjective decisions by calling it aggressive. I think that that was obviously a subjective choice of words, but I would argue that it wasn't opinion, that it wasn't unbalanced or shading things one way or the other."[29] While providing analysis may call for the use of more subjective language, Barabak said the writer still faces the challenge to find "more neutral or interpretative language as opposed to more opinionated language."

- *Morning News* business writer Crayton Harrison wrote about a $300 million agreement among state officials, leaders of the University of Texas at Dallas, and Texas Instruments executives to strengthen research at the school. In the second paragraph of the story, he said, "The financial package, announced Monday, was a rare Triple Crown of government, corporate and academic high rollers who, in a matter of weeks and in the middle of a state budget crunch, made UTD $300 million richer."[30] Harrison said the people involved had commented on their surprise at the cooperation of a corporation, state government, and university officials. "I really wanted to get that message across to the reader that this was kind of an unusual event happening before their eyes. And the Triple Crown word, I think, kind of speaks to that—that's a rare thing to experience."[31] In this case, then, an allusion to a commonly understood sports term shed light on the significance of a business development.

- Karen M. Thomas, a *Morning News* feature writer, did a story about a woman who has overcome obstacles of poverty and illness to help her children. She opened it this way:

> Gayle Punch waits in the baggage-claim area at the Dallas/Fort Worth International Airport, her metal walker pushed to the side of her chair. She has instructed her son, Richmond, 23, to stand so he can see the revolving door through which passengers will arrive. When he sees his sister, she tells him, he must pull her to a standing position.

Since early September, Lauren, 19, has been at Converse College in Spartanburg, S.C., a freshman studying music education. Richmond came several days earlier from Yale University in New Haven, Conn., where he is a graduate student. It's holiday time. Gayle's babies are coming home.

"I see her, Mama," Richmond says. Just as he pulls her up, Lauren rushes into her mother's arms.

"Hi, Mama. I missed my mama. I missed my mama," she says, over and over. Gayle holds on tight.

"Group hug, group hug," Gayle says and she pulls Richmond close. They form a tightknit circle. Folks standing around begin to stare.

Gayle doesn't care. She's on a mission. She wants her children to dream big and live large. She has nurtured them, yelled, coddled and prodded. She has pushed, fought and created pathways for them where there weren't any.[32]

In the final paragraph of this passage, Thomas reflected on Gayle Punch's purpose in life, her desires for her children, and the ways she has tried to clear paths for their success. She said the knowledge that went into that paragraph "came from outside reporting and inside reporting."[33] She talked to Gayle, watched her in action asking for help, and talked to people who became benefactors for her son Richmond.

• Kurt Streeter of the *Times* wrote a narrative about Nadine LeBlanc, a south Los Angeles woman whose grandson was fatally shot, and the transformation in her life in the two years since his death. Streeter included this passage putting the story in broader context:

Huge swaths of Los Angeles are blanketed by just this kind of suffering. Last year, L.A. was the nation's murder capital, with 659 homicides.

Most of the dead leave loved ones behind. The survivors are victims too. Some grieve, some live in denial. Some take on new responsibilities. They raise the children of murder victims, pay off the victims' debts, deal with police.

But some loved ones are different. They refuse to accept the killings. They embark on a mission against violence. They protest. They stuff envelopes. They speak out. And in the process of saving others, they discover something: They also save themselves.

Nadine LeBlanc is one of them. The 63-year-old hairdresser, a short, round-faced woman with broad hips, chestnut skin and dark brown eyes, was desperate for solace after her grandson was killed.

Drawn from scores of interviews and visits over the last two years, this is Nadine's story—the story of one survivor's transformation.[34]

Commenting on this section, Streeter said, "My thinking is in here to try to show how Nadine is typical and unusual at the same time, in a quick way."[35] By providing context for her life, he brought home to readers the broader reality of suffering because of violence.

Reflective passages such as Streeter's and Thomas's shed light on the meaning of individuals' lives in a way that also connects with themes common to the lives of many others. Thomas said reflecting on people in a story may serve readers by connecting to what she called "universal truth" about people. "To air that much of someone's personal story or tale, I would hope there's some greater good to be had in some way, shape, or form. It doesn't have to be some great moral lesson or some great thing. It just has to be something that other people can latch onto no matter who they are"—such as a mother's sacrifice for her children.[36] A narrative that reflects on a person, then, may serve the ethical goods of both truth telling and compassion by showing readers themes common to the lives of many people and building a sense of connection between them and others.

Passages of assessment that address news events and issues rather than the lives of individuals can also serve readers because they may provide greater insight than merely describing sides in a debate or surface activity. Benton of the *Morning News*, talking about education writing, noted that it is important to "analyze the merits of the claims that people make," not just lay them out. For example, giving two sides—saying ten studies support school vouchers and ten say they are a bad thing—and assuming the two sides have equal weight would not help readers. What would help would be to focus on "the two studies that actually sort of looked at it seriously and didn't seem to have an ideological taint to them and seem to be the highest quality."[37] Similarly, Wolinsky of the *Times* said analytical and interpretive stories can help to get closer to the truth of what is happening than what surface appearance might suggest. "Ultimately, it's going to be up to the reporter to tell what they believe is the truth about this, because the truth can be obscured by what you actually see happening in front of you. And so you depend upon someone who is very schooled and has been around the block many times, and knows these people and knows the politics behind it to bring that to you."[38]

Michael Finnegan, who like Barabak covered the 2004 presidential election for the *Times*, said that in political reporting in particular, reporters must cut through "spin." That kind of reporting often involves "sorting through representations by candidates of campaigns that are meant to further the interests of the candidates or campaigns but aren't necessarily consistent with what's true and what's real. A lot of political reporting is sifting through rhetoric for what's real and what isn't real."[39] Again, then, interpretation can give readers greater insight. Different reporters are likely to bring somewhat different perspectives on what "real" is—since judgments about reality are always shaped by the distinctives of one's background—but the experience that reporters such as Finnegan and Barabak bring to their work helps to ensure that their rendering of the real is well grounded.

Even in sports, which on the surface might seem to require less analysis of the meaning of events, interpretation is central to what the audience takes away—especially in a newspaper read long after the game has been shown and the score reported. Bob Yates, the *Morning News* assistant managing editor for sports, said it is important to explain the game people saw and put in perspective why certain things they saw were significant.

> We're reviewing the game. Was this a good game or a bad game? Did this person play well or not play well? Did they have good stats but they didn't really play that well? They weren't there in the clutch—all those kinds of things. That's what the sports page does. The columnists offer straight opinions about it, but the beat writers need to interpret it and I think analysis and interpretation is what we're all about. Those writers have to be more like attorneys and build their case. They have to say that this is important or this is a bad move and then explain why that's the case. We don't want them writing straight opinion pieces. But I think you have to take a point of view. Otherwise it would just sort of ape what happened at the game.[40]

The "value added" by the writer, then, becomes not the clear recounting of facts but the framing of those facts in a way that is meaningful to the reader and adds to his or her perspective.

Opinion

The writing that Yates referred to as "straight opinion" also makes an ethical contribution by directly articulating points of view for readers to consider, confronting them—gently or more sharply—with arguments that may support or challenge their own thinking.

Steve Blow, a Metro section columnist for the *Morning News*, pointed to the value of reflective newspaper opinion writing as a counterpoint to the heated arguments that television often provides.

> I think viewpoint writing is really something very important that we bring to readers in that it contrasts so much against the opinion stuff that they get on television, which tends to be highly emotional, blatant, sort of hot, quick sound bites—almost always paired with somebody with an opposing point of

view so that the emotional rhetoric is up. I think newspaper opinion writing really brings something very valuable to the table, and that is a calmer, a quieter, dispassionate, more in-depth sort of approach to the issues at hand. And so as long as the newspaper fulfills its obligation to provide a wide variety of viewpoints, I think it's tremendously important to help inform the public debate by offering personal perspectives.[41]

Blow also noted the value of seeing arguments that differ from one's own point of view on an issue.

Thinking now as a reader, my view on something a lot of times doesn't really crystallize until I read somebody arguing the other side of something. And then suddenly my own views come into sharper focus because it helps me understand what I see as the fallacies or the weaknesses in the other argument. And so I think if people would allow themselves to read other points of view, not only might they get an enlightenment about that view but it might also help them shape their own, clarify their own opposing views.

This kind of reading to learn varying viewpoints echoes what John Stuart Mill pointed to in the nineteenth century in his discussion of the free exchange of ideas and the clarifying of truth and error as ideas clash.[42] As Blow himself noted, this approach runs against the tendency of some readers today to draw sharp lines of disagreement and to interpret arguments as elements of a culture war. But newspaper opinion pieces that carefully lay out arguments remain a tool for reader learning, even amid the skepticism of many in the audience and the fragmentation of messages in a postmodern world.

Column writing can provide an opportunity for moving, deep personal reflection with broader implications. Al Martinez, a columnist for the *Times* who has worked in journalism for fifty years and contributed to three Pulitzer-winning efforts, said he tries to speak at multiple levels in his columns. He opened one column, written in a fall election season and a time of personal change, this way:

And so September comes, an intermingling of mist on the ocean and heat in the Valley, teasing with its hint of a new season but clinging to the old.

Also arriving, this election year, is an increase in the clanging and banging of presidential campaigning, with its assertions, accusations, recriminations and denials.

Big lies triumph over feeble explanations, and cynical manipulations twist truth into distorted forms. The spin doctors are back, leading us into a looking-glass world where things are never what they seem.[43]

Reflecting on this column, Martinez said:

That particular column I was talking about my granddaughter who's going off to art school in Chicago and also the changing seasons and a kind of changing world, and in the midst of all this change is the election and what we're being subjected to—to all the clanging and the banging of points of view—and that I was hoping—and I think I got that response from both conservatives and liberals who came back at me with understanding. I was talking about change to begin with and feeling overwhelmed by the media in this particular election and the ads and the speeches and the debates and the whole overkill of media response to what was going on.[44]

The powerful wording of the opening drew attention to the noise of the political season, especially in contrast with the peace of the ocean mist. And by opening the column in a way that connected with the political season and the change to fall, Martinez set his later reflections about his granddaughter in broader context.

Another example of deep personal reflection from Martinez's work is a first-person front-page piece he wrote looking back on the Korean War on the fiftieth anniversary of its start. It included this paragraph:

We took the days as they came and moved on from one hill to the next, bearing down on our emotions, keeping them in check. Something within perishes in war. An internal dead zone allows a soldier to face terror that might otherwise break him. Fear abates at the cost of involvement. You come home a different person than the one who left.[45]

Explaining his approach to this paragraph, Martinez said he wanted to give his readers "a better picture of what war was," in contrast to the remote, televised version that people have seen since the first Iraq war in 1991.[46] "I was bringing war a little closer home and what it does to the individual, that it desensitizes, and you have to be a little desensitized in combat to do what you do." By portraying the emotional reality of war from a soldier's point of view, Martinez gave readers more insight than a straight news account would have.

From an ethical standpoint, it is important for a columnist's conclusions to be based on in-depth understanding of an issue. Patt Morrison, another *Times* columnist and veteran reporter, said knowledge and judgment must underlie a column. "I've got twenty-some years of background that you don't see that informs what it is I put in print, on the page. So 800 words in a column represents 80,000 words of thinking of things that I've read, of information that I've run across and filed away, literally or figuratively."[47] The ethical weight of the column rests on the legitimacy of analysis and conclusions based on that knowledge.

Thus, opinion writing—the most overtly analytical approach discussed in this chapter—can provide arguments and perspective in a direct and powerful way. But this kind of writing presents writers a significant ethical challenge because they are using the power of their words to build a case for one side while giving little indication in a brief column of how much or little knowledge underlies their conclusions.

Ways of Doing Better

Despite the lines that the profession draws between labeled analysis and opinion and other writing, it is impossible for journalists to avoid interpreting. Just as the hiddenness of the knowledge underlying opinion columns points to an ethical obligation to ground one's conclusions carefully, the unstated interpretive aspect of pieces that are not labeled interpretation suggests that journalists need to be particularly conscientious in writing and editing interpretive passages and evaluating how stories are framed.

Writers and editors pointed to some ways journalists can approach interpretive writing ethically. These are outlined in the sections that follow.

Watch for Preconceived Notions

Hicks said that in her work at the *Morning News* if she was struggling to get a segment of a story to work, she would sometimes realize she was trying for a conclusion that the material would not back up.

> It may be a valid conclusion, but the material in hand doesn't fully support it. And so the trick then is to be honest with myself and say, either I need to let go of this—of trying to bring home this conclusion at this point in this story—and just write something that's more in accord with the material in hand, or I need to go out and gather new material and try to be not too selective about that new material, make sure that I'm not going out seeking just the things to prove a point that I want to make.[48]

Similarly, Scott Glover, a *Times* investigative reporter who covered the Rampart scandal in the Los Angeles Police Department, said: "I think the difficulty is you become close to the story and you want to make sure that your story is not an editorial. You want to make sure that though it is taking a point of view, that it was reached by balanced, objective reporting and you arrived in an area; you didn't go in with a preconceived notion."[49] He and Matt Lait, his reporting partner,[50] cited an example from the early days of the Rampart scandal.[51] It grew out of a case in which the department disciplined two officers for on-duty contact with a drug user they had stopped and questioned while on patrol. They were both suspended, and the woman later said she was raped—but disappeared and could not be located. The district attorney's office wrote a "reject," a document that spells out allegations and investigative findings. Glover and Lait were curious about whether the officers received special treatment—especially since a video camera showed the two officers at a 7-Eleven buying beer, potato chips, and condoms, and one officer later admitted to having sex with the woman. The reporters decided to file a public records request for all "reject" documents for the past five years. It turned out that more than 350 cases involving about 500 LAPD officers had been sent to the district attorney's Special Investigations Division. Of those, only about 8 percent had been prosecuted, compared with the district attorney's overall 70 percent prosecution rate for the general public. Glover and Lait's story had a point of view based on the fact that the district attorney's office filed no charges despite strong evidence of guilt in dozens of cases. "But the thing is we didn't go in with that point of view," Glover said. "It might have been that we requested these things and that there were twenty of them over a five-year period and we wrote no story whatsoever." Or, he said, it might have been that they found that the filing rate for police cases was just like the rate for the general public. That "makes for an entirely different story or no story."[52]

Preconceived notions are an issue in opinion writing, just as in news. Martinez commented:

> The most basic ethical question in either one, I think, is to get our information right—to get the correct information without it necessarily being the information we want. I mean, when I go searching an issue for a comment, I'll go to the original source if there is one or I'll search through our files or I'll search through online information, and sometimes it doesn't meet my preconceived notion. And my greatest struggle is to put aside that preconceived notion and write from a standpoint of the information that's available, that's true, and yet overlay my opinion on it, which is what I do.[53]

Hicks, Glover and Lait, and Martinez were all transparent about the ethical struggles connected with preconceived notions. Indeed, it would be impossible for writers to avoid carrying some backdrop of opinion and personal perspective into the stories and commentaries that they care about writing.

But their approach to managing their presuppositions offers a good example of the discipline needed to seek and accept the most truthful information possible.

In well-reported stories, it may be ethically appropriate to choose words that frame a source in a sharply critical way. Hicks said: "I have sometimes chosen words deliberately, knowing that they are powerful words and that they will put the source in a light that they don't find flattering. . . . I think that it's a matter of being diligent about the research and the reporting."[54] She noted that bias is inevitable in reporting, but said she would strive for a result that was "sophisticated" and "intellectually honest, and that the way that I am presenting the source is consistent with the material as a whole, with the story as a whole." Hicks said she tried to be "very rigorous in self-critique," but she also acknowledged the importance of editors in providing a cross-check on her perspective. "If I have failed in my self-critique process, it's amazing how many times an editor will say, 'You know, this right here just really doesn't hang together.' And then I've gone off track somewhere and I need to go back and redo it."

Think from the Reader's Vantage Point

Nora Zamichow, who wrote narratives for the *Times* before leaving in 2006, tried to think about what "stepping stones" readers needed to navigate a story. She provided perspective for readers in this paragraph in a story about Jeremy Strohmeyer, who was accused of sexually assaulting and murdering a little girl: "After Jeremy turned 18 on Oct. 11, 1996, early in his senior year, it was as if nobody could tell him what to do. Not his parents, not his friends. Not even Crutch. It was like watching a car speed down an icy road."[55] She said that in deciding when to provide a frame such as this for the reader, she would ask herself:

> Is the reader going to get this? Do I need to help the reader through here? Is there something that I could say that would assist the reader with making the jump from this paragraph to the next one? And I think you start to hear things. Okay, well I may know that and think that because I've met these kids, but maybe the reader doesn't. So what stepping stone can I provide that leads the way?[56]

Zamichow's approach is a good model for questions that carefully evaluate whether an explicit frame is needed to advance reader understanding of a story.

Deepen Background in Areas of Specialty

As the comments of the interviewees show, ethical interpretive writing calls for in-depth reporting. To explain complex matters and evaluate the significance of issues and events, writers need formal or informal background in their areas of specialty. Read of the *Oregonian* is an example of someone who, like many other reporters, developed much of his expertise on the job. His time and experience reporting in Asia laid a foundation for his analysis of the Asian economic crisis and its connection to the Northwest in "The French Fry Connection." But he also gained formal training in international economics through his Nieman Fellowship at Harvard. Not every reporter works at a news organization with the resources to support an academic year away from the newspaper for specialized training. Many will have to background themselves in topics through informal reading, short professional seminars, or courses at local universities. For students still preparing to be journalists, the best approach is to seek out classes in important and complex areas such as science, history, economics, and religion. That kind of preparation will enable them to understand the context of important topics and offer analysis that goes beyond snap judgments or guesswork.

Notes

1. Joshua Benton, "Successes Are Many, Incomplete," *Dallas Morning News*, July 15, 2004, 1A (Collin County Ed.).

2. Mike Drago, interview by the author, July 21, 2004, Dallas.

3. Jamie Gold, interview by the author, October 7, 2004, Los Angeles.

4. James S. Ettema and Theodore L. Glasser, *Custodians of Conscience: Investigative Journalism and Public Virtue* (New York: Columbia University Press, 1998), 11. See also Stephen Klaidman and Tom L. Beauchamp, *The Virtuous Journalist* (New York: Oxford University Press, 1987), 62–66.

5. Robert M. Entman, "Framing: Toward Clarification of a Fractured Paradigm," *Journal of Communication* 43, no. 4 (Autumn 1993): 52 (italics in the original). For a recent discussion of the concept of framing, see Karen S. Johnson-Cartee, *News Narratives and News Framing: Constructing Political Reality* (Lanham, Md.: Rowman & Littlefield, 2005).

6. Chip Scanlan, "The Nut Graf, Part I: Giving Readers a Reason to Care," Poynter Online, www.poynter.org/content/content_view.asp?id=34457 (accessed May 24, 2006).

7. Leo C. Wolinsky, interview by the author, October 7, 2004, Los Angeles.

8. Victoria Loe Hicks, interview by the author, September 14, 2004, Dallas. For a discussion of the value of explicit analysis and commentary in the context of coverage of ethical issues, see David A. Craig, "Covering Ethics Through Analysis and Commentary: A Case Study," *Journal of Mass Media Ethics* 17, no. 1 (2002): 53–68.

9. David Stabler, "Pushed to the Limit," *Oregonian*, June 24, 2002, A1 (Sunrise Ed.), infoweb.newsbank.com.

10. Barry Johnson, interview by the author, June 25, 2004, Portland, Oregon.

11. Sue Goetinck Ambrose, "Folic Acid: Who's Minding the Risks?" *Dallas Morning News*, April 18, 2004, 1A (2nd ed.) infoweb.newsbank.com.

12. Sue Goetinck Ambrose, interview by the author, July 21, 2004, Dallas.

13. Sonia Nazario, telephone interview by the author, March 11, 2005.

14. Drago interview.

15. Henry Fuhrmann, interview by the author, October 4, 2004, Los Angeles.

16. Doug J. Swanson, "Patients' Deaths Haven't Moved State Board to Act," *Dallas Morning News*, July 28, 2002, 1A (2nd ed.), infoweb.newsbank.com.

17. Doug Swanson, interview by the author, July 22, 2004, Dallas.

18. Ted Rohrlich, "City Funds Flow to Check-Bouncing Developer," *Los Angeles Times*, June 14, 2004, A-1 (Home Ed.), infoweb.newsbank.com.

19. Vernon Loeb, telephone interview by the author, October 5, 2004, Los Angeles.

20. Ted Rohrlich, interview by the author, October 7, 2004, Los Angeles.

21. Pam Maples, telephone interview by the author, September 14, 2004.

22. Reese Dunklin, "Convicted Sexual Abuser and Fugitive Works with Kids under His Religious Order's Wing," *Dallas Morning News*, June 20, 2004, 1A (2nd ed.), infoweb.newsbank.com.

23. Maples interview.

24. Loeb interview.

25. For examples of other excellent explanatory pieces with narrative elements, see the winners in the explanatory reporting category of the Pulitzer Prizes at www.pulitzer.org.

26. Richard Read, interview by the author, June 25, 2004, Portland, Oregon.

27. Richard Read, "Fries to Go, Chaos to Come," *Oregonian*, October 20, 1998, A1 (Street Final Ed.), infoweb.newsbank.com.

28. Mark Z. Barabak, "GOP Fires Rhetorical Barrage at Kerry," *Los Angeles Times*, September 2, 2004, A-1 (Home Ed.), infoweb.newsbank.com.

29. Mark Z. Barabak, telephone interview by the author, November 24, 2004.

30. Crayton Harrison, "The Making of a UTD Windfall," *Dallas Morning News*, July 1, 2003, 1A (2nd ed.).

31. Crayton Harrison, interview by the author, July 19, 2004, Dallas.

32. Karen M. Thomas, "Gayle's Gift," *Dallas Morning News*, February 15, 2004, 1E (2nd ed.).

33. Karen M. Thomas, interview by the author, July 22, 2004, Dallas.

34. Kurt Streeter, "Moving Beyond the Pain," *Los Angeles Times*, July 9, 2003, A-1 (Home Ed.), infoweb.newsbank.com.

35. Kurt Streeter, interview by the author, October 8, 2004, Los Angeles.

36. Thomas interview.

37. Joshua Benton, interview by the author, September 13, 2004, Dallas.

38. Wolinsky interview.

39. Michael Finnegan, telephone interview by the author, December 7, 2004.

40. Bob Yates, interview by the author, July 19, 2004, Dallas.

41. Steve Blow, interview by the author, September 14, 2004, Dallas.

42. John Stuart Mill, *Utilitarianism and On Liberty: Including Mill's 'Essay on Bentham' and Selections from the Writings of Jeremy Bentham and John Austin*, ed. Mary Warnock (Oxford, Eng.: Blackwell, 2003), 100–30.

43. Al Martinez, "A Bittersweet Parting, an Empty Nest," *Los Angeles Times*, September 3, 2004, E-14 (Home Ed.), infoweb.newsbank.com.

44. Al Martinez, telephone interview by the author, November 15, 2004.

45. Al Martinez, "A Loss of Innocence . . . A Flight to Freedom," *Los Angeles Times*, June 24, 2000, A-1 (Home Ed.), infoweb.newsbank.com.

46. Martinez interview.

47. Patt Morrison, interview by the author, October 7, 2004, Los Angeles.

48. Hicks interview.

49. Scott Glover, interview by the author, October 4, 2004, Los Angeles.

50. Matt Lait, interview by the author, October 4, 2004, Los Angeles.

51. Scott Glover and Matt Lait, "LAPD Misconduct Cases Rarely Resulted in Charges," *Los Angeles Times*, October 22, 2000, A-1 (Home Ed.), infoweb.newsbank.com.

52. Glover interview.

53. Martinez interview.

54. Hicks interview.

55. Nora Zamichow, "The Fractured Life of Jeremy Strohmeyer," *Los Angeles Times*, July 19, 1998, A-1 (Home Ed.).

56. Nora Zamichow, interview by the author, October 6, 2004, Los Angeles.

CHAPTER SEVEN

Voice

Journalists speak with a range of voices. The detached, institutional news voice reports in measured tones, with little emotion showing in the writing. The narrative writer's voice brings emotion through powerful details and careful pacing. Sometimes an investigative voice of outrage spotlights negligence or wrongdoing with irony and an indignant edge. The columnist's voice engages readers personally and directly, whether through humor, hyperbole, or anger.

Voice is part of the writer's identity and craft. The Poynter Institute's Roy Peter Clark says, "Of all the effects created by writers, none is more important or elusive" than voice.[1] He likes Poynter colleague Don Fry's definition: "Voice is the sum of all the strategies used by the author to create the illusion that the writer is speaking directly to the reader from the page."[2] Clark notes that voice has a number of dimensions—including level of language, person (first, second, or third), use of allusions and figures of speech, sentence structure and length, "distance from neutrality," and the "frames of reference" of the writer (for example, whether he or she uses conventional subject matter and story forms or is experimental).

Voice is also an ethical issue—though it has received little or no attention in scholarly discussion of journalism ethics. Choices about voice may enhance the truthfulness of a story or distort it. Those choices may stir compassion among readers or leave them emotionally detached from important issues and human needs. This chapter explores several facets of voice as they emerge in different kinds of writing: detachment in news writing, emotion in narrative and investigative work, and personal engagement in columns and first-person articles.

Detachment in News Writing

The standard news voice of U.S. mainstream media keeps a distance between the reporter and the viewpoints and feelings of the people he or she is covering, as well as the subject matter itself. The detached, "objective" voice has ethical benefits but also can create ethical difficulties.

The voice of news connects closely with the institutional voice of the newspaper. Whereas features and columns often display the personalities and styles of the writers, news stories—to one degree or another—usually subsume the writer's individual voice under the official, authoritative voice of the organization. John S. Carroll, editor of the *Los Angeles Times* until he retired in 2005, said:

> I think news stories are done to a certain standard, and it isn't individual expression; it is institutional expression. It meets the editor's standards, and it's not necessarily the way the writer would do it if the writer were writing on his own blog. If we had those people on our staff who are writing for blogs, we'd make them do certain things that they don't do in that format. And to me, it's a truthful reflection of what the story is. It's not an individual's story; it's a story reported by an individual but writing to the standards and in the style of the newspaper.[3]

Carroll said he thinks holding to the institutional voice "signals to the reader that we're trying to be factual, we're trying to sort out emotion and opinion on the part of the writer and to give to them as straight as we're capable of."

With the level of suspicion about media bias, as noted in chapter 5, it is a challenge today to convince readers that a news organization is seeking to report truth. And even those who believe that a news outlet is trying to report truthful information may be put off if stories are so devoid of emotion that it seems the writer does not have compassion for the people or issue being covered. However, as Carroll noted, the institutional voice has the potential to communicate a news organization's commitment to being factual and fair.

In political coverage—one of the areas in which the fairness of journalists is most often questioned—a detached voice signals that the writer is not trying to make issue or voting choices for people. Michael Finnegan, a state politics reporter who covered the 2004 presidential campaign for the *Times*, said he considers his voice to be detached. He sees that as appropriate:

I'm not making choices about who's right and who's wrong in a political debate. I'm giving readers all the information I have that's relevant to them making choices, and at the end of the day, if I'm trusted by readers all the way across the political spectrum, then I've done my job right. Or if I'm angering voters all the way across the political spectrum, then maybe . . . I'm doing my job right.[4]

For political writers, credibility with readers is a challenge, given the level of political polarization and distrust of the media. But the effort to lay out information and not take sides does have the potential to give readers a fuller portrayal of the spectrum of views. In that sense, it is a more truthful portrayal—as long as the nuances of positions on issues are clearly communicated.

Aside from allowing a broad portrayal of political positions, the detached news voice—skillfully used—has the more general benefit of simplicity and clarity. Richard Nelson, a copy editor who works with national news at the *Times,* said:

I guess my concern would be that when we're concerned when a writer is overly concentrating on getting away from that detached news voice that we're going to sacrifice the news or the voice. It's not always true. The best ones don't do it that way, but I'm always concerned about the imitators. And if I have to fall on one side or the other, I'd rather have the detached news voice . . . writing that's simply put—clear, to the point, strong, active writing.[5]

When news writing is at its best—not only detached but also clear and easy to navigate—it is also ethically good in that it can advance reader understanding.

The challenge is to rise above the worst elements of standard news writing. Editor and writing coach Bruce DeSilva of the Associated Press, speaking at a narrative journalism conference in 2001, said bad news writing—filled with unfamiliar words ("fueled," "spawned," "fired off") and word orders ("Police yesterday arrested six men")—is "painful to read." Stories in the standard newspaper voice, he said, are "so unnatural, they sound like a foreign language."[6] Getting beyond an ugly version of the news voice is more than a challenge of writing craft; it is an ethical challenge because of the potential to give readers clear information or obscure it.

A detached news voice—despite its air of authority—is not inherently more reliable than other voices. Richard Read, who wrote the *Oregonian's* "French Fry Connection" series as well as other narratives, said:

No matter what you write, it has a voice. And so I think sometimes we kid ourselves into saying these narrative pieces take liberties because you're kind of imposing your voice or a character's voice on the reader when, how can you do that? It becomes more subjective. Well, conventional reporting also has a voice; it's just, again, that we're used to the voice and we're kind of lulled by it. And because it sounds official and it sounds like newspaperese, we tend to just accept it. But it's not necessarily any more reliable; it may be less than the narrative writing because of the lengths to which you've had to go to report a narrative piece.[7]

News writing that is detached, then, may carry the air of authority but, if not well reported, may be ethically weaker than what some might consider "soft" writing.

Taking things to a more philosophical level, Barry Johnson, the *Oregonian's* arts editor, noted that the omniscient third-person voice of news—which is also sometimes part of the voice of narrative—is inherently false in the sense that, as postmodernists would point out, no narrative is truly complete. He said he thinks the omniscient third-person perspective "not only doesn't connect with younger readers but it happens to be false. We're not omniscient. We just pretend that we are. Our philosophical ground is shaky."[8] Johnson was not arguing that well-done news stories are factually false, but his philosophical critique underlines the deeper limitations of the vantage point of the reporter, which are cloaked by what appears to be an all-knowing perspective of the third-person news voice.

News writing may be ethically weak for a more straightforward reason: boring the reader. No truth can be told if people will not stick with a story. Dean P. Baquet, the *Times's* managing editor and more recently editor, said newspapers have an ethical responsibility to be interesting.

> You've got to be read to be part of the national dialogue, to give people the information they need to vote. They pick you up, and do their eyes glaze over after 30 seconds and [do they] smack the paper against the wall because they can't get through the front page? You can adhere to all the other ethical issues you want to, but you failed the first time. And again, that's not a call for becoming the *National Enquirer*. It's just a call for being interesting and being aggressive, and having a voice when you have the right writers, and letting them write.[9]

One of the most basic ethical necessities, then, is to write stories that will draw people in. DeSilva said: "An appealing voice is going to draw you into and all the way through a story on a subject you didn't know you cared about. An unappealing voice can drive readers away from stories that they care about passionately, from subjects that are important to them."[10] Voice—though DeSilva did not discuss it in ethical terms—is therefore an important element in the ethical power of an article because it helps to pull readers into the content of the story.

The detached news voice thus carries ethical strengths and weaknesses. It may signal an effort to seek and communicate truthful information and may give readers a fuller portrayal of the range of views on issues. News writing that is clear and simple (but not simplistic) is ethically good in that it has the potential to help readers understand the political and social world. However, readers' suspicion about media bias and the appearance of being uncaring through a detached voice may blunt the ethical benefits. A weak reporting base and dull or unnatural writing may also undermine the ethical promise of the news voice. In addition, the third-person voice may appear to be more authoritative than it is possible for even the best reporters to be.

Emotion in Narrative and Investigative Work

Outside the realm of the standard news report, emotion becomes a key element in the voice of stories and their engagement with readers. The power of voice—as evident in narratives and some investigative pieces—can convey a complex array of emotions. Mark Kramer, writer-in-residence and director of the Nieman Program on Narrative Journalism at Harvard University, says narrative stories use a variety of "emotion sets." "Private" emotion sets are the province of books and perhaps the *New Yorker*. They "can include emotions that might alienate newspaper readers"—such as "godless rage, impassioned piety, bitterness, prejudice, arrogance, shrillness, sneakiness, hazy softness." They may create rifts in community instead of building it up. "Civic" emotions, in contrast, build community. "They include patriotic feelings, love of children and aged parents, respect for education, anger at criminals, praise for the charitable and job-providing, sorrow for the dying and ill, gratitude toward police and fire fighters, rage at corruption, and many other feelings. It is, in fact, a rich set of emotions, and everyone in town can share in them. They draw a town together."[11] Kramer argues that civic emotions work well in newspapers.

Writers and editors who work with narrative and investigative pieces face choices about how to convey emotions ranging from compassion to outrage. This section explores the ethics of emotion in narrative and, more briefly, investigative writing.

Emotion and Narrative

The narratives discussed in the interviews stir emotions powerfully, as evidenced by readers' response to many of them. But the power of the stories

does not usually come through statements the writer heaps on to push readers toward strong feelings. It emerges instead through other elements of voice
such as detailed description, vivid verbs, careful changes in cadence, and ju-
dicious use of the subjects' voices.

Barry Siegel's *Times* story about a father's agony over the death of the son
he left alone too long during a wilderness trip (discussed in chapter 3) used
an unadorned voice whose power was built on well-chosen details. This paragraph about searcher James Wilkes' horrible discovery is a strong example:

> By the time Wilkes reached the tree, Dino had cleaned off Gage's face. Six
> inches of snow covered the small body. Gage lay in a fetal position, his hands
> clenched, his eyes wide open. His pajama legs were up to his knees; his feet had
> worn through his thin booties. His throat was blue. In his eyes were frozen
> tears.[12]

The simplicity and directness of Siegel's sentences, combined with wrench-
ing details about what Wilkes saw, evoke strong feelings without commentary from the writer.

Similarly, the *Oregonian's* David Stabler used description to let readers feel
the pain in the family of Sam Johnson, the teen cello prodigy whose behavior challenged his strict parents, Gretta and Jeff. For example, Stabler wrote
this passage about a clash between them before Sam started classes at a private school:

> The year got off to a rocky start. A week before classes began, he stayed out all
> night. It wasn't the first time. Sam had stayed out several nights during the
> summer, but this time, Gretta was fed up. She went into his bedroom that
> night and removed his things and replaced them with those of Amelia, his 13-
> year-old sister. If he wasn't going to use his bedroom, he could move into the
> smallest one in the house, she reasoned.
>
> Sam came home the next morning and headed for the kitchen to pour a
> bowl of cereal.
>
> "Oh, no, you're not going to just come in here and eat like nothing hap-
> pened," Gretta recalls saying.
>
> They both agree about what happened next. Sam went upstairs to his room
> and opened the door. He just stared. Everything was gone—his stereo, CDs,
> posters of his idols, basketball bad boys Allen Iverson and Rasheed Wallace.
> He didn't say anything right away, and hung around the house until after sup-
> per, then he went back to his room and began piling Amelia's things in the
> hall. Gretta told him to stop. He swore at her. She slapped him. He lunged as
> if to punch her, but at the last moment, he slammed his fist into the closet
> door, sending it reeling against the wall. He brushed past Gretta and tussled

with Jeff in the hall. Sam lashed out, punching the wall. Then, he ran outside
and headed down the driveway. Jake, 15, his closest brother, ran after him.
"Don't leave!" Jake sobbed. "Why do you always leave?"
Sam kept walking.[13]

Talking about his voice in the story, Stabler said:

I don't know if I consciously thought, well, now I need to heat things up, now
I need to kind of cool things down, no. I think a lot of writing is intuitive, at
least for me. This is a hot story. There are hugely emotional issues at stake. . . .
There's great pain, and I wanted to relay that in the photos and in my voice.
So that's why we have anecdotes. That's why I'm trying to be there. I'm trying
to get readers to be right there and hear them argue and hear him stomp off
into the night with his brother's sobbing in the driveway. "Why do you always
leave?" "Don't leave!" I think when you do that you are emotionally truthful
to the situation. You could write this in a more distant voice, but I don't think
that's truthful. What's more painful or difficult than family life? And so I
wanted the truth of that to seep out of this story. . . . And it comes in word
choices. Active verbs, nothing in passive voice. Sometimes direct quotes. It
comes through indirect characterization, not direct. Direct characterization is
like Charles Dickens saying, "He was an emotional man," or "She was high
strung." You're telling the reader what the person's character is instead of indirect characterization, showing, "He couldn't stop jiggling his leg, and he had
six cups of coffee, and his eyes were blinking ten times a second." That heats
things up. That's crucial in these sort of emotional stories.[14]

Through straightforward, detailed description, this story—like Siegel's—
brings readers face to face with difficult emotions. The truth of the scene
seeps out, as Stabler put it—rather than emerging through summations by
the writer.

Jack Hart, managing editor at the *Oregonian* and the primary editor of narratives at the newspaper, argues that readers feel the emotion of a scene most
strongly through details that enable the reader to experience it:

You can't tell somebody to be emotional. You can't say, "This was really sad.
You're going to understand just how sad it was." They have to experience, at
least in their dream state, things firsthand to have an emotional reaction. Get
down into the reptilian brain when you're dealing with that kind of thing. And
so I'm not so sure that voice, per se, is terribly important to emotional reaction.
Matter of fact, my advice to writers when they're describing an accident, for
example, in which somebody dies is to be as simple and close to the ground as
possible. No adjectives, no adverbs, slow time down, describe in great detail
exactly what happened with visual cues, other sensory cues to put people there.

But don't interject yourself into that. They need to experience it directly to respond emotionally. That's why I just love it when we get letters from people or e-mails saying that they cried. Because that's the hardest thing for a journalist to accomplish usually. Nobody reads a news story from the Mideast in which five Americans were killed that day and cries. And yet it's a terrible tragedy. Sometimes we'll get a level of detail into a funeral story about somebody killed in Iraq that will produce some tears, but usually not even then. That report writing style is great for conveying abstract information, but it's lousy at producing emotion.[15]

Vivid detail, simply conveyed, connects with people's senses in a way that labeling something as sad cannot. By connecting with their senses, writers can stir compassion and other feelings—thereby bringing a story home in a deeper way.

As noted in chapter 3, powerful descriptive passages like this are built on a strong base of reporting. The *Times*'s Sonia Nazario, who wrote "Enrique's Journey," said she does not think of her writing in terms of voice but rather focuses on doing in-depth reporting that yields "amazing material" to work with.

It's like building a house—you're putting one brick on top of the other until you eventually have this strong house, this powerful narrative, and I try to focus a lot on the turning points and the most powerful scenes, the most emotional scenes, so I guess I view it more as letting the story come out and speak for itself in just doing a really good job of reporting it and then trying to build this house.[16]

The power of the voice, then, depends greatly on the strength of the material gathered in reporting. The strong passages these writers produce would be impossible if the reporting were thin.

Often the voices of the characters in the stories are a significant component of the voice of the narrative. Nora Zamichow, in her *Times* story on Jeremy Strohmeyer and the killing of a seven-year-old girl,[17] used several segments of dialogue she or police had had with young people who knew Strohmeyer about their attitudes and actions. They appeared without commentary on her part, allowing troubling statements—such as "I'm not going to get upset over somebody else's life. I just worry about myself first"—to speak for themselves. Zamichow said she likes to think about her writing voice "as lack of voice. What you're hearing more than my voice is their voices, and I feel like I've been most effective when you come away from the story feeling like you know those kids and that you know those people, rather than that you know me."[18]

Barry Horn, a sportswriter for the *Morning News*, showed the power of another tool of voice—verbs—in his story about a son who killed his father after being driven relentlessly toward athletic success. The writing is simple and direct, and much of the power emerges in the verbs—as this passage shows:

> Almost immediately upon the family's return from Colorado, Mr. Butterfield imposed his own strict training regimen on Lance.
>
> He prescribed the boy's diet.
>
> Mornings, he would provide a fistful of vitamins and supplements for the boy to shovel into his mouth. Evenings, he insisted the boy pour weight-gaining shakes down his throat.
>
> Eventually, Mr. Butterfield began checking the boy's bowel movements to determine whether Lance had eaten any foods he had banned from the boy's diet.
>
> And father fed his son steroids.
>
> Mr. Butterfield concocted his own remedies for injuries without regard to what professional trainers and doctors had to say.[19]

The emotion of outrage comes through in the picture Horn paints using verbs such as "shovel," "pour," and "concocted." He said this about his word choice:

> Verbs are very strong words; people think you have to use adjectives. Verbs very often are more descriptive than adjectives. . . . "Shoveled" to me connotes what we're trying to say is here he's forced to take it. Not, the boy didn't sit down and say, "Oh, let me have all the vitamins." They're being shoveled to him, he's got to—he's being force-fed. The boy poured a weight-gaining shake down his throat. The boy's not even having the shakes because he likes them; he's not having the shakes because they're good.[20]

The verbs here are not "neutral"; they are emotionally charged. But Horn said the voice they help create reflected people's attitudes toward Bill Butterfield, a man whom it appeared everyone disliked.

Skillful use of brevity can also stir readers' emotions and keep them engaged in a story. The *Oregonian's* Tom Hallman, Jr., showed the power of change in cadence in his series "Fighting for Life on Level 3," about life in a neonatal intensive care unit. For example, these paragraphs close a scene in which nurse Cathy Pollock-Robinson tried to help save the life of a baby who was fighting to breathe:

> The heart rate shot up to more than 100 and then began falling: 80, 70, 60, 55.
>
> Cathy climbed on a stool to rise above the crowd and get some leverage. She leaned over the isolette and grabbed the baby with both hands as if holding a

mound of clay. She placed her thumbs over the baby's heart and began squeezing.

From her position, Cathy couldn't see the heart monitor. But a nurse had slipped a device for measuring the amount of oxygen in the baby's bloodstream over his right arm. As Cathy pressed down on the heart rhythmically, the device showed oxygen moving through the system. She counted the heart's pulses—a more normal 120 beats a minute. She looked down at the baby's chest.

It began to rise and fall.[21]

Robbie DiMesio, the copy editor who handled the series, said she thinks Hallman's use of short sentences—such as the closing sentence of this scene—helps draw readers in. She noted that the series was long—about 350 inches of copy. "And it read so easily, it just flowed. And you felt like you were reading a book. I think that was what we were going for. They wanted to go for something that was not very newspaper. And I think that this project achieved that."[22] However, Hallman warned against using short sentences too often. "I think earlier in my career I might have gone a little overboard on the short sentences because they are a fun tool. So I'm trying to balance them out and when, almost like a musical score, just to break it up. There is a certain drama or power with those short sentences, but to overuse them takes it away."[23] As with the other devices discussed here, overdoing short sentences blunts the emotional impact and therefore may keep readers from connecting with the themes of the story.

The simplicity of the voices of the narrative writers interviewed frees the emotional power of the subject matter to meet the reader head-on. Richard E. Meyer, the narrative editor at the *Times* who worked with Siegel on the story about the aftermath of Gage Wayment's death and with Nazario on "Enrique's Journey," made a strong case for the ethical benefits of conveying emotion without loading a story with heavily emotional language from the writer. Meyer warned that emotional stories can turn "mawkish, maudlin, purple. You don't want to write a soap opera."[24] Mawkishness,[25] he said, would mean "anything in the writing that has as its explicit text or its implicit subtext, 'Oh, isn't this terrible? The poor boy. Oh my God, Agnes.'" Instead, the writer should view him- or herself as a camera. "I'm going to tell you, reader, what is there, and I'm gonna trust you, reader, to have the emotions. I'm not gonna have the emotions." Meyer sees being maudlin as distorting truth.

Anything that's maudlin is by definition not the truth. It is an exaggeration in truth in a way; it's a distortion of truth. That little boy lying there with the bottom of his booties worn through and a tear frozen on his cheek, that's the truth, that's what was there, that's what the rescuer saw, right? That's what I the camera am going to report to you, right? That's the truth. Now, "Oh my God, isn't that awful? That poor little boy"—that's building on the truth, it's going beyond the truth, and it's easy to go into a distortion when you do that kind of thing.

To Meyer, engaging readers' emotions is important because they are an element of the truth.

But I'm not going to burden you with mine or try to influence you to have a different set than the set you might have, because the emotions you experience as a result of these facts that I'm presenting to you are the real emotions for you. That's your truth—that's the emotional truth you take away from this, right? The emotional truth I take away from this might be the same, it might be different. But when it comes to emotional truth, the readers are the ones that count. Because everyone is gonna have slightly different emotions about this.

Meyer's comments show the complexity of the ethics of emotional stories. Compassion, horror, outrage, and other feelings are not separable from some bare factual truth that the story conveys. Narratives with inherently emotional content—such as stories about the death or difficulties of children or the pain of parents—impart information but also move readers through the emotions wrapped up with the information. But not all readers will be moved in the same way. As Meyer noted, if a writer tries to underline a particular emotion, that steers the reader away from the emotions he or she may naturally feel—and therefore from what, for that reader, is the emotional reality of the scene.

Emotion and Investigative Work

The narrative stories discussed in this book evoke a variety of emotions, but they center on compassion, pain, and sorrow. The investigative projects may evoke compassion or sorrow for victims of wrongdoing, but the focus of the stories is mostly what Mark Kramer called anger at criminals or outrage over corruption. Outrage is a central emotion of the investigative genre,[26] as the title of the 1991 book *The Journalism of Outrage: Investigative Reporting and Agenda Building in America* suggests.[27] As with narrative work, outrage can appear through a voice that does not heap on emotion but reports information straightforwardly. The investigative work discussed in the interviews is not loaded with statements of outrage by the writers, but it does sometimes use dramatic language and irony to drive home the outrageousness of situations or actions.

The interpretive language used to summarize investigative findings (discussed in chapter 6) sometimes implies outrage—as in *Morning News* reporter Doug Swanson's story about the Texas State Board of Medical Examiners, in which he wrote of "routine mercy to doctors whose negligence killed the people they were treating" and "state-sanctioned tolerance for serious medical mistakes."[28] Outrage can also come across in ironic details that emerge through careful reporting. Swanson's story conveyed irony in this passage:

> Dr. Jasbir Ahluwalia of Stephenville had been sued by a husband and wife who alleged that he caused severe and permanent brain damage to their child during delivery. At 6 years, the boy was determined to have the mental functioning of a 4-week-old.
>
> Dr. Ahluwalia settled the suit in 1989 for more than $1.3 million.
>
> In the course of the suit, lawyers for the couple raised questions about the quality of Dr. Ahluwalia's medical training, much of which he received in Uganda.
>
> The medical board took no action.
>
> In March 1991, a Dallas woman sued him, accusing the doctor of perforating her uterus during an abortion. As a result, surgeons had to remove her uterus.
>
> That same year, another Dallas woman sued him. She, too, said he perforated her uterus during an abortion.
>
> Dr. Ahluwalia settled both suits in 1993. The medical board took no action on either one.
>
> In 1995, he was sued by an Erath County woman on whom Dr. Ahluwalia had performed a hysterectomy. She alleged that he mistakenly blocked a ureter with stitches. So severe were the complications that, four months later, another surgeon had to remove her kidney.
>
> Had she known of Dr. Ahluwalia's prior problems, patient Linda Runnels said recently, "I wouldn't have used him for sure."
>
> Her suit was settled. The medical board took no action.
>
> In 1996, Dr. Ahluwalia finally felt the state's regulatory wrath.
>
> The medical board said it acted because Dr. Ahluwalia had lost his privileges at Harris Methodist Erath County Hospital. The privileges had been pulled because he "failed to adequately manage various high-risk pregnancies."
>
> No mention was made of the lawsuits, and the discipline was minimal.
>
> Board members voted to require him to take 50 hours of continuing medical education and keep adequate patient records. And he was ordered to subscribe to the journal *Obstetrics and Gynecology*.
>
> Also, the board said, he must read it.[29]

The irony in Swanson's reference to "the state's regulatory wrath" was clear because he juxtaposed the background on the doctor's problems with the board's light discipline. And by closing the passage by saying the doctor was ordered to read the journal, Swanson used a detail from the order to underline the irony of the board's handling of the case. Pam Maples, Swanson's editor, said:

> Frankly, one of the central missions of good investigative reporting is to reveal the reality when it contradicts with the public persona or statements of a government agency. Anytime they are sort of claiming one thing and doing something radically different, or denying that they are doing it, they are fair game. And it is fair in the story to point out. A lot of investigative reporting sort of lays all of this out but never helps the reader. It just kind of leaves the reader to see the contradiction.[30]

Swanson pointed out the contradiction in a way that drives the point home to the reader without having to label it an irony.

As James S. Ettema and Theordore M. Glasser have noted, irony is a common device in investigative work. They argue that it threatens to breed cynicism among the public and thereby undermine rather than advance discussion of "the true and the good."[31] Their analysis underlines the need to use this device sparingly and not rely on it as the only means to communicate the moral dimension of a story.

Victoria Loe Hicks, one of the authors of the *Morning News*'s "Dallas at the Tipping Point," a project examining Dallas's health compared with that of other large cities, said the voice of outrage "can certainly get very old" and can come across as false.[32] But she saw a place for it in that project. "This is not a stock journalism outrage story, and so I think it's more effective to use the voice of outrage on a non-traditional subject matter than it necessarily would be to use it on the traditional subject matter"—such as poor or oppressed people. The opening story laid out the findings of consulting firm Booz Allen Hamilton about the state of the city. It included strong statements, as this passage early in the story shows:

> Moreover, the numbers suggest that Dallas—lulled by past successes, cushioned by North Texas' robust growth, blinded by a lack of self-examination and hobbled by the legacy of racism and neglect—is at a tipping point, where wrong moves could precipitate a protracted slide.
>
> Crime and troubled schools send families scurrying for the suburbs; employers follow; the tax base and the city budget shrink; city services decline; the drift to the 'burbs accelerates . . .

. . . And Dallas' peril is all the greater, the consultants warned, because a su-
perficial appearance of good health masks its symptoms. The city's malady is
much like a "silent" heart attack, which goes undetected until it's too late for
treatment.

Faced with Booz Allen's diagnosis, city leaders fell back on their habitual
remedies.[33]

Hicks said she felt comfortable making the statement about "habitual remedies" because the four reporters who worked on the project did group interviews
and were able to compare notes on their perception of city leaders' response. "I
also had four years of covering Dallas City Hall, and so I felt quite qualified to
say that this was a behavior pattern that was habitual, and I wanted to convey
that they had not shown themselves well. They had done a poor job of answer-
ing . . . or of dealing with the information that we presented to them."[34] Hicks
saw outrage as the appropriate response from Dallas residents. "We were outraged, and I didn't have any ethical qualms about suggesting through the choice
of words and the writing techniques that we were outraged."

There is a danger that highlighting city government's shortcomings with
an angry edge will indeed breed cynicism among readers, as Ettema and
Glasser might warn, but this approach does grab attention about issues that
might tax the patience of readers if they were presented in a more neutral
voice. The series did go beyond pointing out problems and presented ideas
from other cities that might help Dallas. In doing so, it provides a stronger
ethical model than a series that merely cursed the darkness would have.

Still, as Hicks herself noted, an emotional voice is harder to execute skillfully than a straight news voice. The voice of outrage is best used sparingly—
not only because it may breed cynicism, but also because its overuse may cost
a reporter credibility. Scott Glover, who covers corruption in law enforcement for the *Times*, said: "We may forsake drama for accuracy and fairness,
but in the long run we feel like that kind of keeps us in business. We have a
lot of people who don't like the stories that we write but who will talk to us
because they feel that if we've got it, we've got it—we document it, it's down
the middle and I think it helps us in the long run."[35] His reporting partner,
Matt Lait, said:

I think if you write with kind of an opinion or you are heavy-handed in the
way you present the material, at least for us, you're going to be viewed among
the people that you're collecting information from as a biased, unreliable, not
credible reporter, and it undermines your ability to do your job. We still come
out with very, I think, powerful stories where we don't have to amp it up with
inflammatory language.[36]

Investigative reporters thus face ethical choices that are similar to those of narrative writers. They must decide whether to let the outrage of the situation speak for itself through careful reporting or to underline it for readers through use of dramatic, interpretive language or irony. The straightforward approach lets readers sort out the meaning of the facts and their emotional reactions to those facts, but it may mean that some in the audience miss elements of a situation that are truly outrageous—either because they tune out or because they fail to assemble all the pieces. The more dramatic approach may help them see the bigger picture and stir their anger, but—as Meyer said in discussing emotion in narrative—it may reshape the "emotional truth" that readers take from a story.

Personal Engagement in Columns and First-Person Articles

Narratives and some investigative pieces can connect powerfully with readers by engaging their emotions, but the most direct engagement with readers comes through the voices of columnists—who bring identifiable, ongoing voices to a newspaper—and writers of other first-person pieces that sometimes appear on news pages or elsewhere. This personal engagement comes not only through the use of first person, which sets up more direct communication with readers, but also sometimes through highly emotional statements, humor, hyperbole, or sarcasm.

Steve Blow, a Metro columnist for the *Morning News*, said he thinks directly addressing readers helps communication with them. "I think part of the gift that I'm given as a columnist is my ability to write in first person and that is to speak to the readers in a much more natural way—in a way that they're accustomed to getting information."[37] Although Blow puts a high priority on columns about issues, reactions from readers show that he particularly connects with them when he is personal and writes about his family.

> Time and time again what I hear when I'm out in public is "I love it when you write about your kids. It reminds me so much of my own kids," or that sort of thing. . . . Last night one mentioned the column about taking my daughter off to college. One mentioned a column I wrote, a tribute to my dad on Father's Day. The personal just connects with people. I think in some ways we in journalism have been too hesitant or reluctant to use that. It has to be sparingly—you can't have everybody writing in the first person—but, I don't know, that reluctance to inject ourselves into the news pages in some ways I think has worked against us as a business.

Blow's comments suggest that through both direct address and personal subject matter, readers become engaged in his columns in a way that they might not if his voice and the subject matter it carries were more detached.

Blow sees disclosure of his own feelings—for example, telling readers he choked up during a church service hearing a chorus his children had once sung—as building an emotional bond with readers in a way that third-person objective style does not.

> I think it humanizes. Obviously sort of the whole point of journalism in a lot of ways is to scrub the emotion out of a lot of what we present to people, and so that as a columnist, I am probably a little more willing to share those emotional moments, again, because I see my job in a way as trying to provide balance to the rest of the paper and that we're not that sort of dispassionate, objective third-person approach to life. It's important in the news columns, but at the same time I think that connects with readers and sort of just forms a bond of humanity, if you will, that's important, that makes reading the newspaper more of a shared experience I guess, if you will. Again I find that readers really like those kinds of expressions of honest emotions. They'll say, "Well, you did it to me again. You put a lump in my throat" or "You made me tear up over my breakfast cereal" or whatever. I never want to be calculated about it or just try to yank emotions just for the sake of selling the story, but if I have an honest emotional reaction, I'm gonna sort of feel it's my duty in telling the truth to convey that.

For Blow, honesty about feelings is a matter of telling the truth of a situation more fully. He places a priority on genuineness of voice and believes readers long to hear that kind of genuineness: "I think readers really crave authenticity. That's some of what's missing from politics today. Nobody sounds like themselves. Nobody sounds like they're expressing these genuine, heartful emotions or insights. It all sounds so processed and calculated, and so that may be something that people respond to in a column, that the words sound authentic."

Blow was not the only interviewee who saw first-person writing as in some way more honest than the more formalized, processed voice of objectivity. Hicks included first-person reflection about her feelings in a story[38] (discussed in chapter 1) in which she interviewed a chronic sex offender as part of the Pulitzer-winning 1993 *Morning News* series "Violence Against Women."

> I'm sure that this was what was in my mind even if I hadn't brought it to the forefront . . . that I was particularly unsuited to be an objective observer in that

situation and that to pretend to be an objective observer would be dishonest, and that the reader needed to know just how my reactions and judgments might differ from those of an objective observer. And so by writing it through my own eyes, I hoped to provide them with all the information that they needed to sort out, "Well, you know, I think she misperceived this" or, "Gee, that's interesting that she thought that way, that's really weird"—you know, just sort of spot those areas where I might be bringing bias—I mean that's a good scientific word anyway—bringing bias to bear.[19]

More broadly, reflecting on the place of first person, Hicks echoed the perspective of scholars who have poked holes in the notion of objectivity in expressing her discomfort about the honesty of the objective form.

If I'm really, really honest, I've always been a little bit uncomfortable with that whole third-person objectivity thing. I almost feel like it would be more honest to write in the first person—if there were a way to do it without making oneself the subject of the story. I mean that that, I think, is bad—unless one actually is the subject of the story, then that just gets in the way at a certain point. But I wish that there were something in between almost, a whole different convention of language. And I think that we get more and more toward that the more our journalism becomes, or the more our language becomes, colloquial and not journalese; I think that we're sort of shifting in that direction and I personally think that's a good thing. I think that that real distancing sort of formal journalistic lingo is really not terribly honest about how this process happened. It purports to be more objective than the process really is, I think.

Hicks's comments show considerable sensitivity to the ethical issues wrapped up with the choice of using a more personal, self-disclosing voice. That kind of voice, in stories in which the writer has a strong emotional stake, may be more truthful because it goes underneath the veneer of objective factual reporting to disclose the vantage point of the author.[40]

Morning News managing editor George Rodrigue, who has shared in two Pulitzer Prizes and worked as a foreign correspondent for the paper, sees a place for first person at times in clearly communicating what a reporter is experiencing. "There were things that I saw when I was a foreign correspondent that made me wish I had a way to write about that stuff." For example, learning during the war in Bosnia about a man who had been forced to eat part of another man's flesh provoked a sense of horror that "went beyond, in a way, what a typical news story could convey." Rodrigue said he wished he could have written a piece that conveyed, "you know, sometimes this place is a lot worse in real life than it is in the newspapers." Other kinds of experiences may also be appropriate for first person:

> Sometimes our reporters, for instance, covering schools have experiences or see things that would be maybe not bad for a first-person article. First person just means I saw it myself. It happened to me. I don't particularly want to get into situations where reporters tell us a lot about what they personally think. I don't know why I would care, as a reader. But I sometimes think that we can do a better job of directly conveying what we experience. . . . I think it can just be a more meaningful way of telling the story. It's sort of like just speaking more clearly. But there may be stories that are better spoken more clearly.[41]

The ability to make one's experience an explicit part of the reporting can serve the interest of communicating truthfully by bringing a clearer account to readers—not only factually accurate, but also faithful to the emotional context of the situation and the impressions of the reporter.

Carroll said the *Times* sometimes uses first person in its Column One story, an interesting and unusual piece that runs down the left-hand side of the front page. "If the story is about an individual's experience and the individual is writing it, it makes it more straightforward. Instead of couching it in tortured third-person terms . . . you're just saying, 'Here's what I did and here's what I saw and here's how it affected me.' I think it's actually, in a way, more honest."[42] For Carroll too, then, honesty surfaces as a word that characterizes the first-person voice—at least when it is used to highlight the experience of the writer.

Just as it can express experience more clearly, a personal voice can bring home a larger point in a way that engages readers in the content of the topic. Al Martinez, a *Times* columnist, tries to use good writing to drive home his points. "I think good writing helps establish point of view and truth and fact, and I try to use it and use the rhythms of prose to establish my point, and by so doing I get a lot of conservatives and people who disagree with me reading my work because they like my writing."[43] This passage from a column about the beheading of American civil engineer Jack Hensley in Iraq shows the power of his prose:

> Life goes on in our cities and our neighborhoods in the relative safety of heavy security, but for Hensley and the others who were murdered only because they were in the way of forces beyond their control, there will be no tomorrow.
> They will never again smell a rose or hear a barking dog or make love or have a beer or shop for a new car or rake leaves or celebrate a holiday or hear laughter or cry at a movie or listen to music or sing in a choir or nap on the

couch or attend a concert or picnic on the beach or feel the sun or walk in the rain or hike through the woods.[44]

The length and repetition in the paragraph above emphasized the finality of the deaths in a way that no statistic would. Powerful writing like this, though normally discussed as a matter of craft or rhetoric, also has ethical implications because of its ability to grab the audience and bring home a message.

Martinez considers his voice to be emotional. "That's been both a criticism and praise that I've received, that I write with this emotional voice and the emotion of my presentation overwhelms the facts." But he is also sensitive to the need to evaluate his language for factuality as well as emotion.

> There are times when . . . I can write a column in a couple hours and it takes me the rest of the day to refine it and say what I want. And sometimes I'll soar by something and just fly by it because I love the sound of the words, and then I'll go back and it's very painful for me to change these words because they don't mean what I say or they're so emotional that they're not precisely as factual as I want them to be. And all the substance of a good column, or even a commentary, even a strong commentary, based in, it's got a factual basis, and this is what I try, to maintain that and keep that and still make the writing really good.[45]

For a columnist, then, the power of expression can establish a point in a way that keeps even people who disagree with the argument reading. But both the precision of language and its emotional weight are important ethical considerations.

Patt Morrison, an opinion-page columnist for the *Times*, sees first-person singular as a means to communicate an abstract point in a personal way.

> You're channeling something that's a little bigger than you are. And you're simply using yourself to make a point that people can comprehend, they can get their heads around. We are pattern-seeking creatures. We're creatures who look to the personal rather than the abstract. And so, you can make an abstract point with a personal example. And you do that a lot, certainly, in news and feature coverage, but you can and should do it even more in a column. But the rules should be: Don't be ad hominem. Don't make a campaign or a crusade of it. And don't make it about yourself except insofar as you are the vehicle to make a point.[46]

Her comments echo the concerns of other interviewees about using first-person voice with caution. Commentary that consistently focuses on oneself at the expense of broader points may be more self-indulgent than illuminating. Vivian McInerny, a feature writer for the *Oregonian*, wrote a first-person piece about meeting a man who had served with her oldest brother, who had died in Vietnam.[47] She said it is important to bring home broad themes—as she did in connecting her experience with the pain of those losing loved ones in Iraq. "I do think that the key to writing a first-person piece is that it has to have universal themes or no one does care. Everybody suffers loss. And I think they're really hard to do, and I think they should be done sparingly, and I think we run a lot of bad ones, as many newspapers do. I think just because you can write in the first person doesn't mean you should."[48]

First-person voice enables a writer to reflect in a deep and serious way about experiences such as wartime or personal moments of pain. For less grave topics, humor may also be a component of that voice. Morrison said humor gives her more freedom and can help bring a point home more effectively.

> Women columnists have a particular burden, which is that most people— men in particular but most people—don't like being lectured to by a woman. And so if my name were Peter Morrison and I could put that name on top of it, I could probably write things I couldn't get away with with Patt Morrison on the top of that; so humor becomes a very deft tool which I think gives me ultimately more freedom. It's harder to deliver, especially on very serious topics, and I wouldn't essay that on something really serious. But if you can pull something off with humor, the point becomes more memorable and more tolerable.[49]

Morrison sees humor as a way to get truth across. "Satire is just truth with a smile. And if you can deliver that, people are going to be more inclined to listen to what you say and perhaps even to agree with you than if you were shaking a finger and hectoring." Sometimes her columns use hyperbole to advance an argument. For example, she opened one column during the fall 2004 election season this way:

> First-aid Hollywood-style dictates that the best way to calm a hysterical person is to deliver a sharp slap across the chops. Bogie did it to Bacall's little sister in "The Big Sleep." The passengers in "Airplane!" lined up for a turn at smacking a woman with the screaming meemies.
> When is hysterical America going to slap itself back to its senses?
> This week's e-mails have informed me that George W. Bush must have been equipped with an earpiece or a receiver in his molar during last week's presidential debate because he kept saying "Let me finish" when no one was inter-

rupting him. (Get wise, people; if Bush had had Karl Rove feeding him lines, do you think he would have lost?)

The around-the-bend blogs hollered that John Kerry had illicitly used his own pen at the debates—or was that a cheat sheet in his hand?—and that Kerry won only because someone slipped him the questions beforehand. (Yep, those surprise Iraq questions in a debate on foreign policy sure looked like sucker punches to Bush.)

When did the loonies get off their barstools or off their meds and take over? Aren't Area 51 and Bigfoot enough for them anymore? When did the wackos stop getting transmissions from Saturn in their bridgework and start getting C-SPAN?[50]

Commenting on the hyperbole she used in the last paragraph of the passage, Morrison said:

In order to open the door to the premise that I'm pursuing in here—which is saying the problem is that the difference between opinion and judgment and analysis has all been blurred—you have to kick open the door. You can't just push open the door and peek around the corner. This kicks open the door to the rest of that argument. And it does it in an over-the-top sense that clearly isn't saying people on Paxil are now running the country, or people who are off Paxil are now running the country. But it's over-the-top enough for people to go, "Whoa, what is she talking about here?"[51]

The goal, then, for Morrison is to use hyperbole to engage her audience in the argument she is developing. But once the door is open, she said, it is important "to back off from the hyperbole to make a more rational and sensible point." The ethical choices come in using hyperbole carefully and sparingly.

The ethics of it are making sure that in the rest of the argument that you make, that it's very clear that this is the hyperbolic moment. Otherwise you're crying wolf and everything you write is hyperbole. People are going to stop listening. People are going to stop reading, stop paying attention. But when you take a couple of graphs or a couple of lines that are sort of in-your-face and so over-the-top, you need to use those sparingly or they lose their effect.[52]

Thus humor and hyperbole, like the emotion of Martinez's writing, must be employed judiciously in order to bring a message home in the most ethical manner.

Choices about voice, including use of humor, have interesting implications for connection with younger readers, whose attention newspapers have been fighting to gain and keep in recent years. Michael Arrieta-Walden, the public editor of the *Oregonian* until he became senior editor for online in 2006, said, "I think you find with younger readers that we don't have enough personality. We don't have enough opinion. We don't have enough tone and voice in the paper. And there is a desire for that."[53] But what younger readers like doesn't always go over well with older ones. The newspaper has received sharply differing feedback about a column for commuters that answers questions from readers. Arrieta-Walden said the column was usually somewhat formal until Steve Beaven took it over. Beaven "has made it lively—it's very attractive to younger readers. Our older readers hate it. They just feel like it's disrespectful, it's too snarky."[54] Beaven writes with a sarcastic edge. For example, he opened one column this way:

> They come to us to share their dreams, to whisper their fears, to vent their smoldering anger.
> We are cheaper than a shrink, cooler than your counselor, tastier than your fifth shot of bourbon. We are Back Seat. We care.[55]

Beaven then included a question from a reader:

> Kids these days: I ride the bus to work and have noticed a disturbing trend. How come kids are always swearing on the bus? That ain't right. I saw an elderly lady tell kids to cool it, and they swore at her, too. The driver just sat there. What gives? Can't the driver do something? D.A., Portland

Beaven began his answer by saying:

> Unfortunately, TriMet doesn't employ anyone to ride the bus and wash the little buggers' mouths out with soap. Firing a stun gun at them probably will get you in trouble.

After citing several comments from a TriMet spokeswoman, presented in a more conventional voice, Beaven closed that answer with this advice:

> We suggest pulling that old boom box out of the attic, popping in a Yoko Ono disc and cranking it up to 11. It'll either drown them out or make them move.

At the end of the column, Beaven presented a complaint from another reader and answered with attitude:

> Complaints Dept.: I just had to write about your new format for Back Seat. Is the writer a teenager or a teen wannabe? Does he realize he is not a stand-up comic and he is probably alienating most of your prior readers? Anyone with an I.Q. above room temperature is totally turned off by him.

I used to look to Back Seat for information about the laws here, as I am a retired law enforcement officer from another state and appreciate seeing how
some of your laws are different. No more. I won't waste my time reading that
drivel. Soon I won't even need to get a paper, since you have ruined the
comics, entertainment, editorial page and now metro. Big D, Parts unknown

Sorry, we don't have an Andy Rooney column for you, ossifer. But don't forget Steve Duin. He's crusty. And he hasn't been a teenager since the Hoover
administration.

The sarcastic answer Beaven gave this reader was not likely to win him
any more friends with the older audience. But for younger people who are
bored with newspapers, it may have given them more reason to stick with a
column that also provides information about commuting and thereby serves
its audience. If this kind of writing can engage an audience and supply useful
knowledge, its voice is an ethical plus. However, as Arrieta-Walden noted, it
would serve the older audience to signal clearly that a column such as this
has taken on a different voice from the one to which they were accustomed.

Whether they are written seriously or humorously, columns and other
first-person pieces have the potential to draw readers' interest and engage
their emotions (including their compassion) in ways that news stories written in a detached third-person voice may not. Although truth and objectivity are often wrapped together in professional discussions of journalism
ethics, the voice of columns and other first-person pieces offers some benefits from the standpoint of truth telling. Readers may take away more truth
about life or political issues than they would in a balanced presentation simply because they pay attention thanks to the writer's personal disclosure, humor, or emotive style. In addition, truth may emerge in ways that it would
not in the objective voice. Breaking through the limits of objectivity may
shed more light on who the author is and how that is shaping the story the
reader sees. It may also free the writer to talk more directly and plainly about
his or her experience. At the same time, it is important to truth telling in this
voice that a piece not be so centered on the writer that the reader's view of
the topic is obscured. Ethical use of the power of first person also means
thinking carefully about when and how to use hyperbole or strongly emotional language—not letting them overwhelm or distort the more measured
parts of a column and therefore the truth content of the writing.

Ways to Do Better

As the discussion in this chapter has shown, working with voice across journalistic genres entails choices that have ethical implications. Both detached

and more emotional voices can accomplish good by bringing aspects of truth about life and issues before readers. Engaging voices can stir people's hearts to care about other people and important social issues. The very power of voice means that its use needs to be evaluated carefully. But evaluating carefully does not mean stamping out creative, compelling, and even outrageous voices in knee-jerk fashion. It means thoughtful, open-minded evaluation of the specifics of voice in stories, by both writers and editors. Questions worth asking include:

- Is a formal, detached news voice enhancing clarity of communication or producing dull prose that may drive away readers?
- Are there enough descriptive details in a narrative to engage readers' feelings about the characters and scenes in the story?
- Is strongly emotional language in a narrative leading the reader too much to a particular set of emotions?
- Is a particular investigative story loading on dramatic language to the extent that the language may obscure measured consideration of the facts of the situation?
- Is first person being used in a way that enhances clarity and transparency or puts the focus excessively on the writer?
- Is emotional language in a column helping to engage readers in the substance of the argument or distorting precise communication of some facet of the issue?

It is impossible to answer these questions fully, especially to answer them for the entire range of readers. Research on the impact of voice on audiences would help shed light on what choices have the most positive ethical impact. But absent that research, writers and editors can envision possible responses of readers based on their own responses and those of their colleagues.

It is important for editors to be sensitive to writers' voice—for the sake of stories' ethical impact on readers as well as good relations with writers. Henry Fuhrmann, senior copy desk chief for business and later a deputy business editor at the *Times*, talked about the art of editing and voice:

Too much editing can be thoughtless, in that it ignores what the reporter was trying to achieve in his or her voice. I think voice is very important. In my job, I don't edit as many stories as I used to. I'm more of a supervisor. I supervise thirteen other copy editors and slots. But what I tell them all the time is there's a science of editing and an art of editing, and the science is the blue book. It's our dictionary; it's our stylebook, which is this blue-bindered thing. That's the science of the editing. There are rules and you can follow those. But the art of editing is knowing when to break the rules—knowing when to break the rules, when to decide that not all the rules apply here because this is a different sort of situation. It's knowing that yeah, normally we say X, but here we're going to say Y and it's the reason behind that. And it's getting to figure out what's the most effective way to communicate the particular point to the reader in this particular case. It's the art of editing that makes it fun and challenging.[56]

For copy editors—and other editors, too—handling voice well means being willing to think outside the conventional approaches to style and phrasing. At the same time, it is important to balance sensitivity with skepticism and to read critically. DiMesio, who edits copy at the *Oregonian*, said:

> I think sometimes with a very good writer that it's easy to get sucked into the prose, I guess. It's very easy. And you kind of end up, it's almost being lulled by it, and you don't question—I don't think you put it to him as much. And really be skeptical. If something strikes you as odd, trust your instincts. I have found that whenever I've not trusted my instincts, seems I've regretted it. So if something strikes you as not possible actually or if something just seems—hmmm, this doesn't seem like the proper response to this particular event—you should just bring it up. But again it's a real delicate balance because they are given more license in these types of stories.[57]

Respect for the reporter, DiMesio said, is crucial. "It's not my job to insert my voice into the story, but it is my job to make sure that his voice is as clear as possible."

As with all of the techniques discussed in this book, then, use of voice requires a deft hand and critical thinking by everyone who gets involved in a story.

Notes

1. Roy Peter Clark, "Writing Tool #19: Tune Your Voice," Poynter Online, www.poynter.org/content/content_view.asp?id=68795 (accessed May 24, 2006).

2. Clark, "Tune Your Voice."

3. John S. Carroll, interview by the author, October 6, 2004, Los Angeles.

4. Michael Finnegan, telephone interview by the author, November 26, 2004.

5. Richard Nelson, interview by the author, October 5, 2004, Los Angeles.

6. Bruce DeSilva, Chip Scanlan, and Jon Franklin, "A Love Fest on Narrative Elements," *Nieman Reports* (Spring 2002): 36.

7. Richard Read, interview by the author, June 25, 2004, Portland, Oregon.

8. Barry Johnson, interview by the author, June 25, 2004, Portland, Oregon.

9. Dean P. Baquet, interview by the author, October 5, 2004, Los Angeles.

10. DeSilva, Scanlan, and Franklin, "A Love Fest on Narrative Elements," 36. Mark Kramer also discusses the weaknesses of the news voice in "Narrative Journalism Comes of Age," *Nieman Reports* (Fall 2000): 5–8.

11. Kramer, "Narrative Journalism Comes of Age," 8.

12. Barry Siegel, "A Father's Pain, a Judge's Duty," *Los Angeles Times*, December 30, 2001, A-1 (Home Ed.).

13. David Stabler, "Day One: Lost in the Music," June 23, 2002, A1 (Sunrise Ed.), infoweb.newsbank.com.

14. David Stabler, interview by the author, June 22, 2004, Portland, Oregon.

15. Jack Hart, interview by the author, June 21, 2004, Portland, Oregon.

16. Sonia Nazario, telephone interview by the author, March 11, 2005.

17. Nora Zamichow, "The Fractured Life of Jeremy Strohmeyer," *Los Angeles Times*, July 19, 1998, A-1 (Home Ed.).

18. Nora Zamichow, interview by the author, October 6, 2004, Los Angeles.

19. Barry Horn, "A Father Who Pushed Too Far," *Dallas Morning News*, September 15, 2002, 1A (2nd ed.).

20. Barry Horn, interview by the author, July 20, 2004, Dallas.

21. Tom Hallman, Jr., "Fighting for Life on Level 3," *Oregonian*, September 22, 2003, A1 (Northwest Final Ed.).

22. Robbie DiMesio, interview by the author, June 24, 2004, Portland, Oregon.

23. Tom Hallman, Jr., interview by the author, June 21, 2004, Portland, Oregon.

24. Richard E. Meyer, interview by the author, October 6, 2004, Los Angeles.

25. Meyer credited conversation with Mark Kramer for influencing his thinking on the need to avoid being "mawkish" in narrative writing. Richard Meyer, e-mail message to author, May 24, 2006.

26. Investigative and narrative writing overlap in that investigative work sometimes uses narrative techniques.

27. David L. Protess et al., *The Journalism of Outrage: Investigative Reporting and Agenda Building in America* (New York: Guilford Press, 1991).

28. Doug J. Swanson, "Patients' Deaths Haven't Moved State Board to Act," *Dallas Morning News*, July 28, 2002, 1A (2nd ed.), infoweb.newsbank.com.

29. Swanson, "Patients' Deaths Haven't Moved State Board to Act."

30. Pam Maples, interview by the author, September 14, 2004, Dallas.

31. James S. Ettema and Theodore L. Glasser, *Custodians of Conscience: Investigative Journalism and Public Virtue* (New York: Columbia University Press, 1998), 109.

32. Victoria Loe Hicks, interview by the author, September 14, 2004, Dallas.

33. Victoria Loe Hicks, "Dallas. 'A can-do city,' that's how Dallas loves to see itself—and with good reason. Energy, ambition, vision and hard work have made it the centerpiece of the fastest-growing region in the country. The trouble is, Dallas itself isn't nearly as healthy as the region. And a lack of self-analysis blinds it to that fact," *Dallas Morning News*, April 18, 2004, 3W (2nd ed.), infoweb.newsbank.com.

34. Hicks interview.

35. Scott Glover, interview by the author, October 4, 2004, Los Angeles.

36. Matt Lait, interview by author, October 4, 2004, Los Angeles.

37. Steve Blow, interview by the author, September 14, 2004, Dallas.

38. Victoria Loe, "Confronting Trauma: Question of 'Why?' Haunts Victims of Rape, Physical Abuse," *Dallas Morning News*, June 13, 1993, 1A (Home Final Ed.), infoweb.newsbank.com.

39. Hicks interview.

40. For another example of disclosure of a reporter's vantage point via first person, see Joyce Saenz Harris, "One Who Fell Through the Cracks," *Dallas Morning News*, July 18, 2004, 1A.

41. George Rodrigue, interview by the author, September 14, 2004, Dallas.

42. Carroll interview.

43. Al Martinez, telephone interview by the author, November 15, 2004.

44. Al Martinez, "Hearing a Scream in the Night," *Los Angeles Times*, September 24, 2004, E-10 (Home Ed.).

45. Martinez interview.

46. Patt Morrison, interview by the author, October 7, 2004, Los Angeles.

47. Vivian McInerny, "A Search for Peace," *Oregonian*, November 10, 2003, D1 (Sunrise Ed.), infoweb.newsbank.com.

48. Vivian McInerny, interview by the author, June 23, 2004, Portland, Oregon.

49. Morrison interview.

50. Patt Morrison, "One Nation Off Its Meds," *Los Angeles Times*, October 6, 2004, B-11 (Home Ed.), infoweb.newsbank.com.

51. Morrison interview.

52. Morrison interview.

53. Michael Arrieta-Walden, interview by the author, June 22, 2004, Portland, Oregon.

54. Arrieta-Walden interview.

55. Steve Beaven, "No, I'm Not a Teen; I Don't Swear on the Bus and I Know Foghat," *Oregonian*, December 15, 2003, B3 (Sunrise Ed.).

56. Henry Fuhrmann, interview by the author, October 4, 2004, Los Angeles.

57. DiMesio interview.

CHAPTER EIGHT

The Big Picture

For every highly publicized ethical lapse by a Jayson Blair or a Jack Kelley, thousands of good ethical choices in newsrooms go unnoticed by the public. Some are doubly invisible outside newsrooms because they involve decisions that writers and editors make every day about details and nuances of writing technique. The decisions fall into broad categories—such as choices about description, quotes, and interpretive language—but the decisions about how to use those techniques are matters of detail that conscientious journalists address carefully but quickly. The day-to-day, paragraph-by-paragraph choices are important ethical matters because they go together to influence the picture of the world that the audience takes from news stories, features, analyses, and commentaries.

Ethical Implications of Writing Techniques: A Summary

The substantial body of academic research on journalism ethics in the past two decades—which has also been invisible to the public and many journalists—has shed light on many points of ethical decision in journalistic practice and offered criticism that has been increasingly sophisticated from the standpoint of ethical theory. However, previous scholarly work has paid little attention to the specifics of the low-profile but important choices—often well-considered choices—that journalists make about use of writing techniques.

The insights of the journalists interviewed, along with the evaluation of their comments based on ethical principles and media scholarship, point to specific ethical implications related to all of the techniques discussed:

- Anecdotes: Anecdotes are ethically beneficial in that they can draw readers into stories they might otherwise put aside, thereby bringing some truth to them that they would not have seen. They can simplify issues and show their concrete effect on people. They can provide insight into people's lives and evoke empathy for their needs and difficulties. Anecdotes can, therefore, convey truthful information and insight in a deeper way than would happen without them, and they can stir compassion among readers. On the other hand, they can be engaging but fail to communicate the broader point of a story. They can distort what readers take away about an issue or a person. Powerful but one-sided anecdotes can bias people about an issue without giving them a broader range of perspectives on it, and even ones that are better chosen can, by being so compelling, narrow the focus from a broader issue. At worst, anecdotes can leave room for mistakes or outright falsification.

- Description and attribution: Truthful description rests on careful reporting that corroborates details. Comprehensiveness—though impossible in full—also depends on careful corroboration. Attribution in sensitive matters such as criminal accusations signals fairness, but attribution can at times get in the way of truth telling by making things unclear for readers or even obscuring whether a statement is actually true. Avoiding overattribution can advance truth telling by engaging readers' interest and even stirring their compassion as the story comes to them with greater power. Creative approaches to in-story attribution, attribution through boxes and footnotes, and even first-person narrative can advance both storytelling power and the communication of truthful information. Beyond the issues of corroboration and attribution, leaving in or excluding particular details of description can bias readers for or against a person or an issue in a story. Choices of theme also need to be weighed carefully. Any approach might bias readers in some direction, but careful attention is important particularly when reputation or stereotyping is at issue.

- Quotes and paraphrasing: Quotes have the ethical benefits of revealing the voices and lives of people, potentially enhancing journalists' credibility with their audience, and holding officials accountable for their statements. They also pose ethical challenges. Corroboration presents difficulties, especially when reporters are trying to reconstruct dialogue from people's memory. In addition, many decisions must be made about what quotes to use and how, and about whether to paraphrase. The issues include matters of story advancement, clarity, context and representativeness, balance and bias, and diversity. Emotional or inflammatory quotes are particularly sensitive ethically, as are anonymous quotes. Besides corroboration and choice of quotes, journalists must decide how to render them in print—considering how to condense them accurately, whether to change or edit, and how to signal reconstructions.

- Word choice and labeling: Decisions in this area are complicated by the limitations of language and the differing standpoints of readers. Sensitive choices that came up in the interviews include handling of the word "terrorist," language for the Israeli-Palestinian conflict, and terms and euphemisms related to the Iraq war. The value-ladenness of language and the inescapability of bias, as well as the impact of reader perspectives, are strongly evident in word choice about other sensitive areas such as abortion, political leanings, and taxes—as well as in a host of others such as superlatives and common news words like "controversy." Even seemingly neutral wording can carry ethical liabilities because it implies rejection of the truth of any position or stance represented by a word. But seeking neutrality, though impossible to do fully, has ethical merit. Coupled with wording in voices from different sides, "neutral" wording may provide a fuller portrayal of issues than partisan wording by itself and avoid violating the trust of the audience. But wording in short forms can still fail to convey nuances of meaning.

- Interpretation and analysis: Elements of interpretation and analysis appear in more than just those pieces labeled as analyses or commentaries. No journalist simply says what happened; value choices permeate journalistic writing across genres. Interpretation shows up in unattributed factual statements, in summation of broad findings (especially investigative reporting), in explanation of complex matters (including explanatory narrative), in assessment of meaning or significance through a nut graf or other statements, and through overt statements of opinion. Ethically, the unstated interpretive aspect of pieces that are not labeled as interpretive suggests that journalists need to be particularly diligent in writing and editing interpretive passages and evaluating how stories are framed. Overt opinion writing is ethically challenging because it can use the power of words to build a case for one side while disclosing little about how much or how little knowledge underlies the writer's conclusions.

- Voice: Ethical implications emerge in relation to the detached news voice, narrative and investigative voices, and the voices of columns and other first-person pieces. The detached news voice can signal an earnest search for truthful information and provide a fuller portrayal of the range of views on issues. News writing that is clear and simple can help readers understand the political and social world—but readers' bias concerns and the appearance of being uncaring through the detached voice are problems. A weak reporting base and dull or unnatural writing can also undermine the ethical promise of the news voice, and the omniscient third-person voice can appear more authoritative than it actually is capable of being. Narratives with inherently emotional content convey information but also move readers through the emotions wrapped up with the information. But not all readers will be moved in the same way. Although research is needed to clarify the impact of voice, there is a danger that steering readers emotionally will blunt their emotional experience of a scene. Investigative reporters face ethical choices similar to those of narrative writers. They must decide whether to let the outrage of the situation speak for itself through reporting or to emphasize it through strong language. The straight approach enables readers to sort out what facts mean and what their emotional reactions are, but it can also bore or confuse them. The more dramatic approach can help them see the bigger picture and stir their anger, but it can also reshape readers' emotional connection with the story. Columns and other first-person pieces can engage readers' interest and feelings in ways that news stories written in a detached third-person voice might not. The voice of columns and other first-person pieces offers readers more truth about life or political issues than a balanced presentation simply because the voice grabs their attention. Going outside the objective approach might be more honest in that it can shed more light on who the author is and how that is shaping the story the reader sees. It can also free the writer to talk more directly and plainly about his or her experience. But writers cannot let themselves block the reader's view of the topic. In addition, hyperbole and emotional language need to be weighed for their impact on truthful communication.

Perspectives on Ethics Beyond Specific Techniques

Beyond providing insights about specific techniques, the interviews shed light on several issues:

- Many writers and editors placed truth as a high priority by naming it or related notions as the most important area of ethical challenge in journalistic writing. This may not be surprising given the prominence of this professional value in newsroom discussions and professional codes of ethics in the twentieth century and into the twenty-first. But in light of scholarly recognition of the limitations of seeking truth—as well as the high-profile breaches of truthful reporting in recent years—truth's enduring appearance as a journalistic priority is notable.[1] The pursuit of truth is worth retaining, however constrained it may be by individual perspective, linguistic constraints, and economic and ideological pressures. It is worth retaining because it is a crucial foundation for communication and mutual understanding in a democratic society.

- A few journalists showed sophisticated awareness of objectivity's limitations. The awareness that true objectivity is impossible is significant from a scholarly perspective because it suggests that while objectivity might still be the dominant paradigm for journalistic practice, some mainstream journalists at large news organizations are sensitive to the reality that it is impossible to achieve in full. James Ettema noted two decades ago that some journalists were more perceptive about the limits of "professional values" than scholars often acknowledge.[2] These interviews bear out that observation.

- Journalists at all three newspapers showed sensitivity to matters of fairness and bias to an extent that would surprise the media critics and members of the public who accuse these newspapers and other mainstream media outlets of bias—both liberal and conservative. No one adopted the intellectually naive view that a journalist can act truly free of bias, and no one who discussed the topic argued that one of these newspapers was free of it. But interviewees expressed openness to hearing and reflecting on public complaints about bias, or talked about careful attention to fairness in the writing and editing process—both in general terms and in specifics of stories.

- Many of the reporters supported variations on the idea of read backs. The variations included double-checking quotes with sources, confirming the accuracy of details of scenes and events, checking complex scientific and medical matters, and confirming that a passage rings true with the larger point of what a source is saying. The wide support for read backs is notable because views in the profession on read backs differ sharply. A lengthy piece on the topic in 1996 in the *American Journalism Review* reflected the range of views. On one end of the spectrum was the belief that read backs are worthwhile because they foster accuracy and can yield more information. On the other end was the view that they turn a reporter into "a glorified secretary."[3] The ethical principle of independence calls for caution in approaching read backs. To maintain independence, it is important to make clear to sources that they do not have veto power over the content or framing of a story—a concern about which reporters were sensitive. The need to draw careful lines should not lead to a wholesale rejection of read backs. From the standpoint of truth telling, read backs or variations on them are valuable not only for helping to get factual details right, but also for ensuring that the context is accurate. From the standpoint of compassion, they are particularly valuable for people who are not savvy to the ways of journalists and not used to being in the public eye. Practicing a "no surprises" approach—as *Dallas Morning News* feature writer Beatriz Terrazas put it[4]—toward that kind of person shows ethical sensitivity.

Implications for Journalistic Practice

The interviews and analysis of the ethics of writing techniques suggest several implications for the practice of journalism:

- Read backs and aggressive fact checking by reporters. Kenneth Goodman, a medical ethicist and former journalist, has borrowed the term "standard of care" from medicine and applied it to news coverage of ethical issues.[5] The notion of standard of care is also relevant to fact checking, including read backs. Rigorous fact checking will always be difficult in daily journalism because of time pressures, especially for small publications. But it is as important as proper patient-care protocols are in medicine. Careful fact checking—including context, not just details—is ethically vital from the standpoint of truth telling, but it is also crucial to credibility with the public.

- Editing, at both the assigning editor and copy editor stages, that is both aggressive in questioning fact and context and sensitive to the writer. Good editing includes careful questioning of reporters to unearth inadvertent errors, assumptions about information, weaknesses in sourcing, and unintended (or intended) biases. At the same time, the best editing is open to unorthodox approaches to writing—for example, dialogue embedded in news stories, first-person voice, or attribution handled through a combination of in-story references and accompanying boxes or notes. Stories that are edited both aggressively and artfully have the potential to both communicate truth and stir compassion.

- Constructive, open communication among editors and writers. Animosity or simply lack of communication among copy editors, assigning editors, and reporters can lead to errors of detail or, worse, fabrications. Failure to discuss uses of technique openly can also hold newspapers back from doing innovative work that might engage readers more effectively.
- Cultivation of a nuanced understanding of truth by both writers and editors. Journalists can help guard against assumptions that they have arrived at truth in doing a story—and can pursue a story more thoroughly—if they are sensitive to the limitations of objectivity imposed by personal standpoint and language. At the same time, commitment to as comprehensive, broad, and fair a communication of truth as possible should remain—if not for the sake of truth as a foundational principle, for the social and political value of truthful communication.
- A "both-and" approach that encompasses objective-style reporting and other forms such as extended narratives and first-person stories, with both detached and more emotional or humorous voices. Each of these approaches has its ethical merits, and a mix will draw on the ethical benefits of all of them. With the challenges of keeping an audience in general, as well as the difficulty of drawing in young people specifically, mainstream media—broadcast and web-based as well as print—have a business reason to try a variety of approaches. But as this book has shown, there are ethical reasons, too. Narratives and first-person pieces can powerfully bring home how people are affected by personal difficulties and social problems or connect with them on a less serious level. Objective-style news pieces have a place, though, in providing a broad spectrum of information about social and political issues with which citizens in a democracy must wrestle.
- Greater effort to explain journalists' best practices to the public. The interviews suggest a sharp contrast between the perspectives and practices of many journalists at large mainstream newspapers and the public's stereotypes of journalists as sloppy, biased, and uncaring—though those assumptions have found support in well-publicized cases such as those of Blair and Kelley. It is important to try to educate the public on the best practices of journalism because of the low credibility of journalists in the public eye and the central role of good journalism in fostering communication of information and ideas in a democracy. Efforts to educate the public could include boxes describing how a story was reported. Some publications have taken this approach, but it could be used to include not only who was interviewed but also the nature of reporters' interactions with them. The explanations could include the

sensitivity shown to story subjects—particularly in stories about hurting or vulnerable individuals. In addition, columns by front-line editors about the process by which stories are read and evaluated could aid public understanding. It could be particularly illuminating to many people to hear from middle- and lower-level editors—on both assigning desks and copy desks—because they often evaluate fairness and the nuances of word choice. First-person stories in which journalists are transparent about their interactions with the subjects would also educate readers.

A Final Step Back: Writing Techniques and the Future of Journalism

Journalists cannot escape deadline pressure, whether they work at newspapers, magazines, broadcast outlets, or websites. It is always difficult to take time to reflect on the choices of writing and editing. Conscientious journalism students juggling classes and student or professional media work also have a hard time stopping and focusing on the nuances of technique. It is easy for them to pick up the habits and conventions that produce adequate but not excellent journalism. But stopping to reflect on the ethical implications of writing techniques is vital—not only to achieving personal excellence but also to sustaining the best practices of journalism at a time when the profession faces significant challenges.[6]

At their best, large metropolitan newspapers have for years set a high standard of care in writing and editing. But as profit pressures have grown, even these organizations have faced severe pressure to cut back on resources, putting this standard of excellence at risk. It is important for students, journalists, and those who study journalism[7] to think about what the best practices in the use of writing techniques look like before staff cutbacks and limitations on resources drive away the best practitioners of the craft or further eat into the time to reflect on good work.

This kind of reflection is also important for journalists who practice their craft at broadcast and cable outlets and on websites, and to students who aspire to these jobs. Much of the best storytelling in journalism is done on broadcast newsmagazine programs[8] and on news websites.[9] But these outlets, like metropolitan newspapers, face financial pressures and struggle to compete for the attention of a fragmented and media-saturated audience. Developing and sustaining excellent journalistic practices in broadcasting and on the Internet takes time and effort in the face of these pressures.

Careful thought about the use of writing techniques is vital to the future identity of journalists and of journalism itself. The rise of blogging and citizen journalism[10] has raised questions about who should be called a journalist. Excellence in writing and editing is central to defining journalists' identity, enhancing their ability to convey truth with power and their right to be regarded as trustworthy in the eyes of an increasingly skeptical public. The future of journalism as a distinct profession depends on its ability to maintain and develop practices that uphold high standards of truthfulness while paying compassionate attention to the needs of sources and audiences.

Notes

1. Most interviewees knew that truth might be a matter for discussion in the interviews, but many brought it up not only in discussion of specific techniques but also in questioning about the biggest ethical challenge in journalistic writing.

2. James Ettema, "Journalism in the 'Post-Factual Age,'" *Critical Studies in Mass Communication* 4, no. 1 (March 1987): 82–86.

3. Alicia C. Shepard, "Show and Print," *American Journalism Review* (March 1996), web.lexis-nexis.com.

4. Beatriz Terrazas, interview by the author, July 20, 2004, Dallas.

5. Kenneth Goodman, telephone interview by the author, September 19, 1996. Quoted in David A. Craig, "Covering the Ethics Angle: Toward a Method to Evaluate and Improve How Journalists Portray the Ethical Dimension of Professions and Society" (Ph.D. diss., University of Missouri–Columbia, 1997).

6. For a discussion of standards of excellence, ethics, and the practice of journalism, see Edmund B. Lambeth, *Committed Journalism: An Ethic for the Profession*, 2nd ed. (Bloomington: Indiana University Press, 1992), 72–82. Lambeth's discussion draws on the work of philosopher Alasdair MacIntyre. See Alasdair MacIntyre, *After Virtue* (Notre Dame, Ind.: Notre Dame University Press, 1981).

7. Future evaluation of the ethics of writing techniques could add to the perspectives of this book. For example, additional in-depth interview studies could shed additional light on the practical wisdom of journalists about how they handle ethical choices in writing techniques. Interviews at large and small newspapers, magazines, broadcast outlets, Internet operations, and alternative media outlets could all provide additional ethical perspective. In-depth interviews could also explore views on the sources of the ethical principles the journalists profess and the sources of skepticism over objectivity among those who profess that.

8. See, for example, the Alfred I. duPont-Columbia University Awards in Television and Radio News at www.jrn.columbia.edu/events/dupont (accessed May 24, 2006).

9. See the Online News Association's awards at www.journalist.org/awards (accessed May 24, 2006).

10. For a discussion of citizen journalism, see Steve Outing, "The 11 Layers of Citizen Journalism," Poynter Online, www.poynter.org/content/content_view.asp?id=83126 (accessed May 24, 2006).

Appendix: List of Interviewees

The following people were interviewed for this book between June 2004 and March 2005. For people who changed job roles or left the newspaper after the interviews, their new roles or dates of departure are noted.

Dallas Morning News
Sue Goetinck Ambrose, science writer
Joshua Benton, education writer
Steve Blow, Metro columnist
Frank Christlieb, senior editor on the news copy desk
Berta Delgado, religion writer; left the paper in January 2005
Mike Drago, editor who has worked extensively with education stories
Crayton Harrison, business writer
Victoria Loe Hicks, editorial writer; left the paper in March 2006
Barry Horn, sportswriter
Thomas T. Huang, Texas Living editor
Lisa Kresl, assistant managing editor for Lifestyles
Pam Maples, assistant managing editor for projects
Michael Merschel, assistant features editor
Robert W. Mong, Jr., editor
George Rodrigue, managing editor
Frank Smith, deputy copy desk chief on the news copy desk
Steve Steinberg, features copy editor and writer
Doug Swanson, projects writer

Beatriz Terrazas, feature writer
Karen M. Thomas, feature writer
Bruce Tomaso, religion editor
Bob Yates, assistant managing editor for sports

Los Angeles Times

Dean P. Baquet, managing editor; became editor in August 2005
Mark Z. Barabak, political writer who has covered presidential elections
Glenn F. Bunting, national correspondent
John S. Carroll, editor; retired in August 2005
Laura Dominick, copy editor on the foreign desk
Michael Finnegan, state politics reporter who has also covered presidential campaigns
Don Frederick, national political editor
Henry Fuhrmann, senior copy desk chief for business; became a deputy business editor in May 2005
Scott Glover, investigative reporter
Jamie Gold, readers' representative
Matt Lait, investigative reporter
Vernon Loeb, California investigations editor
Tim Lynch, senior copy chief of the foreign and national desks
Al Martinez, columnist, veteran reporter
Melissa McCoy, assistant managing editor for copy desks; became deputy managing editor for copy desks, design, and production in December 2005
Richard E. Meyer, narrative editor
Patt Morrison, opinion-page columnist, veteran reporter
Sonia Nazario, narrative writer
Richard Nelson, national copy editor
Ted Rohrlich, investigative reporter
Kurt Streeter, narrative writer
Leo C. Wolinsky, deputy managing editor; became managing editor in October 2005
Nora Zamichow, narrative writer; left the paper in January 2006

Oregonian

Jake Arnold, copy editor
Michael Arrieta-Walden, public editor; became senior editor for online in early 2006
Bryan Denson, reporter who has done narrative and investigative writing; assigned full time to investigative team in fall 2004

Robbie DiMesio, copy editor
Andy Dworkin, medical writer
Tom Hallman, Jr., narrative writer
Jack Hart, managing editor, writing coach, and primary editor of narratives
Spencer Heinz, staff writer who has done narrative work
Barry Johnson, arts editor
Vivian McInerny, feature writer
Pat Mullarkey, slot
Seth Prince, copy editor
Richard Read, senior writer for international affairs and special projects
Sandra Mims Rowe, editor
David Stabler, classical music critic who has written narratives

ᖰᕈᖱ

Bibliography

Allen, Barry. *Truth in Philosophy*. Cambridge, Mass.: Harvard University Press, 1993.

Alterman, Eric. *What Liberal Media? The Truth about* Bias *and the News*. New York: Basic Books, 2003.

Aust, Charles F., and Dolf Zillmann. "Effects of Victim Exemplification in Television News on Viewer Perception of Social Issues." *Journalism and Mass Communication Quarterly* 73 (Winter 1996): 787–803.

Beauchamp, Tom L., and James F. Childress. *Principles of Biomedical Ethics*. 5th ed. New York: Oxford University Press, 2001.

Bird, S. Elizabeth, and Robert W. Dardenne. "Myth, Chronicle, and Story: Exploring the Narrative Qualities of News." Pp. 67–86 in *Media, Myths, and Narratives: Television and the Press*, Sage Annual Reviews of Communication Research, vol. 15, edited by James W. Carey. Newbury Park, Calif.: Sage, 1988.

Bok, Sissela. *Lying: Moral Choice in Public and Private Life*. 2nd ed. New York: Vintage Books, 1999.

Brosius, Hans-Bernd, and Anke Bathelt. "The Utility of Exemplars in Persuasive Communications." *Communication Research* 21 (February 1994): 48–78.

Brown, Fred. "Storytelling vs. Sticking to the Facts." *Quill* 90, no. 3 (April 2002): 22–25.

Carey, James W. *Communication as Culture: Essays on Media and Society*. Boston: Unwin Hyman, 1989.

Christians, Clifford G. "The Ethics of Being in a Communications Context." Pp. 3–23 in *Communication Ethics and Universal Values*, edited by Clifford Christians and Michael Traber. Thousand Oaks, Calif.: Sage, 1997.

Christians, Clifford G., John P. Ferré, and P. Mark Fackler. *Good News: Social Ethics and the Press*. New York: Oxford University Press, 1993.

Christians, Clifford, and Kaarle Nordenstreng. "Social Responsibility Worldwide." *Journal of Mass Media Ethics* 19, no. 1 (2004): 3–28.

Christians, Clifford G., Kim B. Rotzoll, Mark Fackler, Kathy Brittain McKee, and Robert H. Woods, Jr. *Media Ethics: Cases and Moral Reasoning.* 7th ed. Boston: Pearson Education, 2005.

Clark, Roy Peter. "The Ethics of Narrative Journalism: A Continuing Debate." Poynter Online. poynteronline.org/content/content_view.asp?id=4718&sid=32.

———. "The Line Between Fact and Fiction." Poynter Online. www.poynter.org/content/content_view.asp?id=3491.

———. "Writing Tool #19: Tune Your Voice." Poynter Online. www.poynter.org/content/content_view.asp?id=68795.

Clark, Roy Peter, and Christopher Scanlan. *America's Best Newspaper Writing: A Collection of ASNE Prizewinners.* 2nd ed. Boston: Bedford/St. Martin's, 2006.

Cooper, Thomas W. *A Time Before Deception: Truth in Communication, Culture, and Ethics.* Santa Fe, N.M.: Clear Light Publishers, 1998.

Craig, David A. "Communitarian Journalism(s): Clearing Conceptual Landscapes." *Journal of Mass Media Ethics* 11, no. 2 (1996): 107–18.

———. "Covering the Ethics Angle: Toward a Method to Evaluate and Improve How Journalists Portray the Ethical Dimension of Professions and Society." Ph.D. diss., University of Missouri–Columbia, 1997.

———. "Covering Ethics Through Analysis and Commentary: A Case Study." *Journal of Mass Media Ethics* 17, no. 1 (2002): 53–68.

———. "The Promise and Peril of Anecdotes in News Coverage: An Ethical Analysis." *Journalism and Mass Communication Quarterly* 80, no. 4 (Winter 2003): 802–17.

Currie, Mark. *Postmodern Narrative Theory.* New York: St. Martin's, 1998.

Denzin, Norman K. "Cultural Studies, the New Journalism, and the Narrative Turn in Ethnography." Pp. 134–49 in *American Cultural Studies,* edited by Catherine A. Warren and Mary Douglas Vavrus. Urbana: University of Illinois Press, 2002.

DeSilva, Bruce, Chip Scanlan, and Jon Franklin. "A Love Fest on Narrative Elements." *Nieman Reports* (Spring 2002): 36–37.

Downie, Leonard, Jr., and Robert G. Kaiser. *The News About the News: American Journalism in Peril.* New York: Alfred A. Knopf, 2002.

Durham, Meenakshi Gigi. "On the Relevance of Standpoint Epistemology to the Practice of Journalism." *Communication Theory* 8, no. 2 (May 1998): 117–40.

"Editors' Letter to the *Washington Post* Staff about Style Book Revisions." Poynter Online. www.poynter.org/content/content_print.asp?id=61247&custom=.

Elliott, Deni. "A Case of Need: Media Coverage of Organ Transplants." Pp. 151–58 in *Risky Business: Communicating Issues of Science, Risk, and Public Policy,* edited by Lee Wilkins and Philip Patterson. New York: Greenwood Press, 1991.

Entman, Robert M. "Framing: Toward Clarification of a Fractured Paradigm." *Journal of Communication* 43, no. 4 (Autumn 1993): 51–58.

Epstein, Edward Jay. *News from Nowhere: Television and the News*. New York: Random House, 1973.

Ettema, James. "Journalism in the 'Post-Factual Age.'" *Critical Studies in Mass Communication* 4, no. 1 (March 1987): 82–86.

Ettema, James S., and Theodore L. Glasser. *Custodians of Conscience: Investigative Journalism and Public Virtue*. New York: Columbia University Press, 1998.

Fisher, Walter R. *Human Communication as Narration: Toward a Philosophy of Reason, Value, and Action*. Columbia: University of South Carolina Press, 1987.

———. "Narration as a Human Communication Paradigm: The Case of Public Moral Argument." *Communication Monographs* 51 (March 1984): 6–7.

Fishman, Mark. *Manufacturing the News*. Austin: University of Texas Press, 1980.

Flesch, Rudolph. *The Art of Readable Writing*. 1st ed. New York: Harper, 1949.

Frank, Russell. "'About This Story': Newspapers Work to Make Narrative Journalism Be Accountable to Readers." *Nieman Reports* (Fall 2002): 49–52.

———. "Wait Before You Narrate." Poynter Online. www.poynter.org/content/content_view.asp?id=4151.

———. "'You Had to Be There' (and They Weren't): The Problem with Reporter Reconstructions." *Journal of Mass Media Ethics* 14, no. 3 (1999): 146–58.

Franken, Al. *Lies and the Lying Liars Who Tell Them: A Fair and Balanced Look at the Right*. New York: Dutton, 2003.

Franklin, Jon. *Writing for Story: Craft Secrets of Dramatic Nonfiction by a Two-Time Pulitzer Prize Winner*. New York: Plume, 1994.

Frus, Phyllis. *The Politics and Poetics of Journalistic Narrative: The Timely and the Timeless*. Cambridge, Eng.: Cambridge University Press, 1994.

Gans, Herbert J. *Deciding What's News*. New York: Vintage Books, 1980.

Gardner, John. *On Becoming a Novelist*. New York: Norton, 1999.

Germer, Fawn. "Are Quotes Sacred?" *American Journalism Review* (September 1995): 34–37.

Gibson, Rhonda, and Dolf Zillmann. "Effects of Citation in Exemplifying Testimony on Issue Perception." *Journalism and Mass Communication Quarterly* 75 (Spring 1998): 167–76.

———. "Exaggerated versus Representative Exemplification in News Reports." *Communication Research* 21 (October 1994): 603–24.

———. "The Impact of Quotation in News Reports on Issue Perception." *Journalism Quarterly* 70 (Winter 1993): 793–800.

Gilligan, Carol. *In a Different Voice: Psychological Theory and Women's Development*. Cambridge, Mass.: Harvard University Press, 1982.

Gitlin, Todd. *The Whole World Is Watching: Mass Media in the Making and Unmaking of the New Left*. Berkeley: University of California Press, 1980.

Goldberg, Bernard. *Bias: A CBS Insider Exposes How the Media Distort the News*. Washington, D.C.: Regnery, 2001.

Hafez, Kai. "Journalism Ethics Revisited: A Comparison of Ethics Codes in Europe, North Africa, the Middle East, and Muslim Asia." *Political Communication* 19, no. 2 (2002): 225–50.

Hamill, Ruth, Timothy DeCamp Wilson, and Richard E. Nisbett. "Insensitivity to Sample Bias: Generalizing from Atypical Cases." *Journal of Personality and Social Psychology* 39 (October 1980): 578–89.

Hammerton, M. "A Case of Radical Probability Estimation." *Journal of Experimental Psychology* 101 (December 1973): 252–54.

Iggers, Jeremy. *Good News, Bad News: Journalism Ethics and the Public Interest*. Boulder, Colo.: Westview Press, 1998.

Iyengar, Shanto. *Is Anyone Responsible? How Television Frames Political Issues*. Chicago: University of Chicago Press, 1991.

Johnson-Cartee, Karen S. *News Narratives and News Framing: Constructing Political Reality*. Lanham, Md.: Rowman & Littlefield, 2005.

Jonas, Hans. *The Imperative of Responsibility: In Search of an Ethics for the Technological Age*. Translated by Hans Jonas with the collaboration of David Herr. Chicago: University of Chicago Press, 1984.

Kahneman, Daniel, and Amos Tversky. "On the Psychology of Prediction." *Psychological Review* 80 (July 1973): 237–51.

Killenberg, G. Michael, and Rob Anderson. "What Is a Quote? Practical, Rhetorical, and Ethical Concerns for Journalists." *Journal of Mass Media Ethics* 8, no. 1 (1993): 37–54.

Kitch, Carolyn. "'Mourning in America': Ritual, Redemption, and Recovery in News Narrative after September 11." *Journalism Studies* 4, no. 2 (2003): 213–24.

Klaidman, Stephen, and Tom L. Beauchamp. *The Virtuous Journalist*. New York: Oxford University Press, 1987.

Koehn, Daryl. *Rethinking Feminist Ethics: Care, Trust and Empathy*. London: Routledge, 1998.

Kohn, Bob. *Journalistic Fraud: How The New York Times Distorts the News and Why It Can No Longer Be Trusted*. Nashville, Tenn.: WND Books, 2003.

Koriat, Asher, Morris Goldsmith, and Ainat Pansky. "Toward a Psychology of Memory Accuracy." *Annual Review of Psychology* 51 (2000): 481–537.

Kovach, Bill, and Tom Rosenstiel. *The Elements of Journalism: What Newspeople Should Know and the Public Should Expect*. New York: Crown Publishers, 2001.

Kozloff, Sarah. "Narrative Theory and Television." Pp. 67–100 in *Channels of Discourse, Reassembled: Television and Contemporary Criticism*, edited by Robert C. Allen. Chapel Hill: University of North Carolina Press.

Kramer, Mark. "Narrative Journalism Comes of Age." *Nieman Reports* (Fall 2000): 5–8.

Lambeth, Edmund B. *Committed Journalism: An Ethic for the Profession*. 2nd ed. Bloomington: Indiana University Press, 1992.

Larrabee, Mary Jeanne, ed. *An Ethic of Care: Feminist and Interdisciplinary Perspectives*. New York: Routledge, 1993.

Lawson, Hilary. "Stories about Stories." Pp. ix–xxviii in *Dismantling Truth: Reality in the Post-Modern World*, edited by Hilary Lawson and Lisa Appignanesi. London: Weidenfeld and Nicolson, 1989.

Layton, Charles. "The Dallas Mourning News." *American Journalism Review* (April–May 2005). www.ajr.org/article.asp?id=3836.

Lee, Tien-Tsung. "The Liberal Media Myth Revisited: An Examination of Factors Influencing Perceptions of Media Bias." *Journal of Broadcasting & Electronic Media* 49, no. 1 (March 2005): 43–64.

Lyon, Don, and Paul Slovic. "Dominance of Accuracy Information and Neglect of Base Rates in Probability Estimation." *Acta Psychologica* 40 (August 1976): 287–98.

MacIntyre, Alasdair. *After Virtue*. Notre Dame, Ind.: Notre Dame University Press, 1981.

Manoff, Robert Karl, and Michael Schudson, eds. *Reading the News*. New York: Pantheon, 1986.

Margolis, Joseph. "Objectivity as a Problem: An Attempt at an Overview." *Annals of the American Academy of Political and Social Science*, vol. 560, "The Future of Fact" (November 1998): 55–68.

Mattingly, Terry. "Religion in the News." *Quill* (July–August 1993): 12–13.

McManus, John H. *Market-Driven Journalism: Let the Citizen Beware?* Thousand Oaks, Calif.: Sage, 1994.

McManus, Kevin. "The, Uh, Quotation Quandary." *Columbia Journalism Review* (May–June 1990): 54–56.

Mieth, Dietmar. "The Basic Norm of Truthfulness: Its Ethical Justification and Universality." Pp. 87–104 in *Communication Ethics and Universal Values*, edited by Clifford Christians and Michael Traber. Thousand Oaks, Calif.: Sage, 1997.

Mill, John Stuart. *Utilitarianism and On Liberty: Including Mill's 'Essay on Bentham' and Selections from the Writings of Jeremy Bentham and John Austin*. Edited by Mary Warnock. Oxford, Eng.: Blackwell, 2003.

Niven, David. "Objective Evidence on Media Bias: Newspaper Coverage of Congressional Party Switchers." *Journalism and Mass Communication Quarterly* 80, no. 2 (Summer 2003): 311–26.

Noddings, Nel. *Caring: A Feminine Approach to Ethics and Moral Education*. Berkeley: University of California Press, 1984.

Patterson, Philip, and Lee Wilkins. *Media Ethics: Issues and Cases*. 5th ed. Boston: McGraw-Hill, 2005.

Pew Research Center for the People and the Press. "News Audiences Increasingly Politicized: Online News Audience Larger, More Diverse." people-press.org/reports/display.php3?ReportID=215.

Pippert, Wesley G. *An Ethics of News: A Reporter's Search for Truth*. Washington, D.C.: Georgetown University Press, 1989.

Protess, David L., Fay Lomax Cook, Jack C. Doppelt, James S. Ettema, Margaret T. Gordon, Donna R. Leff, and Peter Miller. *The Journalism of Outrage: Investigative Reporting and Agenda Building in America*. New York: Guilford Press, 1991.

Putnam, Hilary. *Reason, Truth, and History*. New York: Cambridge University Press, 1981.

Reeder, Allan. "Beyond the Bounds: When to Speak Up, and Why." Poynter Online. www.poynter.org/dg.lts/id.41411/content.content_view.htm. Reprinted from *Copy Editor* (June–July 2003): 1, 6–7.

Rich, Carole. "Ethics of the News Story." Pp. 45–50 in *Journalism Ethics: A Reference Handbook*, edited by Elliot D. Cohen and Deni Elliott. Santa Barbara, Calif.: ABC-CLIO, 1997.

Romano, Carlin. "What? The Grisly Truth About Bare Facts." Pp. 38–78 in *Reading the News*, edited by Robert Karl Manoff and Michael Schudson. New York: Pantheon, 1986.

Rorty, Richard. *Contingency, Irony, and Solidarity*. Cambridge, Eng.: Cambridge University Press, 1989.

Rosen, Jill. "All About the Retrospect." *American Journalism Review* (June–July 2003): 32–35.

——. "Who Knows Jack?" *American Journalism Review* (April–May 2004): 29–38.

Ryan, Michael. "Journalistic Ethics, Objectivity, Existential Journalism, Standpoint Epistemology, and Public Journalism." *Journal of Mass Media Ethics* 16, no. 1 (2001): 3–22.

Scanlan, Chip. "The Nut Graf, Part I: Giving Readers a Reason to Care." Poynter Online. www.poynter.org/content/content_view.asp?id=34457.

Schacter, Daniel L., Kenneth A. Norman, and Wilma Koutstaal. "The Cognitive Neuroscience of Constructive Memory." *Annual Review of Psychology* 49 (1998): 289–318.

Schudson, Michael. *The Power of News*. Cambridge, Mass.: Harvard University Press, 1995.

Serrin, Judith, and William Serrin, eds. *Muckraking! The Journalism That Changed America*. New York: New Press, 2002.

Shepard, Alicia C. "Show and Print." *American Journalism Review* (March 1996). web.lexis-nexis.com.

Smolkin, Rachel. "A Source of Encouragement." *American Journalism Review* (August–September 2005). www.ajr.org/article.asp?id=3909.

Stewart, James B. *Follow the Story: How to Write Successful Nonfiction*. New York: Simon & Schuster, Touchstone, 1998.

Tichi, Cecelia. *Exposés and Excess: Muckraking in America, 1900/2000*. Philadelphia: University of Pennsylvania Press, 2004.

Tuchman, Gaye. *Making News: A Study in the Construction of Reality*. New York: Free Press, 1978.

Valkenburg, Patti M., Holli A. Semetko, and Claes H. de Vreese. "The Effects of News Frames on Readers' Thoughts and Recall." *Communication Research* 26 (October 1999): 550–69.

Walker, Vanessa Siddle, and John R. Snarey, eds. *Race-ing Moral Formation: African American Perspectives on Care and Justice*. New York: Teachers College Press, 2004.

"The *Washington Post's* Policies on Sources, Quotations, Attribution, and Datelines." Poynter Online. www.poynter.org/content/content_print.asp?id=61244&custom=.

White, Hayden. "The Value of Narrativity in the Representation of Reality." *Critical Inquiry* 7, no. 1 (Autumn 1980): 5–27.

Yao, Xinzhong. *Confucianism and Christianity: A Comparative Study of Jen and Agape.* Brighton, U.K.: Sussex Academic Press, 1996.

Zillmann, Dolf, and Hans-Bernd Brosius. *Exemplification in Communication: The Influence of Case Reports on the Perception of Issues.* Mahwah, N.J.: Lawrence Erlbaum, 2000.

Zillmann, Dolf, Rhonda Gibson, S. Shyam Sundar, and Joseph W. Perkins, Jr. "Effects of Exemplification in News Reports on the Perception of Social Issues." *Journalism and Mass Communication Quarterly* 73, no. 2 (Summer 1996): 427–44.

Zillmann, Dolf, Joseph Perkins, and S. Shyam Sundar. "Impression-Formation Effects of Printed News Varying in Descriptive Precision and Exemplifications." *Medienpsychologie: Zeitschrift fur Individual- und Massenkommunikation* 4 (September 1992): 168–85, 239–40.

Index

꧁꧂

About the Author

David Craig is associate professor and director of graduate studies in journalism at the University of Oklahoma. He teaches journalism ethics, editing, and graduate research courses. Craig worked for nine years as a news copy editor at the *Lexington (Ky.) Herald-Leader*. He earned a B.S. in journalism from Northwestern University, an M.A. in communication from Wheaton College, and a Ph.D. in journalism from the University of Missouri–Columbia. He taught editing courses at Northwestern and Missouri. He has been a professor at Oklahoma since 1996.